THE PROMISE OF HIS GLORY

SERVICES AND PRAYERS FOR THE SEASON FROM ALL SAINTS TO CANDLEMAS

Commended by the
House of Bishops of the General Synod
of the Church of England

MOWBRAY

Jointly published by
Church House Publishing
Church House, Great Smith Street, London SW1P 3NZ, England
Mowbray
A Cassell imprint
Villiers House, 41–47 Strand, London WC2N 5JE, England

First published 1991
Reprinted 1991 (twice), 1992 (twice)

Minister's edition   ISBN 0-7151-3741-7 (Church House Publishing)
                     0-264-67220-8 (Mowbray)
People's book   ISBN 0-7151-3738-7 (Church House Publishing)
                     0-264-67263-1 (Mowbray)

The Central Board of Finance is indebted to churches, publishers, and
individuals whose copyright texts have been included with permission in
The Promise of His Glory, either in original or in adapted form. For
further information see Sources and Acknowledgements, pp. 416–419.

Texts for local use. The arrangements which apply to local editions of
Church of England Services from 1 January 1988 cover reproduction on a
non-commercial basis both for a single occasion and for repeated use.
Details are available in a leaflet, *Liturgical Texts for Local Use:
Guidelines and Copyright Information*. This can be obtained by post
(please send stamped addressed envelope) from the Copyright
Administrator, Central Board of Finance, Church House, Great Smith Street
London SW1P 3NZ.

Cover design by Regina M. Rynja OSB
Typeset by Saxon Printing Ltd, Derby
Printed and bound in Great Britain by
Biddles Ltd, Guildford and King's Lynn

CONTENTS

THE PROMISE OF HIS GLORY

This volume of Services and Prayers, covering the season from All Saints' Day to the Presentation of Christ in the Temple, is published with the agreement of the House of Bishops of the General Synod.

The Services and Prayers have been commended by the House of Bishops with the exceptions indicated in this note. Under Canon B 4 it is open to each Bishop to authorize forms of service to be used within his diocese and he may specify that the services should be those commended by the House. If the Bishop gives no directions in this matter a priest remains free, subject to the terms of Canon B 5, to make use of the services as commended by the House.

The Service for Remembrance Sunday printed on pp.84-90 has been authorized since 1984 by the Archbishops of Canterbury and York under Canon B 4 for use in their respective Provinces.

The Prefatory Note to the Appendix (p.369) explains the status of the Calendar and Lectionaries set out there.

October 1990   On behalf of the House of Bishops
                                     ROBERT CANTUAR:
                                                 Chairman

PREFACE

For many people, the season of Christmas is the focal point of their religious observance. For them, the Christmas Carol Service rather than the Easter Vigil provides the ground of their Christian experience. The churches are full for the Midnight Celebration, and people who live in the north of Europe enjoy the contrast between the glow of candlelit churches and the frosty darkness outside – or so the Christmas cards seem to imply. And while the purists may not approve, there is a strong residual sense – in the Church of England at any rate – that the coming of God among us in Christ is as important as his death and resurrection.

For the local congregation, the period which starts some time after the Harvest Festival and ends around the beginning of Lent has its own liturgical programme, though its boundaries and internal coherence seem less sharply defined than the succeeding period of Lent, Holy Week, and Easter.

We believe that this is a season in the Church's year providing many possibilities which the Church at present is only partially in a position to meet.

These are some of the reasons for the appearance of this book of services which we have entitled *The Promise of His Glory*. Many will recognize it as a companion volume to *Lent, Holy Week, Easter: Services and Prayers*, which appeared in 1986 and sold out immediately. We have been encouraged by the way that book has been used for the renewal and deepening of worship in many Churches of very different traditions within and (it may be said) beyond the Church of England.

The Promise of His Glory is, however, more than a collection of texts that will in some measure correspond with *Lent, Holy Week, Easter*. It is true that the Church's year is focused on the celebration of the Incarnation at Christmastide and the Passion and Resurrection at Eastertide, and that each of these celebrations has its own internal rhythms of preparation,

1

celebration, and reflection. But *The Promise of His Glory* is different. Why?

First of all, unlike the Lent, Holy Week, Eastertide sequence, there is no 'chronology' of events in the life of Christ which can be followed strictly. At the centre of *The Promise of His Glory* lies the message of the Incarnation, though the Good News is handled in distinct ways by the four Evangelists. That is why, for instance, the integrity of each Gospel writer is taken seriously in the Patterns for Readings and in the Lectionaries, rather than being jumbled together in a kind of liturgical stew. For instance, the Birth Narratives of Matthew and Luke have different things to say about the Incarnation, and many modern congregations, already familiar with the sum of the parts, welcome having this distinctiveness preached to them.

Secondly, *The Promise of His Glory* does not rely on a series of ancient symbolic rites that originated in the Mediterranean and belong unmistakably (like Ashing, the Palm Procession, Footwashing, and the ceremonies of the Cross) to one tradition. The new book is more comprehensive, for its sources are many and varied, using material from the Eastern as well as the Western Church, and from the reformed as well as the catholic tradition. It is a more innovative collection – and that should provide encouragement to those who regard the productions of liturgical experts as no more than rather fundamentalist exercises in liturgical archaeology!

Thirdly, there is the Christmas which begins with the tinsel-clad shopping days of mid October. This 'winter season' is a relatively new arrival on the scene of the nation's commercial life, and for that reason Christmas has to live at times a double existence. It is solemnly celebrated on the correct day by devout congregations, and yet in practice celebrated in anticipation by millions of people, many on the fringe of religious observance, at carol services and concerts, in schools and civic centres. Many people feel that Christmas is theirs, and not just the Church's, and this sense of ownership is true not only of Christmas: it is true of observances like those of Remembrance Sunday and the New Year, which have a vigorous and continuing existence as part of England's national life.

Fourthly, unlike the Easter cycle, this 'winter season' does not have a single liturgical shape which emerged fairly uniformly in the early centuries, and which the mainstream churches have retained. Nowhere in the Christian past or present is there the kind of consensus around the celebrations of Advent, Christmas and Epiphanytide which surrounds the keeping of Lent, Holy Week and Eastertide. Those who were brought up on the Prayer Book, and then became used to the alternatives offered in the ASB, may be surprised at the wide range of provision. But history does not finally settle even such questions as the relationship between Christmas and Epiphany, let alone the length and significance of Advent. If the past is a bit of a mess, then we do it (and ourselves) a disservice if we expect the present to be uniformly neat and predictable.

In the face of this different kind of world, *The Promise of His Glory* is offered as a new kind of resource to congregations of all traditions in the Church. Some of the material can be used exactly as it is printed, and for most major celebrations we have provided a complete rite. But there are many instances where worship will be more effective if the material is pondered carefully and then adapted to local circumstances.

But however these services and prayers are adapted, it is important to note that the basic provisions reflect the meaning of God's 'promise' as they unfold. Undergirding the whole scheme is the Service of Light, which is bound to have more impact in our own culture during the winter period of shortened days. As a protest, perhaps, against the mechanical provision of uniform illumination, the lighting of living flames and the sharing of candlelight in the darkness of the world has become a universal symbol of our longing for the promised Christ, the Light of the World.

+ COLIN WINTON:
Chairman of the Liturgical Commission

INTRODUCTORY OUTLINE

ALL SAINTS' TIDE

All Saints' tide provides an opportunity to turn away from the ordinary time of the Church year in an autumn month that has its own secular echoes of death and remembering. Sanctity is – in spite of everything – accessible to people, not as a nice idea but as a reality pumped into the blood-stream of the human race by God's action in the lives of his saints. The dark side of that confident rejoicing in our fellowship with the saints is the Church mourning her departed and commending them in faith and trust to God. This commemoration is a proper corrective to the rather forced jollity which is sometimes substituted for a sober confidence in the power of God alone to bring life out of death, light in our darkness. While we rejoice in the heroic example of the saints, we feel the loss of those we know and love, and many people are helped by holding together these two commemorations.

ADVENT

Advent emerges pre-echoed by the 'Sundays of the Kingdom'. *The Promise of His Glory* envisages a different pattern here from that of the ASB calendar, a pattern that is both closer to ancient tradition and at the same time more tuned to the feel of November, with its commemorations of the past amid falling leaves and fading light. Much of Advent – the season of watching and waiting – has been engulfed by the anticipation of Christmas, and in recent years it has seemed a little like a clerical killjoy, frowning at society. To make the Kingship of Christ the focus of some Sundays before Advent links the theme of his universal kingdom with the more nationalistic commemorations of Remembrancetide, and provides for Advent a more resonant context than simply 'preparing for Christmas'. So Advent can now stand out more clearly by challenging, at the same time as valuing, the world Christ comes to judge and save.

CHRISTMAS

Christmas comes with a rich provision of services and prayers, and a careful selection of biblical passages. But we recognize that worship is not confined to the church building – it takes place at home and school, and in the civic centre and superstore as well. In both Advent and Christmastide good use can be made of the Service of Light, the Advent Wreath and the Jesse Tree, along with the Christingle Service: these all find a place as more recent interpretations of the glory we glimpse.

EPIPHANY

In many places Epiphany is a festival that has become increasingly important, and marks a new start after the Christmas break. The highlight of this feast is the Epiphany rite which brings together the Magi, the Baptism of Christ, and the Miracle of Cana – three vivid signs that turn the Church towards reflecting upon the consequences of Christ's coming among us. Epiphanytide provides the opportunity to unpack what this means, reflecting on his ministry and ours, for the Church's mission to the whole world.

CANDLEMAS

Candlemas has been a passenger; a feast in name, but a neglected one. And yet it contains one of the most dramatic Gospel readings in the entire Christmas season. Since the Service of Light is intended to be often repeated as a thread which runs through this whole seasonal reflection on the promise and coming of God's glory, the sharing of the light on this occasion needs extra emphasis. This is just what the Candlemas services do, asking the poignant question, 'Is this day not only the end of Christmas, but also a turning towards Lent?'

APPENDIX: THE CALENDAR AND LECTIONARIES

Basic to our understanding of the provision in *The Promise of His Glory* is a calendrical scheme which is based on an evaluation of the season as a whole. Within the varying patterns in the observance of Advent and Christmastide, the most consistent and widespread tradition includes an extension of the Advent themes back into the period before Advent Sunday, and of the wider revelation themes in Epiphanytide. There has been a careful evaluation of and reflection on the ASB Lectionary and the Calendar which accompanies it. Our proposals, however, which provide a unified approach to the season as a whole, make some important suggestions for the structure, as follows:

ALL SAINTS' TIDE	including an optional Sunday observance and the Commemoration of the Faithful Departed.
A SEASON 'OF THE KINGDOM'	including Remembrancetide and providing a link between All Saints' tide and Advent.
ADVENT	with a change of pace for the last two Sundays.
CHRISTMASTIDE	with a full provision for the twelve days.
EPIPHANYTIDE	with the Baptism of Christ beginning a season focused on turning outwards, and culminating in Candlemas.

Our Lectionary suggestions provide two 'routes' that depart somewhat from the ASB pattern. The first scheme is based on the three-year Roman Catholic Lectionary used worldwide, and in several provinces of the Anglican Communion. (In North America all the mainstream churches use it.) This gives a richer diet of Scripture and avoids a contrived thematic approach by concentrating on one Gospel in each year. The second scheme is more innovative still, giving congregations the opportunity to study books of the Bible regarded as particularly appropriate sequentially, Sunday by Sunday.

'When God chooses to exist within the terms of our environment, a man is what he becomes' (J A Baker, *The Foolishness of God*, p.331). *The Promise of His Glory* is intended to give the Church at large ample opportunity to celebrate that wonderful and yet demanding mystery at a time of the year when the Gospel is in danger of being diminished by trivialization. It is the hope of the Liturgical Commission that God's coming may be celebrated vigorously and reflectively in Bible reading and music, in symbol and movement, prayer and praise, with the help of this publication.

I
THE SERVICE OF LIGHT

A. INTRODUCTION

A living flame is a potent symbol of the victory over darkness, and services involving light have continued to grow in popularity; we should recognize here a deep instinct which has kept hold of an important symbol.

The poet and priest George Herbert records this blessing at the lighting of the lamps as an old custom: 'Praise God who sends us the light of heaven', and he adds 'The parson likes this very much. Light is a great blessing, and as great as food, for which we give thanks.'

It is this tradition – the marking of an important turning point in the day – which indicates the origin of the Service of Light. In the Jewish tradition, a blessing over the lighted candles begins the Sabbath worship on a Friday evening. This in turn echoes the ceremonial lighting of the lamps in the Jerusalem temple morning and evening (Exodus 30. 7-8). This is the tradition out of which the Paschal Candle arose, and not vice versa. The Service of Light was primarily a thanksgiving for the light, and a celebration of Christ our light, performed at home as well as in church. While the theme of resurrection was much more associated with the Morning Office, the Service of Light has been the traditional way of starting Evening Prayer. Indeed such a blessing of God over the evening lamps is one of the earliest strands of Christian liturgical prayer, and may have been the evening prayer of the people of God in the early centuries. This tradition survived vestigially in the Book of Common Prayer in the Third Collect, 'Lighten our darkness, we beseech thee, O Lord; and by thy great mercy . . .' And the early tradition has been picked up again in the ASB with the use of the ancient hymn 'O gladsome light'.

The Service of Light which follows is based on this ancient use, and may precede Evening Prayer, which then might appropriately begin with the Psalms for the Day; or it may begin a service of prayer and praise, with readings and music, as in a traditional Carol Service; or a pattern of readings and periods of silent prayer, concluded by a Collect, as in a traditional Vigil Service; ending in each case with the Proclamation of the Gospel of the festival being celebrated, together with a Canticle or hymn of praise, the concluding Collect and the Dismissal.

The use of silence is an important ingredient in a Vigil Service, or a more reflective rite. Periods of silence should follow the Readings and precede the Psalm or Collect.

These elements – the Service of Light, the meditative Word Service, and the concluding Gospel Proclamation and Dismissal – may be used in any appropriate combination.

The Service of Light is particularly appropriate in Advent and Epiphanytide, and on the vigils of major festivals, such as All Saints and Candlemas, or for some other specific cause. The Word Service may take a variety of forms, and a number of outlines are suggested here.

The concluding Gospel Proclamation is particularly appropriate, whether the Service of Light has been used or not, at Vigils and with Evening Prayer on Saturdays throughout the year as part of the Church's preparation for Sunday.

The Service of Light, followed by the Sunday Readings concluding with the Gospel, a Canticle, and a Collect, makes a suitable service for Saturday evening in private homes. When a meal follows, a blessing over food may conclude the service.

The Service of Light, followed by a number of Readings interspersed with chants, responsories, and canticles or hymns, and concluding with the Proclamation of the Gospel, is appropriately followed by Baptism and Confirmation, especially at All Saints' tide, in Advent, at the Epiphany, and at the Vigil of the Feast of the Baptism of the Lord. Such a Vigil Service may also form an appropriate introduction to a Vigil Eucharist.

B. THE SERVICE OF LIGHT

NOTES

1 **The President** While the president of the rite may be either a priest or a deacon, there is a long tradition of the deacon making the Acclamation of Light, as well as reading the Gospel. 'President' and 'Minister' indicate these complementary roles.

2 **The Light** This may be a large candle (especially in Eastertide, the Paschal Candle), or a cluster of candles, set near the Lectern, or the candles on the Holy Table. On certain occasions, it may be appropriate for the congregation to hold candles.

3 The hymn 'O gladsome light' (section 3) may be sung either as the lights are lit, or after the Acclamation (section 4) as a corporate response.

ORDER OF SERVICE

1 In the darkness, the president may say

Either

The Lord is my light and my salvation.
The Lord is my light and my salvation.
The Lord is the strength of my life.
The Lord is my light and my salvation.
Glory be to the Father, and to the Son,
  and to the Holy Spirit.
The Lord is my light and my salvation.

or one of the following.

You, O Lord, are my lamp:
You turn our darkness into light.   *Psalm 18. 28*

With you, O Lord, is the well of life:
In your light shall we see light.   *Psalm 36. 9*

Your word is a lantern to my feet
and a light upon our path.   *Psalm 119. 105*

In the beginning was the Word,
and the Word was with God, and the Word was God.
He was in the beginning with God;
all things were made through him,
and without him was not anything made that was made.
In him was life, and the life was the light of men.
The light shines in the darkness,
and the darkness has not overcome it.   *John 1. 1-5*

Give thanks to the Father,
who has delivered us from the dominion of darkness
and made us partakers
in the inheritance of the saints in light.   *Colossians 1. 12-13*

2   A minister brings in a light, and says

Jesus Christ is the Light of the world:
a light no darkness can quench.

3   While the candles are lit and the light is shared, this or another
hymn may be sung.

> **O gladsome light of the holy glory of the immortal
>   Father,**
> **heavenly, holy, blessed Jesus Christ.**
>
> **Now that we have come to the setting of the sun
> and behold the light of evening,
> we praise you, Father, Son, and Holy Spirit.**
>
> **For it is right at all times to worship you
>   with voices of praise,
> O Son of God and giver of life.
> Therefore all the world glorifies you.**   *1†*

See Appendix, p.43, for alternative translations and other
suitable hymns and chants.

4   *Minister*   Let us give thanks to the Lord our God.
          He is worthy of all thanksgiving and praise.

---

† Numbers in right-hand margin refer to Sources and Acknowledgements
(pp.416-419).

a   *At All Saints' Tide*
    Blessed are you, Lord our God, King of the universe:
    to you be glory and praise for ever!
    We rejoice in the glorious splendour of your majesty.
    For you have given us a share
    in the inheritance of the saints in light.
    In the darkness of this passing age
    your saints proclaim the glory of your kingdom.
    Chosen as lights in the world,
    they surround our steps as we journey on
    towards that eternal city of light
    where they sing the triumphal song.
    Open our eyes to behold your glory
    and free our tongues to join our song with theirs:
    For great and wonderful are your deeds,
        O Lord God Almighty;
    just and true are your ways, O king of the ages.
    To you be praise and glory, now and for ever.   **Amen.**

b   *In Advent*
    Blessed are you, Lord our God, King of the universe,
    eternal creator of light and darkness.
    In this season of Advent,
    when the sun's light is swallowed up
    by the growing darkness of the night,
    you renew your promise to reveal among us
    the splendour of your glory,
    made flesh and visible to us in Jesus Christ your Son.
    Through the prophets
    you teach us to hope for his reign of peace.
    Through the outpouring of his Spirit,
    you open our blindness to the glory of his presence.
    Strengthen us in our weakness;
    support us in our stumbling efforts to do your will,
    and free our tongues to sing your praise.
    For to you all honour and blessing are due,
    now and for ever.   **Amen.**

From *Praise God in Song*, © GIA Publications Inc.   2

13

c   *In Advent*

Blessed are you, Lord our God, King of the universe,
eternal creator of day and night.
Now, as darkness is falling,
hear the prayer of your faithful people.
Wash away our transgressions,
cleanse us by your refining fire,
and make us temples of your Holy Spirit.
May we live in watchfulness
as we wait for the coming of your Son Jesus Christ,
who shall judge the world and all its works.
Rouse us from the sleep of sin
and make us ready to enter your kingdom
where songs of praise for ever sound.
For you are the true light, who lightens everyone,
and the new heavens and the new earth
join to sing your praise
now and for evermore.   **Amen.**

d   *For Christmas*

Blessed are you, Lord our God, Judge of all the earth:
your word endures for ever in heaven.
Yet in the stillness of midnight
the almighty Word
leapt down from his royal throne
and was born in the likeness of men.
In him, the Word made flesh, was life,
a life that is the light of men:
it brings to light what is hidden in dark
and the darkness will never quench it.
Rejoice in the light, you people of God.
For by his light shall the nations walk
till the whole earth is filled with his praise
and every tongue confesses that Jesus Christ is Lord
to the glory of God the Father.   **Amen.**   *3*

e   *For Christmas*

Blessed are you, Lord our God, King of the universe:
to you be glory and praise for ever!
In the beginning you laid the foundation of the earth,
and the heavens are the work of your hands;
yet in your tender compassion
you visit us with your salvation.
For when the time had fully come
you sent forth your Son, born of a woman,
to bring light to those who sit in darkness,
who walk in the shadow of death.
He is the first-born of all creation,
the offspring of David;
he is the bright and morning star.
In him the light shines on;
the darkness is put to flight.
So we your people, beholding your glory,
join the praises of earth and heaven
as all creation shouts for joy:
Glory to God, glory to God,
glory to God in the highest.   **Amen.**

f   *For the New Year*

Blessed are you, Lord our God, King of the universe:
to you be glory and praise for ever!
You give the sun for light by day,
the moon and the stars to govern the night;
in the changing year, your light never fails.
At the beginning you laid the foundations of the earth,
and the starry heavens are the work of your hand:
they shall perish, worn out like a garment;
but you are the same, and your years will never fail.
Teach us to number our days;
receive us into your merciful protection,
that we may walk in the light,
and be led to the perfect vision of glory,
where with the saints of every age and nation
you live and reign in majesty for ever.   **Amen.**

g   *At Epiphany*

Blessed are you, Lord our God, King of the universe:
to you be glory and praise for ever!
From the rising of the sun to its setting
your name is proclaimed in all the world.
When the time had fully come,
your unconquered Sun of Righteousness
in whom the fullness of your glory dwells
called us out of darkness into his own marvellous light.
You gave him as a light to the nations,
and by the outpouring of his anointing Spirit
you establish us as your royal priesthood.
According to the riches of his glory
may we be strengthened through his Spirit
that, rooted and grounded in love,
our lives may be a witness to your truth,
and our lips never cease to proclaim your praise,
now and for ever.   **Amen.**

3

h   *In Epiphanytide*

Blessed are you, Sovereign God, gentle and merciful:
to you be glory and praise for ever!
You dwell in unapproachable light
but make visible the mystery of your presence.
Your Spirit brooded over the chaos;
your Word brought light out of darkness;
your wisdom delights in the created world;
daily your Spirit renews the face of the earth.
When we turned away to darkness and chaos,
like a mother you would not forsake us.
You cried out like a woman in labour
and rejoiced to bring forth a new people.
In your Son you delivered us from darkness
to the gentle rule of your love.
Your Spirit brings light into our darkness;
through your kindness healing dawns upon the world;
your grace gives joy to those who walk in shadow;
your light fills our life with song.
Blessed are you, Sovereign God, light of the world.
Amen.

i *At Candlemas*

Blessed are you, Lord our God, King of the universe:
to you be glory and praise for ever!
You are our light and our salvation
and we your children wait for your loving kindness
in the midst of your temple.
In your Christ, born of the Virgin Mary,
there has sprung up a light for the righteous
and joyful gladness for those who are faithful.
As we, like Simeon and Anna, welcome him with joy,
presented before us as light of all the world,
may we be filled with his Spirit and made a living temple
to the praise and glory of your holy name.
And, as we join our praises with theirs,
grant us a quiet night and a perfect end
now and for ever. **Amen.**

j *For the Blessed Virgin Mary*

Blessed are you, Lord our God, King of the universe:
to you be glory and praise for ever!
In the greatness of your mercy you chose the Virgin Mary
to be the mother of your only Son.
In her obedience the day of our redemption dawned
when by the overshadowing of your Holy Spirit
he took our flesh and dwelt in the darkness of her womb.
In her your glory shines as in the burning bush,
and so we call her blessed with every generation.
With her we rejoice in your salvation
and ponder in our hearts the mystery of your love.
May we bear with her the piercing sword of sorrow
in hope that we like her may share the joy of heaven.
As now we join our praise with hers, blessed among all
    women,
create in us a heart of love obedient to your will,
for you are Lord and you are our God for ever. **Amen.**

k   *General*

Blessed are you, Lord our God, King of the universe!
Your word brings on the dusk at evening,
your wisdom creates both night and day.
You determine the cycles of time,
arrange the succession of seasons,
and establish the stars in their heavenly courses.
Lord of the starry hosts is your name.
Living and eternal God, rule over us always.
Blessed be the Lord, whose word makes evening fall.
Amen.

From *Praise God in Song*, © GIA Publications Inc.   2

l   *General*

Blessed are you, Sovereign God, source of light,
giver of all things good!
In your presence wisdom has prepared a feast;
she calls the foolish to leave the way of darkness;
she welcomes us with truth and goodness.
In Jesus your light has shone out;
his cross has brought peace to the sinful.
Your Spirit has opened our hearts;
with all the saints we share your light.
Refuge of the weary, hope of the dying,
blessed are you, Sovereign God, light in the darkness.
Amen.

5   If desired, one of the following PSALMS may be used.

PSALM 141

I call to you, O Lord; come to me quickly:
hear my voice when I cry to you.

Let my prayer rise before you as incense:
the lifting up of my hands as the evening sacrifice.

Set a guard over my mouth, O Lord:
keep watch over the door of my lips.

Let not my heart be turned towards evil:
to busy myself with those who do wickedly.

Let my prayer rise before you as incense.

To you, Lord God, I turn my eyes:
I take refuge in you; do not leave me defenceless.

Glory to the Father, and to the Son, and to the Holy Spirit:
as it was in the beginning, is now,
and shall be for ever.   **Amen.**

Let my prayer rise before you as incense.

President   As our penitent prayer rises before you,
                   O Lord,
               so may your mercy come down upon us
               to cleanse our hearts and set us free
               to sing your praise, now and for ever.   **Amen.**

or
PSALM 134

Come, bless the Lord, all you servants of the Lord:
who stand by night in the house of the Lord.

**Lift up your hands in the holy place
and bless the Lord.**

May the Lord bless you from Zion
he who made heaven and earth.

Lift up your hands and bless the Lord.

Glory to the Father, and to the Son, and to the Holy Spirit:
as it was in the beginning, is now,
and shall be for ever.   **Amen.**

Lift up your hands and bless the Lord.

President   May God, to whom we lift our hearts,
               kindle in us the fire of his love.   **Amen.**

6   If neither of the foregoing Psalms is used, the president
     concludes the Service of Light with one of the following.

19

(1)   May God, who gives us the light of his grace,
grant that we may come to behold
    the light of his glory.   **Amen.**

(2)   Grant us your light, O Lord,
that the darkness of our hearts being done away,
we may be brought at the last
    to the light which is Christ.   **Amen.**   *47*

(3)   Eternal Light, shine into our hearts;
eternal Goodness, deliver us from evil;
eternal Power, be our support;
eternal Wisdom, scatter the darkness of our
    ignorance;
eternal Pity, have mercy on us;
that with all our heart and mind and strength
    we may seek your face
    and be brought by your infinite mercy
    to your holy presence;
through Jesus Christ our Lord.   **Amen.**   *4*

(4)   Yours is the day, O Lord, and yours is the night.
Let Christ the Sun of Righteousness abide
    in our hearts
to drive away the darkness of evil thoughts:
for he is our God for ever and ever.   **Amen.**   *48*

7   Where Evening Prayer follows, it may appropriately begin with the Psalm(s) of the day.

At a Vigil Service or Carol Service the first Reading follows at once (see the following section, C, Patterns for Readings).

C. PATTERNS FOR READINGS, WITH PSALMS, CANTICLES, AND COLLECTS

1 ALL SAINTS

1	Genesis 12. 1-8 Psalm 113	The Call of Abraham
2	Daniel 6. (1-15) 16-23 Psalm 116. 1-9	Daniel is delivered from the lions' den.
3	Ecclesiasticus 44. 1-10, 13-14 *or* Isaiah 56. 3-8 Psalm 148	Let us now praise famous men.
4	Isaiah 43. 1-7 Psalm 91. 9-16	I have called you by name, you are mine.
5	Hebrews 11. 32 – 12. 2 Canticle: 35	Surrounded by so great a cloud of witnesses. A Song of the Redeemed
6	Revelation 21. 1-4, 22 – 22. 5	The Jerusalem above

CANTICLE: 38   A Song of the Lamb

GOSPEL: Matthew 5. 1-11   The Beatitudes

COLLECT
Almighty and everlasting God,
you have kindled the flame of love
   in the hearts of the saints.
Grant to us the same faith and power of love,
that, as we rejoice in their triumphs,
we may be sustained by their example and fellowship;
through Christ our Lord.   *4*

When this pattern is used for a Vigil for an apostle or other saint, the Collect on p.38 is used.

2 A VIGIL FOR PRISONERS AND THOSE WHO SIT IN DARKNESS

1	Isaiah 43. 1-7 Psalm 46. 1-4, 11-12	I have called you by name, you are mine.
2	Psalm 107. 1-3, 10-16 Psalm 130	When they cried to the Lord, he delivered them from their distress.
3	Isaiah 61. 1-3, 11 Psalm 146	The spirit of the Lord is upon me.
4	Isaiah 42. 5-9 Psalm 43	Bring the prisoners out of darkness.
5	Isaiah 62. 1-7, 10-12 *or* Micah 4. 1-5 Psalm 85. 1-7	You shall be called Sought Out, a city not forsaken. They shall beat their swords into ploughshares.
6	Ephesians 2. 11-22	He is our peace, who has made us one.

CANTICLE: 28   Song of Zechariah (Benedictus)

GOSPEL: Matthew 25. 31-end I was in prison and you visited me.

COLLECT
God of tender compassion and mercy,
whose Son is the morning star
and the sun of righteousness;
let him shine in the darkness
and shadows of this world,
that we may serve you in freedom and peace;
through Jesus Christ our Lord.

3 ADVENT 1: THE KING AND HIS KINGDOM (Matthean)

1	Zechariah 9. 9-10	Rejoice greatly, for your king comes.
	Psalm 72. 1-8	
2	Jeremiah 23. 5-6	I will raise up for David a righteous branch.
	Psalm 21. 1-7	
3	Psalm 118. 19-29	Open me the gates of righteousness.
	Psalm 24	
4	Isaiah 9. 2, 6-7	The people that walked in darkness have seen a great light.
	Psalm 28. 7-10	
5	Isaiah 7. 10-15	Behold, a virgin shall conceive and bear a son.
	Psalm 132. 10-16	
6	Romans 12. 1-2; 13. (8) 11-14	Salvation is nearer to us now than when we first believed.

CANTICLE: 41   Song of the Church (Te Deum)

GOSPEL: *In Advent*   Matthew 25. 1-13
             At Christmas   Matthew 1. 18-25

COLLECT
O Lord,
you have set before us the great hope
   that your kingdom shall come on earth,
and have taught us to pray for its coming:
give us grace to discern
   the signs of its dawning,
and to work for the perfect day
when your will shall be done on earth
   as it is in heaven;
through Jesus Christ our Lord.   4

4   ADVENT 2: LOOKING FOR THE LIGHT

1	Genesis 1. 1-5	And God said: Let there be light.
	Psalm 136. 1-9	
2	Psalm 13	Give light to my eyes, lest I sleep in death.
	Psalm 43	
3	Isaiah 45. 2-8	I form light and create darkness.
	Psalm 97	
4	Baruch 4. 36 – 5. 9	Look to the east.
	or Isaiah 60. 1-5a	
	Psalm 84. 8-12	
5	Isaiah 9. 2-3, 6-7	The people that walked in darkness have seen a great light.
	Psalm 36. 5-10	
6	1 Thessalonians 5. 1-11, 23-24	You are not in darkness, brethren, for you are all sons of light.
	CANTICLE: 12	Song of the New Jerusalem
	GOSPEL: Luke 12. 35-40	Let your loins be girded and your lamps burning.
	or	
	John 3. 16-21 etc.	I am the light of the world.

COLLECT
Lord our God,
on the first day of creation
you made the light that scatters all darkness.
Let Christ, the light of lights,
hidden from all eternity,
shine at last on your people
and free us from the darkness of sin.
Fill our lives with joy
as we go out to welcome your Son at his coming.
We ask this in the name of Jesus the Lord.

5   ADVENT 3: THE FORERUNNER

1	Exodus 3. 1-6 Psalm 99	The burning bush
2	Isaiah 40. 1-11 Psalm 103. 8-17	A voice cries in the wilderness: Prepare the way of the Lord.
3	Isaiah 52. 7-10 Psalm 147. 1-6	How beautiful on the mountains
4	Malachi 3. 1-5 Psalm 97	Behold, I send my messenger to prepare the way before me.
5	Isaiah 61. 1-3, 11 Psalm 146	The spirit of the Lord is upon me.
6	Philippians 4. 4-7	The Lord is at hand.
	CANCICLE: 28	Song of Zechariah (Benedictus)
	GOSPEL: Luke 1. 5-25	The birth of John the Baptist is foretold.

COLLECT
Almighty and everlasting God,
whose servant and prophet John the Baptist
bore witness to the truth
   as a burning and shining lamp:
Lead us to bear witness to your Son,
who is the eternal light and truth,
and lives and reigns with you and the Holy Spirit,
now and for ever.

6 CHRISTMASTIDE 1 : GOOD NEWS FOR THE POOR (Lukan)

These Readings are also suitable on Christmas Eve.

1	Micah 5. 2-4	Bethlehem, from you shall come forth a ruler.
	Psalm 89. 1-4	
2	Isaiah 35	The wilderness and the dry land shall be glad.
	Psalm 126	
3	Haggai 2. 5b-9	I will fill this house with splendour.
	or	
	Jeremiah 22. 13-16; 23. 5-6	Your Father judged the cause of the poor.
	Psalm 96. 7-12	
4	Isaiah 11. 1-9	There shall come forth a shoot from the stump of Jesse.
	Psalm 132. 10-16	
5	Isaiah 52. 7-10	How beautiful on the mountains
	or	
	Isaiah 40. 1-11	A voice cries in the wilderness: Prepare the way of the Lord.
	Psalm 85. 8-13	
6	Philippians 2. 5-11	He took the form of a servant.
	CANTICLE: 29	Song of Mary (Magnificat)
	GOSPEL: *In Advent*	
	Luke 1. 26-38	The Annunciation
	At Christmas	
	Luke 2.1-20	The Birth of Jesus

COLLECT
Almighty God,
who by your grace called the blessed Virgin Mary
and opened for all the door
of infinite mercy and eternal light:
Fill us with your grace,
that, through our obedience and faith,
the world may rejoice in your mercy
and walk in your light;
for the sake of Jesus Christ our Lord.

7   CHRISTMASTIDE 2: The Gospel of Luke

In Christmastide Readings 1 and 4 might be omitted. This pattern of readings might also be used before Christmas, when Readings 6 and 7 (and possibly 5) might be omitted. But there is virtue in reading the whole infancy narrative with hymns, songs, and canticles interspersed.

1	Luke 1. 5-25	The Annunciation to Zechariah
2	Luke 1. 26-38	The Annunciation to Mary
3	Luke 1. 39-56 *or* 39-49 *if The Song of Mary is used as a Canticle*	The Visit of Mary to Elizabeth
4	Luke 1. 57-80 *or* 57-67 *if The Song of Zechariah is used as a Canticle*	The Birth of John
5	Luke 2. 1-7	The Birth of Jesus
6	Luke 2. 8-20	The Shepherds
7	Luke 2. 22-40 *or* 22-28 *if The Song of Simeon is used as a Canticle*	The Presentation in the Temple
	Canticle: 28	Song of Zechariah (Benedictus)
	Canticle: 29	Song of Mary (Magnificat)
	Canticle: 30	Song of Simeon (Nunc Dimittis)

FINAL READING: Titus 2. 11-14; 3. 3-7

COLLECT
Almighty and everlasting God,
you have stooped to raise fallen humanity
through the child-bearing of blessed Mary.
Grant that we who have seen your glory
     revealed in our human nature,
and your love made perfect in our weakness,
may daily be renewed in your image,
and conformed to the pattern of your Son,
Jesus Christ our Lord.   4

8 CHRISTMAS EVE
PATTERN FROM KING'S COLLEGE, CAMBRIDGE

This pattern is traditionally introduced by the Bidding Prayer below.

1	Genesis 3. 8-15	The Fall
2	Genesis 22. 1-19 or 22. 15-18	The Promise to Abraham
3	Isaiah 9. 2, 6-7	The Prophecy of the Messiah's Birth
4	Isaiah 11. 1-9	The Prophecy of the Messiah's Kingdom of Peace
	or Micah 5. 2-4	The Messiah will be born in Bethlehem.
5	Luke 1. 26-38	The Annunciation to Mary
	or Isaiah 60. 1-6, 19	The Coming of the Glory of the Lord
6	Matthew 1. 18-23	The Birth of Emmanuel
	or Luke 2. 1-7	The Birth of Jesus
7	Luke 2. 8-16	The Shepherds go to the Manger.
8	Matthew 2. 1-11	The Magi are led by the star to Jesus.
9	John 1. 1-14	The Incarnation of the Word of God

Beloved in Christ, be it this Christmastide our care and delight to hear again the message of the angels, and in heart and mind to go even unto Bethlehem and see this thing which is come to pass, and the Babe lying in a manger.

Therefore let us read and mark in Holy Scripture the tale of the loving purposes of God from the first days of our disobedience unto the glorious Redemption brought us by this Holy Child.

But first, let us pray for the needs of the whole world; for peace on earth and goodwill among all his people; for unity and brotherhood within the Church he came to build, and especially in this city (town, village) of . . .

and diocese of . . .

And because this of all things would rejoice his heart, let us remember, in his name, the poor and helpless, the cold, the hungry, and the oppressed; the sick and them that mourn, the lonely and the unloved, the aged and the little children; all those who know not the Lord Jesus, or who love him not, or who by sin have grieved his heart of love.

Lastly, let us remember before God all those who rejoice with us, but upon another shore, and in a greater light, that multitude which no man can number, whose hope was in the Word made flesh, and with whom in the Lord Jesus we are for ever one.

These prayers and praises let us humbly offer up to the Throne of Heaven, in the words which Christ himself hath taught us:

> **Our Father,**
> **which art in heaven,**
> **hallowed be thy name;**
> **thy kingdom come;**
> **thy will be done;**
> **in earth as it is in heaven.**
> **Give us this day our daily bread.**
> **And forgive us our trespasses,**
> **as we forgive them that trespass against us.**
> **And lead us not into temptation;**
> **but deliver us from evil;**
> **for thine is the kingdom,**
> **the power and the glory,**
> **for ever and ever. Amen.**

May the Almighty God bless us with his grace; Christ give us the joys of everlasting life, and unto the fellowship of the citizens above may the King of Angels bring us all.   **Amen.**

CONCLUSION
The Lord be with you
and with thy spirit.

COLLECT

O God, who makest us glad with the yearly remembrance
of the birth of thy only Son Jesus Christ.
Grant that, as we joyfully receive him for our Redeemer,
so we may with sure confidence behold him
when he shall come to be our judge;
who liveth and reigneth with thee and the Holy Ghost,
one God, world without end.   **Amen.**   6

BLESSING

May he who by his incarnation gathered into one
things earthly and heavenly,
bestow upon you the fullness
   of inward peace and goodwill;
and the blessing of God almighty,
the Father, the Son, and the Holy Ghost,
be upon you and remain with you always.   **Amen.**

9   CHRISTMASTIDE 2 : THE NEW CREATION (**Johannine**)

This pattern may also be used appropriately at other times of
the year to prepare for a celebration of the creation.

1	Proverbs 8. 22-31	The Lord created me at the beginning of his work.
	Psalm 33. 1-11	
2	Genesis 1. 1-5	In the beginning, the Lord created the heavens and the earth.
	Psalm 19. 1-6	
3	Isaiah 55. 6-11	Seek the Lord while he may be found.
	Psalm 19. 7-14	
4	Isaiah 65. 17-25	Behold, I create new heavens and a new earth.
	Psalm 147. 1-6	
5	Revelation 22. 1-15	The Lord God will be their light.
	Psalm 148	
6	Hebrews 1. 1-12	He reflects the glory of God and bears the very stamp of his nature.

or 1 John 4. 7-14 | Let us love one another, for love is of God.

CANTICLE: 33 | A Song of Redemption

GOSPEL: John 1. 1-14 | In the beginning was the Word.

COLLECT
Almighty God,
you have shed upon us
the new light of your incarnate Word,
giving us gladness in our sorrow,
your presence in our isolation.
Fill our lives with your light
until they overflow with gladness and praise;
through Christ our Lord.   *4*

10 NEW YEAR'S EVE

1 Proverbs 8. 22-31 | The Lord created me at the beginning of his work.

   Psalm 8

2 Ecclesiastes 3. 1-15 | There is a time and a season for all things.

   Psalm 90. 1-11

3 Ecclesiastes 12. 1-8 | Remember now your Creator.
   Psalm 102. 18-28

4 Job 38. 1-21; 42. 1-2, 5-6 | Before the majesty of God, I am dumb.

   Psalm 39

5 Deuteronomy 30. 11-20 | I have set before you life and death . . . therefore choose life.

   Psalm 73. 21-29

6 Revelation 21. 1-14, 22-24 | Behold, I make all things new.

   CANTICLE: 15 | Song of the New Creation

   GOSPEL: John 3. 1-12 | You must be born anew.
            or
            John 8. 50-58 | Before Abraham was, I am.
            or
            John 8. 12-19 | I am the light of the world.

COLLECT
God and Father of our Lord Jesus Christ,
whose years never fail,
and whose mercies are new each returning day:
let the radiance of your Spirit renew our lives,
warming our hearts and giving light to our minds;
that we may pass the coming year
in joyful obedience and firm faith;
through him who is the beginning and the end,   *4*
your Son Christ our Lord.   *56*

11   THE VIGIL OF EPIPHANY

1	Genesis 1. 1-5	Let there be light.
	Psalm 98	
2	Isaiah 60. 1-6, 19	Arise, shine, for your light has come.
	Psalm 67	
3	Isaiah 49. 6b-13	I will give you as a light to the nations.
	Psalm 113	
4	Baruch 4. 36 – 5 end	Look to the East.
	or	
	Isaiah 41. 8-20	You are my servant, I have chosen you.
	Psalm 96	
5	Isaiah 9. 2-3, 6-7	The people that walked in darkness have seen a great light.
	Psalm 145. 1-7	
	or	
	Haggai 2. 5b-9	I will fill this house with splendour.
	Psalm 27. 1-8	
6	Revelation 21. 22 – 22. 5	The temple of the Lamb
	CANTICLE: 34	A Song of God's Grace
	GOSPEL: Matthew 2. 1-12	The Magi at the Birth of Jesus

COLLECT
Almighty and everlasting God,
who drew the Gentiles to your brightness
and made known to them the one who is our true light,
the bright and morning star:
fill the whole world, we pray, with your glory,
and by the radiance of your splendour
reveal yourself to your faithful people;
through Jesus Christ our Lord.

12 VIGIL OF THE BAPTISM OF THE LORD

These Readings are suitable at any Vigil service outside Lent
and Eastertide, in preparation for the celebration of Baptism
and/or Confirmation. On these occasions it is suggested that at
least three Old Testament Readings are used.

1	Genesis 7. 1-5, 11-18; 8. 6-18; 9. 8-13 Psalm 93	Noah and the Flood
2	Isaiah 43. 15-19 Psalm 36	The Lord makes a way in the sea, a path in the mighty waters.
3	1 Samuel 16. 1-13 Psalm 89. 19-29	The anointing of David
4	2 Kings 5. 1-14 Psalm 42. 1-7	The cleansing of Naaman in Jordan
5	Isaiah 55. 1-11 Psalm 19. 7-14	My word shall not return to me empty.
6	Ezekiel 36. 24-28 Psalm 139. 1-11	A new heart and a new spirit
7	Isaiah 42. 1-9 Psalm 40. 1-7	Behold my servant, my chosen in whom my soul delights.
8	Colossians 2. 6-12	You have come to fullness of life in him, who is the head of all.

CANTICLE: 4		Song of Salvation *or* I Saw Water (p.229)
GOSPEL:	Mark 1. 1-11 *or*	The Baptism of Christ
	John 3. 1-12 (21)	Born of water and the Spirit

COLLECT

Almighty God,
who at the baptism of your blessed Son Jesus Christ
   in the river Jordan
revealed the glory of his divine nature:
let the light of his presence shine in our hearts,
and his glory be shown forth in our lives;
through the same Jesus Christ our Lord.   7

13   A VIGIL FOR THE MISSION OF THE CHURCH (1)
IN ADVENT OR AT ST ANDREW'S-TIDE

1	Lamentations 2. 1, 9, 13, 14, 19 *or*	Cry out in the night before the Lord.
	Isaiah 2. 12-21 Psalm 4	God opposes the proud.
2	Isaiah 9. 2a-7 Canticle: 4	Light in the dark
3	Isaiah 11. 1-5 (6-9), 10 Psalm 67	The reign of the Messiah
4	Matthew 4. 12-22 Canticle: 34	Jesus calls the disciples.
5	Acts 8. 26-39 Canticle: 38	Philip meets the Ethiopian eunuch.
6	Acts 17. 22-31	Jesus preached at Athens
	CANTICLE: 29	Song of Mary (Magnificat)
	GOSPEL: Matthew 25. 1-13 *or*	The wise and foolish virgins
	John 1. 35-42	Andrew brings Peter.

COLLECT
Almighty God,
who gave such grace to your *apostles*
that *they* readily obeyed the call of your Son:
give us, who are called by your holy Word,
grace to follow without delay
and to tell the good news of your kingdom;
through Jesus Christ our Lord.   *8* *

or

God of tender compassion and mercy,
whose Son is the morning star
    and the sun of righteousness,
let him shine in the darkness
    and shadows of this world,
that we may serve you in freedom and peace;
through Jesus Christ our Lord.

14 A VIGIL FOR THE MISSION OF THE CHURCH (2)
AT EPIPHANY OR AT THE CONVERSION OF ST PAUL

1	Genesis 49. 8-12	A universal king from Judah
	or	
	Exodus 12. 42-49	Foreigners and the Passover
	Responsory: 1	
	(Ps. 89)	
2	Isaiah 49. 1-6	A light to the nations
	Responsory: 8	
	(Ps. 96)	
3	Acts 9. 1-6	The conversion of St Paul
	Canticle: 8	Song of the Covenant
4	Galatians 2. 11-21	Conflict at the admission of the Gentiles
	Canticle: 13	Song of the Bride
5	Ephesians 3. 1-13	The secret revealed: Gentiles are welcomed
	Canticle: 35	Song of the Redeemed

6	Revelation 21. 9-14, 22-25	The glory of the nations enters the city of God.
	or	
	2 Corinthians 5. 13 – 6. 2	The love of Christ for all
	CANTICLE: 30	The Song of Simeon (Nunc Dimittis)
	GOSPEL: Matthew 2. 1-11	The Visit of the Magi
	or	
	Luke 9. 1-6	Preaching the Gospel

COLLECT

God of hope,
by your Spirit you make known your truth.
Remember the many who, though created in your image,
have known neither you nor the dying of your Son,
their Saviour Jesus Christ;
and grant that by the prayers and labours of your Church
they may be delivered from ignorance and unbelief
and brought to worship you;
through him who is the resurrection and the life of all,
Jesus Christ our Lord.

15 THE VIGIL OF CANDLEMAS

1	Exodus 12. 51; 13. 1-2, 11-16	Consecrate to me all the first-born.
	Responsory: 25	Search the scriptures
2	Leviticus 12. 6-8	The Law of Purification
	Responsory: 26	From the Virgin Mary
3	Isaiah 6. 1-8	I saw the Lord, and his train filled the temple.
	Canticle: 33	A Song of Redemption
4	Isaiah 19. 1-4, 19-21	In that day the Egyptians will worship with sacrifice.
	Responsory: 27	Simeon takes in his arms
5	Haggai 2. 1-9	I will fill this house with splendour.

	Responsory: 28	Zion, adorn the bridal chamber
6	Hebrews 10. 1-10	We have been sanctified through the offering of the body of Jesus Christ.
	Canticle: 30 *or* Psalm 40. 8-13	Song of Simeon (Nunc Dimittis)

GOSPEL: Luke 2. 22-40   The Presentation in the Temple

COLLECT
God our Father,
whose Son was revealed to Simeon and Anna
as the light of the nations, and the glory of Israel:
grant that, guided by your Holy Spirit,
we may live by the light of faith
until we come to the light of glory;
through Christ our Lord.   *8**

16   APOSTLES AND EVANGELISTS

1	Joshua 5. 13-15	What does my Lord bid his servant?
	Psalm 138	
2	Daniel 12. 1b-3	Those who are wise shall shine like the brightness of the firmament.
	Psalm 34. 1-10	
3	Ezekiel 37. 1-14	I will put my spirit within them and they shall live.
	Psalm 104. 26, 29-36	
4	Wisdom 3. 1-9	The souls of the righteous are in the hand of God.
	Psalm 116. 10-18	
5	Isaiah 55. 10-11	My word shall not return to me empty.
	Psalm 19. 7-14	
6	Romans 10. 11-18	How are they to hear without a preacher?

CANTICLE: 41   Song of the Church (Te Deum)

GOSPEL   *In Eastertide*
Matthew 28. 16-20 Go therefore and make disciples.

Out of Eastertide
Luke 9. 1-6, 23-27 He sent them out to preach the kingdom of God and to heal.

In Eastertide
John 20. 1-18   The Resurrection

COLLECT

Almighty God,
who chose your servant *N* to be an *apostle*,
that *he* might bring those who were wandering
   in darkness and error
to the true light and knowledge of your word:
let us so walk in that light,
that we may come at last
   to the light of everlasting life;
through the merits of Jesus Christ
your Son our Lord.

17 THE BLESSED VIRGIN MARY

1	Genesis 3. 1-20 Psalm 25. 1-9	Eve was the mother of all who live.
2	Genesis 21. 1-6a Psalm 113	God has given me cause to laugh.
3	Isaiah 7. 10-14 Psalm 36. 5-10	A young woman shall bear a son.
4	Zephaniah 3. 14-18a	The Holy One is in the midst of you.
	Canticle: 27	Song of Hannah
5	Galatians 4. 1-7	God sent his Son, born of a woman.
	Responsory: 25	Search the scriptures

6   Revelation 11. 19 – 12. 6   A woman adorned with the sun

CANTICLE: 29   The Song of Mary (Magnificat)

GOSPEL   *In Advent*
       Luke 1. 26-38   Behold the handmaid of the Lord.

       After Christmas
       Luke 2. 22-40   A sword will pierce through your own soul also.

       In Lent
       John 19. 25-27   Son, behold your mother.

COLLECT

Almighty God,
who by your grace
   called the blessed Virgin Mary
and opened for all the door
of infinite mercy and eternal light:
fill us with your grace,
that, through our obedience and faith,
the world may rejoice in your mercy
and walk in your light;
for the sake of Jesus Christ our Lord.

Other patterns of readings may be found in, for example,
Carols for Today, edited by Michael Perry.

D. AT THE CONCLUSION:
THE GOSPEL PROCLAMATION

On Saturday evenings at the end of Evening Prayer, at the conclusion of Vigil Services, or at the end of an evening service before any great festival, the Gospel may be proclaimed as follows.

1   ACCLAMATION

The Gospel Reading may be introduced by one of these Acclamations.

We proclaim not ourselves, but Christ Jesus as Lord,
And ourselves as your servants for Jesus' sake.

For the God who said 'Let light shine out of darkness'
has caused his light to shine within us

To give the light of the knowledge of the Glory of God
in the face of Jesus Christ.

or

May the God of our Lord Jesus Christ,
the all-glorious Father,
give us the spiritual powers of wisdom and vision.

May God enlighten our inward eyes
that we may know clearly the hope of our calling,

The wealth of glory his promise holds out for us,
the wondrous majesty with which he clothes us.

2   THE GOSPEL

Hear the words of the Gospel according to . . .
Glory to Christ our Saviour.

After the Gospel

This is the Gospel of Christ.
Praise to Christ our Lord.

3   THE CANTICLE

A HYMN or CANTICLE may be sung.

If THE GOSPEL PROCLAMATION follows a Pattern of Readings at a
Vigil Rite, this may be The Song of Mary (Canticle 29) or a
seasonal Canticle from Chapter VII, or one suggested in the
Pattern of Readings.

The following are especially suitable on Saturday evenings.

1   SONG OF TIMOTHY

Here are words you may trust:

Remember Jesus Christ, risen from the dead.
He is our salvation, our eternal glory.

If we die with him, we shall live with him.
If we endure we shall reign with him.

If we deny him, he will deny us.
If we are faithless, he keeps faith.

For he has broken the power of death
**And brought life and immortality to light
through the Gospel.**

or

2   THE SONG OF THE CHURCH (Te Deum): Canticle 41

3   A SONG OF REDEMPTION (Colossians 1. 15-20):
     Canticle 33

4   THE BEATITUDES (Matthew 5. 3-12a): Canticle 31

5   PSALM 150

4   THE COLLECT

This may be a Collect for the Service of Light (see Chapter VIII, Part A) or the Collect for the Sunday or Feast Day following, as appropriate.

5   THE BLESSING

President   Let us bless the living God:

He was born of the Virgin Mary,
Revealed in his glory,

Worshipped by angels,
Proclaimed among the nations,

Believed in throughout the world,
Exalted to the highest heavens.

Blessed be God, our strength and
    our salvation,
Now and for ever.   Amen.

or

President   Grant us salvation, O Lord:
O Lord, grant us the victory.

Blessed is he who comes
in the name of the Lord:
We bless you from the house of the Lord.

Blessed be God, our light and our salvation,
Now and for ever.   Amen.

or a seasonal Blessing from the provision for the Eucharist may be used.

APPENDIX TO SERVICE OF LIGHT

ALTERNATIVE HYMNS

O gladsome light, O grace	NEH 247 (p.262 below)
or Hail, gladdening light	AMNS 58
or Light of gladness (Christopher Idle)	HTC 277

At All Saints' Tide and for Saints' Days

Glory to thee, O God, for all thy saints in light	AMNS 363
He wants not friends	AMNS 183, NEH 371
Jerusalem thou city blest	NEH 228
Who are these, like stars appearing?	AMNS 323, NEH 231

In Advent

Awake, awake, fling off the night	AMNS 342
Creator of the stars of night	AMNS 23, NEH 1
O come, O come thou dayspring bright (from O come, O come Emmanuel)	AMNS 26, NEH 11
O splendour of God's glory bright (adapted)	EH 52

At Christmas

God of God, Light of Light (v.2 of Adeste fideles)	AMNS 34, NEH 30
Come, thou redeemer of the earth (adapted by Stanbrook)	NEH 19

After Christmas

O Trinity of blessed light	AMNS 5, NEH 54
The race that long in darkness pined	AMNS 52, NEH 57
Brightest and best of the sons of the morning	AMNS 47, NEH 49

General

Light's abode, celestial Salem	AMNS 185, NEH 401
O Christ, who art the light and day	NEH 61
Thou whose almighty word	AMNS 180, NEH 466
Be thou my vision, O Lord of my heart	AMNS 343, NEH 339
Christ whose glory fills the skies	AMNS 4, NEH 234
All praise to thee in light array'd	See over

Taizé Chants

Misericordias Domini
Laudate omnes gentes
In darkest night

Key

EH	English Hymnal	AMNS	Hymns Ancient and Modern New Standard
NEH	New English Hymnal	HTC	Hymns for Today's Church

SONGS AND CHORUSES

All praise to thee, in light array'd
Who light thy dwelling-place hast made:
A boundless ocean of bright beams
From thy all-glorious Godhead streams.

Bless'd angels, while we silent lie,
You hallelujahs sing on high;
You joyful hymn the Ever-blest
Before the throne, and never rest.

I with your choir celestial join
In off'ring up a hymn divine;
With you in heaven I hope to dwell,
And bid the night and world farewell.

My soul, when I shake off this dust,
Lord, in thy arms I will entrust;
O make me thy peculiar care,
Some mansion for my soul prepare.

O may I always ready stand,
With my lamp burning in my hand!
May I in sight of heaven rejoice,
Whene'er I hear the bridegroom's voice.

Shine on me, Lord, new life impart,
Fresh ardours kindle in my heart;
One ray of thy all-quick'ning light
Dispels the sloth and clouds of night.

Praise God, from whom all blessings flow,
Praise him, all creatures here below;
Praise him above, ye heav'nly host,
Praise Father, Son, and Holy Ghost.

Thomas Ken

II
ALL SAINTS' TIDE

A. INTRODUCTION

The period around All Saints' Day directs the thoughts of
Christians towards 'the communion of saints, the forgiveness of
sins and the life everlasting'. We have included provision for this
season in *The Promise of His Glory*, partly for the practical
reason that it falls within the period of the year we are covering
and has implications for the calendar in the pre-Advent period,
but mainly because there is an important theological connection
between our celebration of the saints and our reflection on God's
judgement on us. In other words, All Saints' and Advent belong
together, and the one informs the other.

While many people think of the saints as examples of 'virtuous
and godly living', this hardly does justice to the biblical insight
that in our pilgrimage through this world 'we are surrounded by
so great a cloud of witnesses'. Sanctity is not so much about hero-
worship as about accessibility; the saints are the real men and
women of every age in whose lives we can glimpse heaven in our
midst. They are our partners in prayer:

> Before thy throne we daily meet
> As joint-petitioners to thee;
> In spirit each the other greet,
> And shall again each other see.   *(Richard Baxter)*

But there is a dark side to our standing before the throne of God.
While we are called to be saints, we know ourselves to be sinners.
We have tried to build on that and to make All Saints' Day the
turning point from the 'green season' of Pentecost to the darker
mood of the Commemoration of the Faithful Departed on 2
November, and the month that follows. In November there are a
number of commemorations, of which Remembrance Sunday is
the most obvious, which combine with the natural feeling of
autumn days to focus on a sense of the coming end. By linking
All Saints' tide with Advent through the provision made for the
Sundays of the Kingdom (see Chapter III), we have continued the

theme of All Saints and the Commemoration of the Faithful Departed. By this means there is a natural move from a season of reflection on the Church in time to one meditating on the Church's destiny in eternity.

The Calendar for this period is set out in the Introduction and in the Appendix, with the suggestion that the last Sunday in October (which the ASB calendar calls The Ninth Sunday Before Christmas) be kept as the Dedication Festival unless a particular date is known, or else, following the Lutheran tradition, as Reformation Sunday, with particular thanksgiving for the Bible as the word of God. *The Promise of His Glory* makes no further provision beyond that found in the ASB for Harvest with its twin themes of Creation and Eschatology. It is not yet clear where liturgical meditation on Creation is best treated. Some would wish to take up the theme on the Sunday in One World Week (for which readings are provided on p. 381). All Saints' Day may be kept on the first Sunday in November if it is transferred from 1 November, or this Sunday may be kept as a Sunday in All Saints' Tide. The remaining Sundays in November, of which Remembrance Sunday is the first, are designated Sundays of the Kingdom, linking All Saints' tide to Advent proper.

The principal service for All Saints' tide is the Eucharist of All Saints' Day, whether kept on 1 November or the first Sunday in November. Although there is seasonal material for use at many points in the service, the only structural change from Holy Communion Rite A is in the position of the penitential section. Biblical acclamations lead into the Gloria at the beginning, making that an inappropriate place for the Confession, and the special Intercession leads without interruption into the Peace, making the Confession inappropriate at that point also. The rite allows for the omission of the Prayers of Penitence entirely on this day but, for those who wish to retain them, two places are suggested, either as a preparation before the rite begins or before the Prayers of Intercession.

There is also provision for the Eucharist on 2 November, The Commemoration of the Faithful Departed. There are those who are hesitant about having a separate Commemoration of the Faithful Departed on the day after All Saints' Day, and there is indeed a danger if the dead are placed in supposedly neat categories. The All Saints' Day collect affirms that God has knit together his elect 'into one communion and fellowship'. Nevertheless, psychologically and liturgically, there is a need for a day that is seen to be about our own departed, rather than the heroes of the faith, and that acknowledges human grief and fragility in a way that would hardly find a place when we celebrate the triumphs of the great ones on All Saints' Day. For this reason a Eucharist for the Commemoration of the Faithful Departed has been included. This is the context in which the unity of the living and the departed in the body of the risen Christ is both celebrated and proclaimed, and while we are sensitive to the theological difficulties that some have in relation to prayer for the Christian dead, we have provided words and options that will enable everyone to use this service with a good conscience. We have also tried to hold in a proper balance the confident proclamation of the Easter faith and the sobering reality of death and judgement that brings us to our knees before the majesty of God, whose grace alone can save.

The distinctive feature of the rite is a Commemoration, which is placed immediately after the Distribution of Communion (although we allow it at an earlier point). Here there is provision for names to be read (and perhaps candles might be lit by members of the congregation). The Commemoration is placed here to emphasize our union with the departed within the body of Christ: as we feed on his broken body, so we are made one by his risen life. Here is an opportunity for those who have been bereaved in the previous year to remember their departed family and friends in prayer.

Conscious that a eucharistic setting will not always be appropriate in ministry to the bereaved, we have provided another form for this season, a service of Word and Prayer.

For many twentieth-century Christians the All Saints' tide period is extended to include Remembrance Sunday. In the suggested Calendar and Lectionary (see Appendix) we have sought to make it easier to observe this without cutting across a developing lectionary pattern, and we have reprinted the form of service approved ecumenically for use on that day. As an alternative, the provision for the Commemoration of the Faithful Departed may be suitable for use on Remembrance Sunday.

B. THE EUCHARIST OF ALL SAINTS

THE PREPARATION

1   The PRAYERS OF PENITENCE printed at section 15 may be used
    here or may be omitted.

2   A HYMN may be sung.

3   THIS SENTENCE is used.

Rejoice, people of God, praise the Lord. Let us keep the feast
in honour of all God's saints, in whose victory the angels
rejoice and glorify the Son of God.

4   The president welcomes the people.

May the joy and peace of heaven be with you.
The Lord bless you.

To our God belong victory, glory, and power,
for right and just are his judgements.
Praise our God, all that serve him:
those who fear him, both small and great.
The Lord Almighty has claimed his kingdom:
let us exult, rejoice, and give him glory.

5   GLORIA IN EXCELSIS is said.

Glory to God in the highest,
and peace to his people on earth.

Lord God, heavenly King,
almighty God and Father,
we worship you, we give you thanks,
we praise you for your glory.

Lord Jesus Christ, only Son of the Father,
Lord God, Lamb of God,
you take away the sin of the world:
have mercy on us;
you are seated at the right hand of the Father:
receive our prayer.

For you alone are the Holy One,
you alone are the Lord,
you alone are the Most High,
Jesus Christ,
with the Holy Spirit,
in the glory of God the Father.   Amen.

6   The president says THE COLLECT.

Let us pray that we may be strengthened by our
communion with all the saints.

Silence may be kept.

Almighty God,
you have knit together your elect
into one communion and fellowship
in the mystical body of your Son, Christ our Lord.
Give us grace so to follow your blessed saints
in all virtuous and godly living,
that we may come to those unspeakable joys
which you have prepared for those who truly love you;
through Jesus Christ our Lord,
who is alive and reigns with you and the Holy Spirit,
one God, now and for ever.   **Amen.**   8†

THE MINISTRY OF THE WORD

7   Either two or three READINGS FROM SCRIPTURE follow, the last of
which is the Gospel.

8   **Sit**

THE FIRST READING

At the end the reader may say

This is the word of the Lord.
Thanks be to God.

† Numbers in right-hand margin refer to Sources and Acknowledgements
(pp. 416-419).

9 **Stand**

THIS CANTICLE may be used.

Great and wonderful are your deeds,
Lord God the Almighty:
just and true are your ways, O King of the nations.

Who shall not revere and praise your name, O Lord?
for you alone are holy.

All nations shall come and worship in your presence:
for your just dealings have been revealed.

**To him who sits on the throne and to the Lamb:
be praise and honour, glory and might,
for ever and ever.   Amen.**

8

10 **Sit**

THE SECOND READING

At the end the reader may say

This is the word of the Lord.
Thanks be to God.

11 **Stand**

A CANTICLE, A HYMN, or A PSALM may be used.

12 THE GOSPEL

When it is announced

Glory to Christ our Saviour.

At the end the reader says

This is the Gospel of Christ.
Praise to Christ our Lord.

13 **Sit**

THE SERMON

14 Stand

THE NICENE CREED

Let us give glory to God as we confess the faith in which
the saints rejoice.

We believe in one God,
the Father, the almighty,
maker of heaven and earth,
of all that is,
seen and unseen.

We believe in one Lord, Jesus Christ,
the only Son of God,
eternally begotten of the Father,
God from God, Light from Light,
true God from true God,
begotten, not made,
of one Being with the Father.
Through him all things were made.
For us men and for our salvation
he came down from heaven;
by the power of the Holy Spirit
he became incarnate of the Virgin Mary,
    and was made man.
For our sake he was crucified under Pontius Pilate;
he suffered death and was buried.
On the third day he rose again
in accordance with the Scriptures;
he ascended into heaven
and is seated at the right hand of the Father.
He will come again in glory
to judge the living and the dead,
and his kingdom will have no end.

We believe in the Holy Spirit,
the Lord, the giver of life,
who proceeds from the Father and the Son.
With the Father and the Son he is worshipped
    and glorified.
He has spoken through the Prophets.

We believe in one holy catholic
and apostolic Church.
We acknowledge one baptism for the
forgiveness of sins.
We look for the resurrection of the dead,
and the life of the world to come.   Amen.

THE PRAYERS

15   PRAYERS OF PENITENCE may be said.

Christ calls us to share the heavenly banquet of his love
with all the saints in earth and heaven. Knowing our
unworthiness and sin, let us ask from him both mercy and
forgiveness.

Almighty God, our heavenly Father,
we have sinned against you,
through our own fault,
in thought and word and deed,
and in what we have left undone.
For your Son our Lord Jesus Christ's sake,
forgive us all that is past;
and grant that we may serve you in newness of life
to the glory of your name.   Amen.   8

Other confessions may be used.

President
Almighty God,
who forgives all who truly repent,
have mercy upon *you*,
pardon and deliver *you* from all *your* sins,
confirm and strengthen *you* in all goodness,
and keep *you* in life eternal;
through Jesus Christ our Lord.   **Amen**.   8

16   THE PRAYERS OF INTERCESSION

Biddings may precede this form, which should be used
without interpolation. Silence may be kept after each section.

United in the company of all the faithful and looking for the coming of the kingdom, let us offer our prayers to God, the source of all life and holiness.

Merciful Lord, strengthen all Christian people by your Holy Spirit that we may live as a royal priesthood and a holy nation to the praise of Christ Jesus our Saviour.
Lord, have mercy.

Bless *N* our bishop, and all ministers of your Church, that by faithful proclamation of your word we may be built on the foundation of the apostles and prophets into a holy temple in the Lord.
Lord, have mercy.

Empower us by the gift of your Holy and Life-giving Spirit that we may be transformed into the likeness of Christ from glory to glory.
Lord, have mercy.

Give to the world and its peoples the peace that comes from above, that they may find Christ's way of freedom and life.
Lord, have mercy.

Hold in your embrace all who witness to your love in the service of the poor and needy; all those who minister to the sick and dying; and all who bring light to those in darkness.
Lord, have mercy.

Touch and heal all those whose lives are scarred by sin or disfigured by pain, that, raised from death to life in Christ, their sorrow may be turned to eternal joy.
Lord, have mercy.

Remember in your mercy those gone before us who have been well-pleasing to you from eternity; preserve us who live here in your faith, guide us to your kingdom, and grant us your peace at all times.
Lord, have mercy.

Hasten the day when those who fear you in every nation
will come from east and west, from north and south, and
sit at table in your kingdom.
Lord, have mercy.

And so we give you thanks for the whole company of your
saints in glory, with whom in fellowship we join our
prayers and praises; by your grace may we, like them, be
made perfect in your love.
Blessing and glory and wisdom,
thanksgiving and honour and power,
be to our God for ever and ever.   Amen.

THE PEACE

17 **Stand**

May the God of peace make you perfect and holy, that you
may be kept safe and blameless in spirit, soul, and body,
for the coming of our Lord Jesus Christ.

The peace of the Lord be always with you.
And also with you.

A minister may say

Let us offer one another a sign of peace.

and all may exchange a sign of peace.

THE PREPARATION OF THE GIFTS

18 The bread and wine are placed on the holy table.

19 The president may praise God for his gifts in appropriate
words to which all respond

Blessed be God for ever.

20 The offerings of the people may be collected and presented.
These words may be used.

Yours, Lord, is the greatness, the power,
the glory, the splendour, and the majesty;
for everything in heaven and on earth is yours.
All things come from you,
and of your own do we give you.

21   At the preparation of the gifts A HYMN may be sung.

THE EUCHARISTIC PRAYER

22   The president takes the bread and cup into his hands and
replaces them on the holy table.

23   The president uses one of the authorized Eucharistic Prayers
with one of these PROPER PREFACES.

And now we give you thanks
for the hope to which you call us in your Son,
that following in the faith of all your saints,
we may run with perseverance
   the race that is set before us,
and with them receive the unfading crown of glory.

or

And now we give you thanks, most gracious God,
surrounded by a great cloud of witnesses
and glorified in the assembly of your saints.
The glorious company of apostles praise you.
The noble fellowship of prophets praise you.
The white-robed army of martyrs praise you.
We, your holy Church, acclaim you.
In communion with angels and archangels,
and with all those who have served you in every age
and worship you now in heaven,
we raise our voice to proclaim your glory,
for ever praising you and saying:

Holy, holy, holy Lord,
God of power and might,
heaven and earth are full of your glory.
Hosanna in the highest.
Blessed is he who comes in the name of the Lord.
Hosanna in the highest.

The president continues the Eucharistic Prayer using one of the authorized texts.

THE COMMUNION

24 THE LORD'S PRAYER is said in one of the following forms.
As our Saviour has taught us, so we pray:

Our Father in heaven, *or*	Our Father, who art in heaven,
hallowed be your name,	hallowed be thy name;
your kingdom come,	thy kingdom come;
your will be done,	thy will be done;
on earth as in heaven.	on earth as it is in heaven.
Give us today our daily bread.	Give us this day our daily bread.
Forgive us our sins	And forgive us our trespasses,
as we forgive those	as we forgive those
who sin against us.	who trespass against us.
Lead us not into temptation	And lead us not into temptation;
but deliver us from evil.	but deliver us from evil.
For the kingdom, the power,	For thine is the kingdom,
and the glory are yours	the power, and the glory,
now and for ever. Amen.	for ever and ever. Amen.

25 The president breaks the consecrated bread, saying

We break this bread
to share in the body of Christ.
**Though we are many, we are one body,
because we all share in one bread.**

26 Either here or during the distribution one of the following ANTHEMS may be said.

**Lamb of God, you take away the sins of the world:
have mercy on us.**

**Lamb of God, you take away the sins of the world:
have mercy on us.**

**Lamb of God, you take away the sins of the world:
grant us peace.**

or

Jesus, Lamb of God: have mercy on us.
Jesus, bearer of our sins: have mercy on us.
Jesus, redeemer of the world: give us your peace.

27   Before the distribution the president says

I heard the voice of a great multitude crying,
Alleluia!
The Lord our God has entered into his kingdom.
Blessed are those who are called to the supper of the Lamb.

28   The president and people receive the Communion. Any
authorized words of distribution may be used. During the
distribution HYMNS and ANTHEMS may be sung. The Alternative
Service Book provision is followed for consecration of
additional bread and wine and for disposing of what remains.

AFTER COMMUNION

29   The president says

You have come to Mount Zion and to the city of the living
God, the heavenly Jerusalem, to the spirits of the just,
made perfect, and to Jesus, the mediator of a new
covenant.

30   **Silence** may be kept and A HYMN may be sung.

31   Either or both of these prayers is said.

32   God, the source of all holiness
and giver of all good things:
may we who have shared at this table
as strangers and pilgrims here on earth
be welcomed with all your saints
to the heavenly feast
   on the day of your kingdom;
through Jesus Christ our Lord.   **Amen.**

or

33   **We thank you, Lord,**
that you have fed us in this sacrament,
united us with Christ,
and given us a foretaste of the heavenly banquet.
Amen.   9

34   THE DISMISSAL

The president may say THIS BLESSING.

May God, who kindled the fire of his love in the hearts of
the saints, pour upon you the riches of his grace.   **Amen.**

May he give you joy in their fellowship and a share in their
praises.   **Amen.**

May he strengthen you to follow them in the way of
holiness and to come to the full radiance of glory.   **Amen.**

And the blessing of God Almighty, the Father, the Son,
and the Holy Spirit, be upon you and remain with you
always.   **Amen.**

35   *Minister*   Go in peace to love and serve the Lord.
                          In the name of Christ.   **Amen.**

or

      Minister   Go in the peace of Christ.
                          Thanks be to God.

36   The ministers and people depart.

C. A THANKSGIVING FOR THE HOLY ONES OF GOD

This Litany of Thanksgiving is appropriate for various occasions. It is particularly suitable for use at Morning or Evening Prayer at All Saints' tide.

V   Let us bless the Lord.
R   **Thanks be to God.**

For Abraham and Sarah, our ancestors in faith,
journeying into the unknown, yet trusting God's promises:

For Jacob, deceitful younger brother, yet chosen by God,
father of those called by no virtue of their own:

For Moses the lawgiver and Aaron the priest,
who led the people of Israel to freedom and the
    promised land:

For Esther and Deborah, saviours of their nation,
and for all who dare to act courageously at God's call:

For Isaiah, John the Baptist and all the prophets,
who spoke your truth no matter the cost:

For Mary the Virgin, full of grace,
called to be the Mother of the Lord:

For Andrew and John and the first disciples,
who left all to follow Jesus:

For Mary Magdalene, Salome and Mary,
first witnesses of the resurrection,
and for all who bear witness to Christ:

For Peter and Paul and all the apostles,
who preached the gospel to Jew and Gentile:

For the writers of the gospels,
and for all who bring the faith of Christ alive for each
    generation:

For Stephen and Alban and the whole army of martyrs,
who have faced death for love of Christ:

For Augustine and Aidan, Boniface and Patrick,
and for all who have carried the gospel to this and
   other lands:

For Aelred and Bernard,
and for all who live and teach the love of God:

For Anselm and Richard Hooker,
and for all who reveal to us the depths of God's wisdom:

For Benedict and Francis, Hilda and Bede,
and for all who deepen our common life in Christ:

For Julian of Norwich and Teresa of Avila,
and for all who renew our vision of the mystery of God:

For Thomas Cranmer
and all who reform the Church of God;

for Thomas More
and all who hold firm to its continuing faith:

For Gregory and Dunstan, George Herbert and
   John Keble,
and for all who praise God in poetry and song:

For Lancelot Andrewes, John Wesley, and
   Charles Simeon,
and for all who preach the word of God:

For William Wilberforce and Josephine Butler,
and for all who work to transform the world:

For Monica and for Mary Sumner,
and for all who nurture faith in home and family:

For the martyrs and peacemakers of our own time,
who shine as lights in the darkness:

For all the unsung heroes of our faith,
whose names are known to God alone:

For all those in our own lives
who have brought us to this time and place
and shown to us the way of holiness:

(For NN . . .)

Let us praise them with thankful hearts:
And glorify our God in whom they put their trust.

THE LORD'S PRAYER

THE COLLECT FOR ALL SAINTS' DAY

May the infinite and glorious Trinity,
the Father, the Son, and the Holy Spirit,
direct our life in good works,
and after our journey through this world,
grant us eternal rest with the saints.   **Amen.**

D. THE EUCHARIST FOR THE COMMEMORATION OF THE FAITHFUL DEPARTED

THE PREPARATION

1   A HYMN, A CANTICLE, or A PSALM may be sung.

2   One of these SENTENCES may be used.

I am the resurrection, and I am the life; those who believe in me, though they die, yet shall they live, and whoever lives and believes in me shall never die.

or

We look not to the things that are seen but to the things that are unseen; for the things that are seen are transient but the things that are unseen are eternal.

3   The president welcomes the people.

The grace and mercy of our Lord Jesus Christ be with you.
The Lord bless you.

PRAYERS OF PENITENCE

4   PRAYERS OF PENITENCE are said. This form may be used.

Minister
God has shone in our hearts to give the light of the knowledge of his glory in the face of Christ. But we have this treasure in earthen vessels to show that the transcendent power belongs to God and not to us.

As we acknowledge our human frailty, we call to mind our sins of word, deed, and omission, and confess them before God our Father.

Silence is kept.

Either

5   **Father eternal, giver of light and grace,**
    we have sinned against you and against our neighbour,
    in what we have thought,
    in what we have said and done,
    through ignorance, through weakness,
    through our own deliberate fault.
    We have wounded your love,
    and marred your image in us.
    We are sorry and ashamed,
    and repent of all our sins.
    for the sake of your Son Jesus Christ,
        who died for us,
    forgive us all that is past;
    and lead us out from darkness
    to walk as children of light.   Amen.   *8*

President
Almighty God,
who forgives all who truly repent,
have mercy upon *you*,
pardon and deliver *you* from all *your* sins,
confirm and strengthen *you* in all goodness,
and keep *you* in life eternal;
through Jesus Christ our Lord.   **Amen.**   *8*

    or

6   You raise the dead to life in the Spirit:
    Lord, have mercy.
    Lord, have mercy.

    You bring pardon and peace to the sinner:
    Christ, have mercy.
    Christ, have mercy.

    You bring light to those in darkness:
    Lord, have mercy.
    Lord, have mercy.

    May almighty God have mercy on us,
    forgive us our sins,
    and bring us to everlasting life.   **Amen.**   *10*

7   The president says THE COLLECT.

Let us pray for the peace and well-being of the whole
Church.

Silence may be kept.

O God,
the maker and redeemer of all believers:
grant us, with all the faithful departed,
the sure benefits of your Son's
    saving passion and glorious resurrection;
that in the last day,
when you gather up all things in Christ,
we may with them enjoy the fullness of your promises;
through Jesus Christ our Lord,
who is alive and reigns with you and the Holy Spirit,
one God, now and for ever.   **Amen.**   8*

or

Heavenly Father,
in your Son Jesus Christ
you have given us a true faith and a sure hope.
Strengthen this faith and hope in us all our days,
that we may live as those who believe in
    the communion of saints,
    the forgiveness of sins,
    and the resurrection to eternal life;
through your Son Jesus Christ our Lord.   **Amen.**   8

THE MINISTRY OF THE WORD

8   Either two or three READINGS FROM SCRIPTURE follow, the last of
     which is the Gospel.

     Sit

9   THE FIRST READING

     At the end the reader may say

     This is the word of the Lord.
     Thanks be to God.

10   THIS CANTICLE, or A PSALM or A HYMN may be used.

Response   **The ransomed of the Lord shall return with singing.**

1   The wilderness and the dry land shall rejoice:
    the desert shall burst into song;

2   They shall see the glory of the Lord:
    the splendour of our God.

The ransomed of the Lord shall return with singing.

3   Strengthen the weary hands:
    make firm the feeble knees.

4   Say to the anxious:
    Be strong, fear not!

5   Your God is coming with judgement:
    coming with judgement to save you.

The ransomed of the Lord shall return with singing.

11   **Sit**

THE SECOND READING

At the end the reader may say

This is the word of the Lord.
Thanks be to God.

12   A CANTICLE, A HYMN, or A PSALM may be used.

13   **Stand**

THE GOSPEL

When it is announced

Glory to Christ our Saviour.

At the end the reader says

This is the Gospel of Christ.
Praise to Christ our Lord.

14   **Sit**

THE SERMON

THE PRAYERS

15 THE COMMEMORATION OF THE FAITHFUL DEPARTED (sections 29-34) may be used at this point in the service.

16 PRAYERS OF INTERCESSION are said. This form may be used.

Minister
In peace let us pray to the Lord.

Jesus, Bread from Heaven,
you satisfy the hungry with good things:
grant us a share with all the faithful departed
in the banquet of your kingdom.

Hear us, risen Lord,
our resurrection and our life.

Jesus, the Light of the World,
you gave the man born blind the gift of sight
and opened the eyes of his faith:
bring those in darkness
to your eternal light and glory.

Hear us, risen Lord,
our resurrection and our life.

Jesus, Son of the Living God,
you summoned your friend Lazarus from death to life:
raise us at the last to full and eternal life with you.

Hear us, risen Lord,
our resurrection and our life.

Jesus, Crucified Saviour,
in your dying you entrusted each to the other
Mary your mother and John your beloved disciple:
sustain and comfort all who mourn.

Hear us, risen Lord,
our resurrection and our life.

Jesus, our Way and Truth and Life,
you drew your disciple Thomas from doubt to faith:
reveal the resurrection faith to the doubting
and the lost.

Hear us, risen Lord,
our resurrection and our life.

President
May God in his infinite love and mercy bring the whole
Church, living and departed in the Lord Jesus, to a joyful
resurrection and the fulfilment of his eternal kingdom.
Amen.

THE PEACE

17 **Stand**

Jesus says: Peace I leave with you. My peace I give to you.
Not as the world gives give I unto you. Do not let your
hearts be troubled, neither let them be afraid.

The peace of the risen Christ be always with you.
And also with you.   *10*

A minister may say

Let us offer one another a sign of peace.

and all may exchange a sign of peace.

THE PREPARATION OF THE GIFTS

18 The bread and wine are placed on the holy table.

19 The president may praise God for his gifts in appropriate
   words to which all respond

   Blessed be God for ever.

20 The offerings of the people may be collected and presented.
   These words may be used.

   Yours, Lord, is the greatness, the power,
   the glory, the splendour, and the majesty;
   for everything in heaven and on earth is yours.
   All things come from you,
   and of your own do we give you.

21 At the preparation of the gifts A HYMN may be sung.

THE EUCHARISTIC PRAYER

22   The president takes the bread and cup into his hands and replaces them on the holy table.

23   The president uses one of the authorized Eucharistic Prayers with one of these PROPER PREFACES.

And now we give you thanks because
through him you have given us
    the hope of a glorious resurrection;
so that, although death comes to us all,
yet we rejoice in the promise of eternal life;
for to your faithful people life is changed,
    not taken away;
and when our mortal flesh is laid aside,
an everlasting dwelling place
    is made ready for us in heaven.   8

or

And now we give you thanks
through Jesus Christ our Lord.
In him who rose from the dead
our hope of resurrection dawned.
The sting of death has been drawn
by the glorious promise of his risen life.   *10**

THE COMMUNION

24   THE LORD'S PRAYER is said in one of the following forms.

As our Saviour has taught us, in faith and trust we pray:

Our Father in heaven,	*or*	Our Father, who art in heaven,
hallowed be your name,		hallowed be thy name;
your kingdom come,		thy kingdom come;
your will be done,		thy will be done;
on earth as in heaven.		on earth as it is in heaven.
Give us today our daily bread.		Give us this day our daily bread.
Forgive us our sins		And forgive us our trespasses,
as we forgive those		as we forgive those
who sin against us.		who trespass against us.

| Lead us not into temptation
but deliver us from evil. | And lead us not into temptation;
but deliver us from evil. |
| For the kingdom, the power,
   and the glory are yours
now and for ever.   Amen. | For thine is the kingdom,
   the power, and the glory,
for ever and ever.   Amen. |

25 The president breaks the consecrated bread, saying

Jesus is the living bread which came down from heaven:
if anyone eats of this bread, they will live for ever.
Lord, give us this bread always.

26 Either here or during the distribution one of the following
ANTHEMS may be said.

**Lamb of God, you take away the sins of the world:
have mercy on us.**

**Lamb of God, you take away the sins of the world:
have mercy on us.**

**Lamb of God, you take away the sins of the world:
grant us peace.**

or

**Jesus, Lamb of God: have mercy on us.
Jesus, bearer of our sins: have mercy on us.
Jesus, redeemer of the world: give us your peace.**

27 Before the distribution the president says

I am the bread of life, says the Lord;
Whoever comes to me will never hunger;
Whoever believes in me will never thirst.

I am the vine: you are the branches.
May we dwell in him as he lives in us.   *11*

28 The president and people receive the Communion. These
words of distribution should be used.

The Body of Christ keep you in eternal life.   **Amen.**

The Blood of Christ keep you in eternal life.   **Amen.**

During the distribution HYMNS and ANTHEMS may be sung. The Alternative Service Book provision is followed for consecration of additional bread and wine and for disposing of what remains.

A COMMEMORATION OF THE FAITHFUL DEPARTED

29 Glory and honour and power:
are yours by right, O Lord our God;

**For you created all things:
and by your will they have their being.**

Glory and honour and power:
are yours by right, O Lamb who was slain:

**For by your blood you have ransomed for God
a kingdom of priests from every race and language,
from every people and nation.**

30 The names of those to be remembered may be read aloud. Silence may be kept after each name, or group of names, or after all the names have been read.

THESE WORDS are used.

This is the will of him that sent me
that I should lose nothing of all that he has given me,
and I will raise them up at the last day.

31 One or more of the three sections that follow (32-34) are used.

32 Lord God, creator of all,
you have made us creatures of this earth,
but have also promised us a share in life eternal.
According to your promises,
may all who have died in the peace of Christ
share with your saints in the joy of heaven
where there is neither sorrow nor pain,
but life everlasting.
Alleluia! Amen.

4*

33 *Either*

Grant to us, Lord God,
to trust you not for ourselves alone,
but for those also whom we love
and who are hidden from us by the shadow of death;
that, as we believe your power to have raised
our Lord Jesus Christ from the dead,
so may we trust your love to give eternal life
to all who believe in him;
through Jesus Christ our Lord,
who is alive and reigns with you and the Holy Spirit,
one God, now and for ever. **Amen.**   4

or

†**Give rest, O Christ, to your servants with your saints,**
where sorrow and pain are no more,
neither sighing, but life everlasting.

You only are immortal, the creator and maker of all:
and we are mortal, formed from the dust of the earth,
and unto earth shall we return.
For so you did ordain when you created me, saying,
'Dust thou art, and unto dust shalt thou return.'
All we go down to the dust;
and weeping o'er the grave we make our song:
Alleluia, alleluia, alleluia.

Give rest, O Christ, to your servants with your saints,
where sorrow and pain are no more,
neither sighing, but life everlasting.

34 This prayer may be said by all.

Hear us, O merciful Father,
as we remember in love
those whom we have placed in your hands.
Acknowledge, we pray, the sheep of your own fold,

---

† This ancient hymn of the Orthodox Church recalls our mortality, and
prays for the living and the departed as they are bound together in the dying
and rising of Christ.

lambs of your own flock,
sinners of your own redeeming.
Enfold them in the arms of your mercy,
in the blessed rest of everlasting peace,
and in the glorious company of the saints in light.
Amen.   12*

THE CONCLUSION

35 A HYMN may be sung.

36 The president may say this prayer.

God of love,
may the death and resurrection of Christ,
which we have celebrated in this eucharist,
bring us, with the faithful departed,
into the peace of your eternal home.
We ask this in the name of Jesus Christ,
our rock and our salvation.   **Amen.**   11

37 THE DISMISSAL

The president may say one of these BLESSINGS.

The God of peace,
who brought again from the dead our Lord Jesus,
    that great shepherd of the sheep,
make you perfect in every good work to do his will;
and the blessing of God almighty,
the Father, the Son, and the Holy Spirit,
be upon you and remain with you always.   **Amen.**

or

May God give to you and to all those whom you love
his comfort and his peace,
his light and his joy,
in this world and the next;
and the blessing of God almighty,
the Father, the Son, and the Holy Spirit,
be upon you and remain with you always.   **Amen.**   13

38 *Either*

Minister   Go in the peace of Christ. (Alleluia!)
Thanks be to God. (Alleluia!)

or

Minister   Neither death nor life
can separate us from the love of God
in Jesus Christ our Lord.
Thanks be to God. (Alleluia! Alleluia!)

39 The ministers and people depart.

E. A SERVICE OF PRAYERS AND READINGS IN COMMEMORATION OF THE FAITHFUL DEPARTED

This service may be used as an alternative to the Eucharist for the Commemoration of the Faithful Departed, or on the anniversary of a death; or it may be used as the outline for a Memorial Service or a Service of Thanksgiving.

THE INTRODUCTION

1   In the name of Christ, who died and was raised by the glory of the Father, we welcome you: grace, mercy and peace be with you all.

2   The minister may introduce the service with these or other words.

We meet this day to remember *N*, to renew our trust and confidence in Christ, and to pray that together we may be one in him, through whom we offer our praises to the Father.

Then the minister says†

I have set the Lord always before me:
He is at my right hand, and I shall not fall.

Show us your mercy, O Lord:
And grant us your salvation.

For with you is the well of life:
And in your light shall we see light.

3   A HYMN may be sung now or after this Acclamation.

4   THE ACCLAMATION

Blessed are you, Lord our God, lover of souls:
you uphold us in life and sustain us in death:

† For an alternative see p.82.

to you be glory and praise for ever!
For the darkness of this age is passing away
as Christ the bright and morning star
brings to his saints the light of life.
As you give light to those in darkness
who walk in the shadow of death,
so remember in your kingdom your faithful servants,
that death may be for *them* the gate to life
and to unending fellowship with you;
where with your saints you live and reign
one in the perfect union of love
now and for ever. **Amen.**

THE LITURGY OF THE WORD

5   THE FIRST READING

One of the following passages may be read.

Isaiah 51. 1-3, 9-16	Sorrow and sighing shall flee away.
Lamentations 3. 22-26, 31-33	The Lord's mercies are new every morning: great is your faithfulness.
Wisdom 3. 1-9	The souls of the righteous are in the hand of God.
Romans 8. 31b-end	What shall separate us from the love of God?
1 Corinthians 15. 20-28	Christ has been raised from the dead.
1 Corinthians 15. 51-57	O death, where is your victory?
2 Corinthians 4. 7-18	We look not to the things that are seen, but to the things that are unseen.
Revelation 21. 1-7	God will wipe away every tear.

6   THE PSALM

One of the following Psalms is said or sung.

23; 27; 42; 43; 90; 116; 118. 19-end; 121; 130; 139. 1-18.

If these are said in a responsorial form the following responses are appropriate.

Psalm 23   Lord, remember me in your kingdom.

or   Though I walk through the valley of the shadow of death I shall fear no evil.

Psalm 27   One thing have I asked of the Lord, that I may dwell in the house of the Lord.

Psalm 42   My soul is athirst for God, thirsting for the living God.

Psalm 43   Send out your light and your truth that they may lead me.

Psalm 90   Teach us to number our days, that we may apply our hearts to wisdom.

Psalm 116   I will walk in the presence of the Lord in the land of the living.

Psalm 118   Open for me the gates of righteousness: I will enter and offer thanks to the Lord.

Psalm 121   My help comes from the Lord: who has made heaven and earth.

Psalm 130   In the Lord's word is my hope.

Psalm 139   The darkness is no darkness with you; the night is as clear as the day.

7   THE GOSPEL

Stand

Before the Gospel the reader says

Hear the words of the Holy Gospel according to . . .
Glory to Christ our Saviour.

One of the following Gospels is read.

Luke 23. 39-43   Today you will be with me in paradise.

John 6. 35-40   I am the bread of life.

John 11. 17-27   I am the resurrection and the life.

John 14. 1-6   I am the way, the truth, and the life.

John 17. 24-26   Father, I want those you have given me to be with me where I am.

John 20. 1-9   The Resurrection

At the end the reader says

This is the Gospel of Christ.
Praise to Christ our Lord.

8   AN ADDRESS may follow, and/or A HYMN or ANTHEM may be sung.

THE PRAYERS

9   Blessed be the Lord, the God of Israel:
He has come to his people and set them free.

He has raised up for us a mighty Saviour:
born of the house of his servant David.

In the tender compassion of our God:
the dawn from on high shall break upon us,

To shine on those who dwell in darkness
and the shadow of death:
and to guide our feet into the way of peace.

10 Let us pray.

Either

Almighty God, you have knit your chosen people together in one communion, in the mystical body of your Son, Jesus Christ our Lord. Give to your whole Church in heaven and on earth your light and your peace.

Lord, hear us;
Lord, graciously hear us.

Grant that all who have been baptized into Christ's death and resurrection may die to sin and rise to newness of life, and that through the grave and gate of death we may pass with him to our joyful resurrection.

Lord, hear us;
Lord, graciously hear us.

Grant to us who are still in our pilgrimage, and who walk as yet by faith, that your Holy Spirit may lead us in holiness and righteousness all our days.

Lord, hear us;
Lord, graciously hear us.

Grant to your faithful people pardon and peace, that we may be cleansed from all our sins and serve you with a quiet mind.

Lord, hear us;
Lord, graciously hear us.

Grant to all who mourn a sure confidence in your loving care, that casting all their sorrow on you, they may know the consolation of your love.

Lord, hear us;
Lord, graciously hear us.

May we have strength to meet the days ahead in the joyful expectation of eternal life with those we love.

Lord, hear us;
Lord, graciously hear us.

Help us, we pray, in the midst of things we cannot understand, to believe and trust in the communion of saints, the forgiveness of sins, and the resurrection to life everlasting.

Lord, hear us;
Lord, graciously hear us.

Grant us grace to entrust *N/those whom we remember* to
your never-failing love which sustained *them* in this life.
Enfold *them* in the arms of your mercy, and remember
them according to the favour you bear for your people.

Lord, hear us;
Lord, graciously hear us. *11**

or

What no eye has seen, nor ear heard, nor human heart
conceived, God has prepared for those who love him.

God of all consolation,
in your unending love and mercy
you turn the darkness of death
into the dawn of new life.

Show compassion to your people in their sorrow.
Be our refuge and our strength
to lift us from the darkness of grief
to the peace and light of your presence.

Your Son our Lord Jesus Christ
by dying for us, conquered death,
and by rising again, restored life.

May we then go forward eagerly to meet him,
and after our life on earth
be reunited with our brothers and sisters
where every tear will be wiped away.
We ask this through Jesus Christ our Lord.   **Amen.**   *11**

11   **Our Father in heaven,**   *or*   **Our Father, who art in heaven,**
    hallowed be your name,   **hallowed be thy name;**
    your kingdom come,   **thy kingdom come;**
    your will be done,   **thy will be done;**
    on earth as in heaven.   **on earth as it is in heaven.**
    Give us today our daily bread.   **Give us this day our daily bread.**
    Forgive us our sins   **And forgive us our trespasses,**
    as we forgive those   **as we forgive those**
        who sin against us.   **who trespass against us.**

Lead us not into temptation
but deliver us from evil.
For the kingdom, the power,
  and the glory are yours
now and for ever.   **Amen.**

And lead us not into temptation;
but deliver us from evil.
For thine is the kingdom,
  the power, and the glory,
for ever and ever.   **Amen.**

12 Lord Christ our Redeemer, in the day of your coming raise us up, and set us at your right hand in the day when your greatness shall appear. Keep the living by your grace, and give resurrection to the dead. We ask this in your name, O Lord our resurrection and our life.   **Amen.**

13 A HYMN may be sung.

THE COMMEMORATION

14 You, Christ, are the King of glory,
the eternal Son of the Father.

You overcame the sting of death
and opened the kingdom of heaven to all believers.

You are seated at God's right hand in glory.
We believe that you will come to be our judge.

**Come then, Lord, and help your people,
bought with the price of your own blood;
and bring us with your saints
to glory everlasting.**

15 Hear us, O merciful Father,
as we remember in love *N*
whom we have placed in your hands.
Acknowledge, we pray, a sheep of your own fold,
a lamb of your own flock,
a sinner of your own redeeming.
Enfold *him/her* in the arms of your mercy,
in the blessed rest of everlasting peace,
and in the glorious company of the saints in light.
Amen.

12*

16 The eternal God is your dwelling place,
and underneath are the everlasting arms.
Blessed is the Lord,
our strength and our salvation.

THE BLESSING

17 The Lord bless you and keep you,
the Lord make his face to shine upon you
and be gracious to you,
the Lord lift up the light of his countenance upon you
and give you peace.
And the blessing of the God almighty,
the Father, the Son, and the Holy Spirit,
be upon you and remain with you always.   **Amen.**

or

18 According to the riches of God's glory,
may we be strengthened with might
through the Spirit in our inner being,
and may Christ dwell in our hearts through faith,
that being rooted and grounded in love,
we may have power to comprehend with all the saints
what is the breadth and length and height and depth,
and to know the love of Christ
which surpasses knowledge,
that we may be filled with all the fullness of God.   **Amen.**
Ephesians 3. 16-19

ADDITIONAL PRAYER

Help us, Lord, to receive and understand your gospel,
so that we may find light in this darkness,
faith in our doubts,
and comfort for one another in your saving words.
We ask this through Christ our Lord.   **Amen.**

Let us pray also for those who mourn
   our *brother's / sister's* death;
comfort them in their sorrow.
Lord, hear our prayer.

Fill the emptiness in their hearts
with the presence of your love.
Lord, hear our prayer.

Increase their faith and strengthen their hope.
Lord, hear our prayer.

Let us pray also for ourselves
in our pilgrimage through life;
strengthen us and keep us faithful in your service.
Lord, hear our prayer.

Fill our hearts with the hope for heaven.
Lord, hear our prayer.

ALTERNATIVE RESPONSES

In place of the responses in section 2, the minister may use
the following.

As a father cares for his children:
so does the Lord care for those who fear him.

For he himself knows whereof we are made:
he remembers that we are but dust.

Our days are like the grass:
we flourish like a flower of the field.

When the wind goes over it, it is gone:
and its place shall know it no more.

But the merciful goodness of the Lord endures
for ever on those who fear him:
and his righteousness on children's children.

Psalm 103. 13-17

F. REMEMBRANCE SUNDAY

INTRODUCTION

Remembrance Sunday is observed on the second Sunday in November, generally the Sunday nearest to 11 November.

Since 1968, a Service for Remembrance Sunday has been commended for general use by the Archbishops of Canterbury, of York, and of Wales, the Cardinal Archbishop of Westminster, and the Moderator of the Free Church Federal Council. This service was reissued in 1984 with modest updating of the language and a fresh choice of hymns. The 1984 text is set out below. *14*

The proposed Lectionary (see Appendix) provides psalms and readings for the Holy Communion and Morning and Evening Prayer. These are appropriate both for the season and for those wishing to incorporate Remembrance Sunday themes into the main services. As a general rule these psalms and readings should not be altered. There is a further provision of psalms and readings which are suitable for special Services of Remembrance.

On occasions when local circumstances particularly require it, the Bishop may order that features of the special service, as well as the psalms and readings, be incorporated into the Holy Communion, or Morning or Evening Prayer, as follows.

	The Holy Communion	*Morning Prayer*	*Evening Prayer*
Introduction	After section 2	Section 1	Section 24
Penitence	Sections 4-8 or 23-28	Sections 3-6	Sections 26-29
Intercession	Sections 20-21	Section 23	Section 46
Commitment	Sections 51-52	Section 23	Section 46
Remembrance	After section 2 or at sections 20-21	Section 1	Section 24

An Order for Remembrance Sunday

All stand while the minister reads

1   THE INTRODUCTION

We are here to worship Almighty God, whose purposes
are good; whose power sustains the world he has made;
who loves us, though we have failed in his service; who
gave Jesus Christ for the life of the world; who by his Holy
Spirit leads us in his way.

As we give thanks for his great works, we remember those
who have lived and died in his service and in the service of
others; we pray for all who suffer through war and are in
need; we ask for his help and blessing that we may do his
will, and that the whole world may acknowledge him as
Lord and King.

2   HYMN

3   LESSON

4   HYMN

5   **ACT OF PENITENCE**

The minister says

Let us confess to God the sins and shortcomings
     of the world;
its pride, its selfishness, its greed;
its evil divisions and hatreds.
Let us confess our share in what is wrong,
and our failure to seek and establish that peace
which God wills for his children.

After a short silence, all say

Most merciful God,
we confess that we have sinned
in thought, word, and deed.
We have not loved you with our whole heart.
We have not loved our neighbours as ourselves.

**In your mercy
forgive what we have been,
help us to amend what we are,
and direct what we shall be;
that we may do justly, love mercy,
and walk humbly with you;
through Jesus Christ our Lord.   Amen.**

The minister stands and says

Almighty God, have mercy upon us,
pardon and deliver us from all our sins,
confirm and strengthen us in all goodness,
and keep us in life eternal;
through Jesus Christ our Lord.   **Amen.**

6   **INTERCESSION**

Special intentions may be inserted at appropriate points.

The minister says

Let us pray for the peace of the world:
for statesmen and rulers, that they may have wisdom to
know and courage to do what is right . . .

for all who work to improve international relationships,
that they may find the true way to reconcile people of
different race, colour, and creed . . .

and for men and women the world over, that they may
have justice and freedom, and live in security and peace . . .

Here follows a short silence.

Lord, in your mercy
Hear our prayer.

Most gracious God and Father,
in whose will is our peace:
turn our hearts and the hearts of all to yourself,
that by the power of your Spirit
the peace which is founded on righteousness
may be established throughout the whole world;
through Jesus Christ our Lord.   **Amen.**

Let us pray for all who suffer as a result of war:

for the injured and the disabled,
for the mentally distressed,
and for those whose faith in God and man has been
weakened or destroyed . . .

for the homeless and refugees,
for those who are hungry,
and for all who have lost their livelihood and security . . .

for those who mourn their dead,
those who have lost husband or wife,
children or parents,
and especially for those who have no hope in Christ
to sustain them in their grief . . .

Here follows a short silence.

Lord, in your mercy
Hear our prayer.

Almighty God, our heavenly Father,
infinite in wisdom, love, and power:
have compassion on those for whom we pray;
and help us to use all suffering
in the cause of your kingdom;
through him who gave himself for us on the cross,
Jesus Christ your Son, our Lord.   **Amen.**

If there is a collection, it is taken during the hymn which
follows.

7   HYMN

8   SERMON

9   HYMN

ACT OF REMEMBRANCE

10   All stand while the minister says

Let us remember before God,
and commend to his sure keeping
   those who have died for their country in war;
   those whom we knew, and whose memory we treasure;
   and all who have lived and died
   in the service of mankind.

Here follows **The Silence**.

Then the minister says

Almighty and eternal God,
from whose love in Christ we cannot be parted,
either by death or life:
hear our prayers and thanksgivings
for all whom we remember this day;
fulfil in them the purpose of your love;
and bring us all, with them, to your eternal joy;
through Jesus Christ our Lord.   **Amen.**

ACT OF COMMITMENT

11   The minister, or some other person appointed, says

Let us pledge ourselves anew to the service of God
   and our fellow men and women:
that we may help, encourage, and comfort others,
and support those working for the relief of the needy
   and for the peace and welfare of the nations.

All say together

**Lord God our Father,
we pledge ourselves
to serve you and all mankind,
in the cause of peace,
for the relief of want and suffering,
and for the praise of your name.**

Guide us by your Spirit;
give us wisdom;
give us courage;
give us hope;
and keep us faithful
now and always.   Amen.

12   THE LORD'S PRAYER

13   NATIONAL ANTHEM

14   BLESSING

Note on the use of the service and the observance of the Two Minutes Silence

This order has been prepared for use at any time on Remembrance Sunday, not necessarily when the Two Minutes Silence is observed. If it is used in the morning it can be so timed that the Act of Remembrance is reached at 11 a.m. without any alteration of the order. Alternatively, the Act of Remembrance may be taken out of the order and used first at 11 a.m. followed by the rest of the service. Where a brief observance is required, as at a War Memorial, the Act of Remembrance may be used, followed by the Act of Commitment, the Lord's Prayer, and the Blessing. If desired, the Act of Remembrance may take the form printed below.

ACT OF REMEMBRANCE (Alternative Form)

All stand while the minister says

Let us remember before God,
and commend to his sure keeping:
    those who have died for their country in war;
    those whom we knew, and whose memory we treasure;
    and all who have lived and died
    in the service of mankind.

The list of those to be remembered by name may then be read.

Then may be said

They shall grow not old as we that are left grow old:
Age shall not weary them, nor the years condemn.
At the going down of the sun and in the morning
We will remember them.

And all repeat

We will remember them.

Here follows **The Silence**.

Then the Last Post and the Reveille may be sounded.

Then the minister says

Almighty and eternal God,
from whose love in Christ we cannot be parted,
either by death or life:
Hear our prayers and thanksgivings
for all whom we remember this day;
fulfil in them the purpose of your love;
and bring us all, with them, to your eternal joy;
through Jesus Christ our Lord.   **Amen.**

SUPPLEMENTARY TEXTS

THE NATIONAL ANTHEM may be sung in the following form.

God save our gracious Queen,
Long live our noble Queen,
God save the Queen.
Send her victorious,
Happy and glorious,
Long to reign over us:
God save the Queen.

Thy choicest gifts in store
On her be pleased to pour,
Long may she reign.
May she defend our laws,
And ever give us cause
To sing with heart and voice,
God save the Queen.

Nor on this land alone –
But be God's mercies known
From shore to shore.
Lord, make the nations see
That men should brothers be,
And form one family
The wide world o'er.

THIS THANKSGIVING may be used.

We offer to almighty God our thanksgiving for the many blessings with which he has enriched our lives.

For the Queen and her family, and all who under her bear the responsibility of government:
Thanks be to God.

For those who serve in the Armed Forces of the Crown on sea and land and in the air:
Thanks be to God.

For doctors, nurses, chaplains, and all who minister to those in need or distress:
Thanks be to God.

For the unity of our people within the Commonwealth:
Thanks be to God.

For the sacrifices made, especially in two world wars, whereby our peace has been preserved:
Thanks be to God.

For the Royal British Legion:
Thanks be to God.

THIS BLESSING may be used.

God grant to the living, grace; to the departed, rest; to the Church, the Queen, the Commonwealth, and all mankind, peace and concord; and to us and all his servants, life everlasting; and the blessing of God almighty, Father, Son, and Holy Spirit, come down upon you and remain with you always.   **Amen.**

III
ADVENT

A. INTRODUCTION

The provision for Advent, and the weeks that precede it, is one of the most distinctive contributions of *The Promise of His Glory*. No one can pretend that the Church is unaffected by the spirit of the age, that is, by the anticipation of Christmas. The result of this is that Christmas carols crowd out the keeping of Advent, and the Church hardly has time for the 'earnest looking forward' – for the watching and waiting for the coming of the King in his kingdom now. Throughout Advent we are preoccupied with the pastness of the past in our concentration on preparing for Christmas with everyone else.

While Advent shares with Lent a spirit of restraint, preparation and penitence, the provision in this book hopes to restore to the Church the distinctive eschatological thrust of Advent, with its expectant longing for the coming of Christ's kingdom in power and the spirit of penitence which that engenders. At the same time we need to use creatively the stubborn popular conception of Advent as a lead into the Christmas festival.

So while we have retained a four-week Advent as such, the tradition of an Advent of variable length, or of some preliminary Sundays with an Advent flavour, is also reflected in our provision. The main thrust of our proposals is that the Pentecost 'green' season comes to an end with a 'white' feast day, All Saints' Day, celebrated on the first Sunday in November. Then there is a change of mood. Our proposal is that instead of one Sunday (Stir-up Sunday) before Advent with a feeling of looking forward in expectation, there should be three. This is a pattern that is both closer to ancient tradition (Stir-up Sunday is a left-over from a five-week Advent in the Middle Ages), and at the same time more tuned to the feel of November, so full of commemorations of the past.

We have designated these Sundays 'Sundays of the Kingdom' and allocated to them readings which reflect the Messianic hope of the Old Testament and the coming of the Kingdom of Christ in the New Testament. This note is struck by the three-year Roman Catholic Lectionary, which includes the observance of a feast of Christ the King on the Sunday before Advent. The Taizé calendar, too, makes provision for a season of the Kingdom, although it is observed earlier in the year.

The first of these Sundays will usually be Remembrance Sunday, and the lections we have provided for that day are more in keeping with the Remembrance theme than those in earlier lectionaries. The Sunday before Advent has been given material celebrating the kingship of Christ. Some may wish to celebrate this as a festival, but our preference is to explore this kingship theme rather more in terms of the darker mood of approaching Advent and of the one who comes as King and Judge.

Experience of the ASB's Ninth to Fifth Sundays before Christmas, with their Old Testament themes but still within a 'green' season, has not been entirely satisfactory. The Ninth Sunday often falls at the schools' half-term, and that pattern is then interrupted by both All Saints' tide and Remembrance Sunday. Nor has that pattern, though it has had fairly widespread commendation through the Joint Liturgical Group, been taken up elsewhere in the Anglican Communion. While some will be content to follow the pattern of the ASB or BCP Calendar though drawing on the resources of this chapter for Advent, and some will wish to use the provision of Lectionary 2 (see Appendix) to explore the themes and scriptures of the season in a different way, others – and this is the logic of our provision – will wish to move to a more full-scale adoption of the Advent ethos straight after All Saints' Sunday than the ASB's five Sundays encouraged. This could include a change of liturgical colour to the Advent colour, the use of the more penitential options in the liturgy, and the choice of hymns of an eschatological character.

Advent itself has a change of gear: the last two Sundays, focused on the forerunners John the Baptist and Mary the Mother of the Lord, look forward to the particularity of the Incarnation. If these two weeks are unduly dominated by the demands of Christmas, there remain in our proposals some four or five weeks beforehand to treat the eschatological themes. But whatever calendar and lectionary routes are followed, there is the period from Advent 3 to the Feast of the Baptism of our Lord (Epiphany 1) where local preferences should give way to a common core.

We have not provided one major Advent rite in the same way as can be provided for some feast days, for instance for All Saints' Day and for the Presentation. Our principal concern is that the whole season should have a flavour of its own. Rich provision has been made of eucharistic propers, sets of readings, collects, canticles, and responsories for use throughout the season, in the hope that local selection will be made imaginatively.

Nevertheless, in many churches there is one major Advent liturgy usually, though not necessarily, celebrated on Advent Sunday itself. This could be eucharistic: with the full use of the Advent eucharistic propers a fine and distinctive Advent Eucharist could be celebrated. But there is already a widespread practice of a non-eucharistic Advent rite, often in the form of an Advent Carol procession, making full use of prophetic scriptures and some ancient Advent texts. We have provided for this in a number of ways in the section that follows, and can envisage a characteristic Advent liturgy built on the Light Service and Vigil pattern together with the use of the Advent introductions, collects, endings, and solemn blessings.

Many Advent liturgies in current use depend on the darkness/light theme, and several of our patterns are consonant with this. But there are other themes that churches would do well to explore, especially when the light theme is to be fully developed at Candlemas. Many of the forms of Advent Service that have been popularized in recent years have also had too much of the feel of a first Christmas Carol Service about them. While we recognize a 'change of gear' in mid-Advent, when with the forerunners, John the Baptist and Mary the Mother of the Lord, the Church begins to look forward to the celebration of the Nativity, there is no need for such overlap: Advent has strong themes and material of its own, and the many Patterns for Readings in Chapter I should be explored.

In *Lent, Holy Week, Easter* the Church was given two penitential rites as part of a response to a feeling that modern liturgy had not provided sufficient opportunity for Christian people to reflect on human failure and sin. In *The Promise of His Glory* we have provided two more, both with an Advent flavour. The first is a reflection on The Four Last Things, and more appropriate to the first part of Advent; the second is based on the Great Advent Antiphons, and strikes a note of hope and expectancy as much as penitence, setting human sin in a more cosmic and less individual context. Both can be used in a variety of ways, but are probably at their best as reflective corporate liturgies of penitence in preparation for Christmas.

Provision is also made for some popular Advent customs to be used as effectively as possible by the Church. The Advent Wreath and the Jesse Tree have potential both in the church building itself and in the homes of Christian people, as well as in schools.

B. VIGIL SERVICES AND CAROL SERVICES IN ADVENT

1 THE SERVICE OF LIGHT

In the Service of Light in Advent in section 1, either the first option or the first, second, or fourth of the alternatives are particularly suitable. In section 4, options b and c are particularly suitable, as is j (For the Blessed Virgin Mary).

2 BIDDING PRAYERS AND INTRODUCTIONS

1   As we enter, eager and expectant, into this solemn season of Advent, looking forward to the birth of the Christ child, let us renew in ourselves that vision of God's perfect kingdom which is the end of all our strivings and the consummation of God's loving purposes for us.

In sorrow and penitence we confess our failures and shortcomings, and seek pardon for those sins which frustrate his redemptive purposes and hinder the advent of his reign of love.

So in prayer, praise, and song do we give voice to the hope set forth in the Scriptures, that his kingdom shall come; and, as we prepare for that day to dawn upon us from on high, so we commend ourselves and the whole human family to his keeping.

May he guide us into the way of peace, give light to those who sit in darkness and the shadow of death, and kindle in us the fire of his love.

Amen. Come, Lord Jesus.   15*†

† Numbers in right-hand margin refer to Sources and Acknowledgements (pp.416-419).

2   In the name of God, who has delivered us from the
     dominion of darkness, and transferred us to the kingdom of
     his beloved Son, we welcome you: grace to you and peace.

     We are gathered together to proclaim and receive in our
     hearts the good news of the coming of God's Kingdom, and
     so prepare ourselves to celebrate with confidence and joy the
     birth of our Lord and Saviour Jesus Christ. We pray that we
     may respond in penitence and faith to the glory of his
     Kingdom, its works of justice and its promise of peace, its
     blessing and its hope.

     And as we seek to renew our allegiance to God's loving
     purpose, we pray for all who at this time especially need his
     pity and protection: the sick in body, mind or spirit; those
     who suffer from loss of dignity or loss of hope; those who
     face the future with fear, or walk in the shadow of death.

     May God, of his grace and mercy, grant to all his people a
     new trust in his good providence and a new obedience to his
     sovereign word, for to him is most justly due all glory,
     honour, worship, and praise, world without end.   **Amen**. *16*

3   In the name of God, who has delivered us from the
     dominion of darkness and made a place for us in the kingdom
     of his beloved Son, we welcome you: grace to you and peace.

     As we meet to celebrate anew the coming of God's
     Kingdom, we hear revealed the mystery of God's loving
     purpose for us – how that when we were far off, he met us in
     his Son and brought us home; how he humbled himself to
     take our human nature, that we might share his divine glory.

     Let us then so celebrate this coming with our carols and
     hymns of praise, that our lives may be charged with his life;
     that we may bear witness to his glory and so bring light to
     those who sit in darkness. So first we pray for those among
     whom the Christ was born: the poor and helpless, the aged
     and young children; the cold, the hungry, and the homeless;
     the victims of poverty, injustice, and oppression, the sick and
     those who mourn, the lonely and the unloved; those in
     despair or in the shadow of death.

Then, as we hear again the message of peace on earth and goodwill among all his people, we pray for the leaders of the nations, that all may be inspired to work together for the establishment of justice, freedom, and peace the world over.

And that we may bear true witness to this hope in a divided world, we pray for the peace and unity of Christ's body, the Church universal, that the whole earth may live to praise his name.

Finally, as we rejoice with the saints in heaven and on earth, we remember all who have gone before us with the sign of faith, whose hope was in the Word made flesh, Jesus Christ our Lord, through whom we offer up our prayers for the coming of his Kingdom, in the words he himself has taught us, saying:

Our Father in heaven,	*or*	**Our Father, who art in heaven,**
hallowed be your name,		**hallowed be thy name;**
your kingdom come,		**thy kingdom come;**
your will be done,		**thy will be done;**
on earth as in heaven.		**on earth as it is in heaven.**
Give us today our daily bread.		**Give us this day our daily bread.**
Forgive us our sins		**And forgive us our trespasses,**
as we forgive those		**as we forgive those**
who sin against us.		**who trespass against us.**
Lead us not into temptation		**And lead us not into temptation;**
but deliver us from evil.		**but deliver us from evil.**
For the kingdom, the power,		**For thine is the kingdom,**
and the glory are yours		**the power, and the glory,**
now and for ever. Amen.		**for ever and ever. Amen.**

And may the Lord when he comes find us watching and waiting, now and at all times. **Amen.** *3*

4 It is time for us to wake out of sleep, for deliverance is nearer to us now than it was when first we believed. It is far on in the night; day is near. Let us therefore cast off the deeds of darkness and put on our armour as soldiers of the light.

The grace and peace of God our Father and the Lord Jesus Christ be with you.
And also with you.

My brothers and sisters, we enter today the solemn season of Advent in which the Church bids us prepare to celebrate the coming of Christ; a coming that we recall in the Child of Bethlehem; a coming that we experience in the gift of his Spirit, in the bread of the Eucharist, in the joy of human lives that are shared; a coming we wait for when God gathers up all things in Christ. Let us in this holy season reflect on the coming of Christ who brings light to the world. Let us leave behind the darkness of sin, walk in the light that shines on our path, and renew within ourselves the hope of glory to which he beckons us. And as we turn towards the light, let us have on our hearts all those who see no light, for whom all is darkness and despair. Let us pray that they too may be illumined by Christ who is our light.   17

The whole congregation prays silently, after which the president draws the prayers together in the Collect for Advent Sunday.

Almighty God,
give us grace to cast away the works of darkness
and put on the armour of light,
now in the time of this mortal life,
in which your Son Jesus Christ
    came to us in great humility;
so that, at the last day,
when he shall come again in his glorious majesty
    to judge the living and the dead,
we may rise to the life immortal;
through him who is alive and reigns
    with you and the Holy Spirit,
one God, world without end.   **Amen.**   8

3 PATTERNS OF READINGS

The following Patterns of Readings from Chapter I, C are suitable in Advent.

(2)   A Vigil for Prisoners and those who sit in darkness
(3)   The King and his Kingdom
(4)   Looking for the Light
(5)   The Forerunner
(6)   Good News for the Poor

The first Pattern is particularly suitable for Vigils of Prayer for prisoners and refugees, for all who wait in darkness with hope and longing for a changed order. Patterns 3 and 4 are more suitable in the early part of Advent, Pattern 5 in the week of Advent 3 and Pattern 6 in the week of Advent 4. Pattern 15 may also be suitable.

4 CONCLUSIONS

1   Restore us, O Lord God of hosts:
Show the light of your countenance, and we shall be saved.

Will you not give us life again
That your people may rejoice in you?

Show us your mercy, O Lord,
And grant us your salvation. *11*

2   Blessed be the Lord, the God of Israel.
He has come to his people and set them free.

Hosanna to the Son of David,
Blessed is he who comes in the name of the Lord.
Hosanna in the highest.

Blessed is the coming Kingdom of our father David.
Hosanna in the highest.

Blessed be the name of the Lord.
Now and for ever.   Amen.

3   Blessed be God, Father, Son, and Holy Spirit,
and blessed be his Kingdom, now and for ever.

Blessed is the king who comes in the name of the Lord.
Peace in heaven and glory in the highest.

4   We wait for your loving kindness, O God,
in the midst of your temple.

The glory of the Lord shall be revealed
and all flesh shall see it together.

Show us your mercy, O Lord,
and grant us your salvation.

5   We wait for your loving kindness, O God,
in the midst of your temple.

Our help is in the name of the Lord,
who made heaven and earth.

Let us bless the Lord.
Thanks be to God.

6   The night is far spent, the day is at hand.
Let us therefore cast off the works of darkness
and put on the armour of light.

Come, O Lord, comfort the soul of your servant.
Even so, Lord, come.

The light of life send upon us;
the joy of peace send upon us;
the gladness of goodwill send upon us.

**In judgement and justice draw near,
in your merciful loving kindness draw near,
with the blessing of peace draw near.**

O wisdom of God, sweetly ordering all things,
flowing from the glory of the Almighty,
making all things new, kind to all,
making them friends of God.

**Come and comfort the soul of your servant,
for to you do I lift up my soul.**

O Lord Jesus Christ, come
at evening time, with light,

And in the morning, with your glory,
to guide our feet into the way of peace.

He who receives our prayers says:
Surely I come quickly.
I am the root and offspring of David,
I am the bright and morning star.
Amen. Even so come, Lord Jesus.

7   May God the Father, who loved the world so much that he
    sent his only Son, give you grace to prepare for eternal life.
    Amen.

    May God the Son, who comes to us as Redeemer and
    Judge, reveal to you the path from darkness to light.
    Amen.

    May God the Holy Spirit, by whose working the Virgin
    Mary conceived the Christ, help you bear the fruits of
    holiness.   **Amen.**

    And the blessing of God Almighty,
    the Father, the Son, and the Holy Spirit,
    be upon you and remain with you always.   **Amen.**   *13*

C. PENITENTIAL RITES IN ADVENT

1. The Four Last Things
A Service of Preparation for the End

The eschatological themes of Advent have traditionally been summarized under the title The Four Last Things – Death, Judgement, Heaven and Hell. Our Calendar and Lectionary proposals (see Introductory Outline and Appendix) make it possible for these themes to be treated at any time between the First Sunday of the Kingdom and the Second Sunday in Advent, thus avoiding the last two Sundays before Christmas with their incarnation and annunciation themes. While the readings provided on those Sundays signal some treatment of the Four Last Things, there should be provision for particular liturgies which highlight them.

We offer here the outline of such a liturgy. It is modelled on the form of a Vigil, but it may be adapted to the form of Antecommunion, or the Office, or it may be combined with the Eucharist, or shaped to make a Service of Penitence.

NOTES

1 If it is desired to combine this service with the Holy Communion, it may end at section 9 and the Holy Communion begin immediately at the Peace.

2 **At a Service of Penitence** the service is used as far as section 6. Then follows an Act of Penitence (sections 7 and 8 or Appendix B), suitable prayers, and the conclusion (sections 10 and 11).

3 **Hymns** may be sung at any suitable point.

INTRODUCTION

1   The Book of the Gospels is brought into the church and placed on the holy table or a reading desk.

2   The minister greets the people.

Blessed be God: Father, Son, and Holy Spirit,
And blessed be his Kingdom, now and for ever.   Amen.

or

Grace and peace from God our Father
and the Lord Jesus Christ be with you.
And also with you.

3   The minister addresses the people in these or similar words.

In Advent we look forward. We rekindle the eager hope and fear with which the Old Testament prophets looked forward to the coming of the promised Messiah; we prepare ourselves to celebrate his birth at Christmas.

When the Lord Christ came to live among us, he taught us to look forward to the hour when we shall each be called from this world through death: the crowning point of every life, when we appear before him for judgement.

He taught us also, and above all, to see our lives in his divine perspective, to long for the day when he will come again, the point beyond which all looking forward will cease, for time will have come to an end. Then all will be united and perfected in heaven, save what has been lost to hell.

Today let us meditate on these four last things: death, judgement, heaven, and hell. Let us examine our preparation for death and eternal life, in order that we may be strengthened in hope, moved to thank God for his grace, and inspired to deeper penitence and greater love.

4   THIS RESPONSORY, or one from Chapter VII (11-14), is used.

Let us call on God's loving mercy.

Turn to us again, O God our Saviour,
and let your anger cease from us.

Lord, have mercy.
Lord, have mercy.

Show us your mercy, O Lord,
and grant us your salvation.

Christ, have mercy.
Christ, have mercy.

Your salvation is near for those who fear you,
that glory may dwell within our land.

Lord, have mercy.
Lord, have mercy.   *3*

5   Stir up your power, Lord,
and with great might come among us;
and, because we are sorely hindered by our sins,
let your bountiful grace
    speedily help and deliver us;
through Jesus Christ our Lord,
who is alive and reigns with you and the Holy Spirit,
one God, now and for ever.   **Amen.**   *4*

or

Grant us, Lord,
the wisdom and the grace to use aright
the time that is left to us here on earth.
Lead us to repent of our sins,
the evil we have done and the good we have not done;
and strengthen us to follow the steps of your Son,
in the way that leads to the fullness of eternal life;
through Jesus Christ our Lord.   **Amen.**   *8*

THE WORD OF GOD

6   Readings, together with psalms, canticles and hymns and
prayers are used as required. The final reading is from the
Gospels. Silence should be kept after each reading, and then
follows the psalm, biddings, and prayer. (For the Collects see
Chapter VIII.) A sermon may be preached.

READINGS AND PRAYERS

Old Testament

1   Job 19. 21-27
    Psalm 27 (1-10, 16-end)
    Collect: 38

2   Isaiah 25. 6-9
    Psalm 23
    Collect: 24

3   Wisdom 3. 1-9
    Psalm 116 (1-9)
    Collect: 31

4   Wisdom 4. 7-15
    Psalm 25 (10-end)
    Collect: 32

New Testament

1   Romans 8. 14-23
    Psalm 42 (1-7)
    Collect: 22

2   Romans 8. 31b-39
    Psalm 130
    Collect: 36

3   Romans 14. 7-12
    Psalm 103 (8-17)
    Collect: 30

4   1 Corinthians 15. 20-26
    Psalm 118 (14-21)
    Collect: 34

5   2 Corinthians 4. 16 – 5. 10
    Psalm 90 (1-6, 10-12, 14,
    16-17)
    Collect: 37

6   Philippians 3. 10-end
    Psalm 139 (1-11, 17-18,
    23-24)
    Collect: 39

7   1 Thessalonians 4. 13-18
    Psalm 121
    Collect: 35

8   Revelation 20. 11-end
    Psalm 143 (1-10)
    Collect: 40

9   Revelation 21. 1-7
    Psalm 63 (1-9)
    Collect: 31

10   Revelation 21. 22 – 22. 5
    Psalm 122
    Collect: 23

Gospel

1   Matthew 25. 1-13

2   Matthew 25. 31-end

3   Luke 12. 35-40

4   John 5. 19-25

5   John 14. 1-6, 27

RESPONSE

7   PENITENCE

This act of penitence is used, or a selection made from Appendix B, pp.124-127.

† Man that is born of woman
has but a short time to live;
We have our fill of sorrow.
We blossom like a flower, and then wither.
We slip away like a shadow, and do not endure.

Holy God, holy and mighty,
holy and merciful Saviour,
abandon us not to the bitterness of eternal death.

In the midst of life we are in death;
where can we turn for help?
Only to you, O Lord,
justly angered by our sins.

Holy God, holy and mighty,
holy and merciful Saviour,
abandon us not to the bitterness of eternal death.

Lord, you know the secrets of our hearts;
shut not your ears to our prayers,
but spare us, O Lord, and forgive us.

Holy God, holy and mighty,
holy and merciful Saviour,
abandon us not to the bitterness of eternal death.

O eternal and merciful Judge,
in life and when we come to die,
let us not fall away from you.

Holy God, holy and mighty,
holy and merciful Saviour,
abandon us not to the bitterness of eternal death.

† *or*

Those born of woman
have but a short time to live.
We have our fill of sorrow . . .

8   The minister prays

O Lord God,
whose mercies are sure and full and ever new:
grant us the greatest of them all,
the Spirit of your dear Son;
that in the day of judgement
we may be presented to you
if not blameless, yet forgiven,
if not successful, yet faithful,
if not holy, yet persevering,
deserving nothing, but accepted in him
who pleads our cause and redeemed our lives,
even Jesus Christ our Lord.   **Amen.**

9   Other prayers may be said. The Litany for Holy Dying
(appended to this service) is particularly appropriate. If it is
not used, other intercessions and thanksgivings may be
appropriate, and the Lord's Prayer is said.

CONCLUSION

10   **God and Father of our Lord Jesus Christ,**
bring us to the dwelling which your Son
is preparing for all who love you.
Give us the will each day
to live in life eternal.
Let our citizenship be in heaven
with your blessed and beloved,
the whole company of the redeemed,
and with countless angels,
praising, worshipping, and adoring him
who sits upon the throne for ever and ever.   **Amen.**

11   To him who is able to keep us from falling and to present
us without blemish before the presence of his glory with
rejoicing, to the only God, our Saviour through Jesus
Christ our Lord, be glory, majesty, dominion, and
authority, before all time and now and for ever.   **Amen.**

or

12 May the God of peace himself sanctify you wholly; and
may your spirit and soul and body be kept sound and
blameless at the coming of our Lord Jesus Christ; and may
the blessing of God almighty, Father, Son, and Holy Spirit,
come down upon you and remain with you always.
Amen.

APPENDIX : THE LITANY FOR HOLY DYING 4

God the Father
have mercy on us.

God the Son
have mercy on us.

God the Holy Spirit
have mercy on us.

Holy, blessed, and glorious Trinity
have mercy on us.

God, who took the form of a servant, and shared the life
of suffering and sorrow,
have mercy on us.

God, who raised the daughter of Jairus, the son of the
widow of Nain, and Lazarus at Bethany,
have mercy on us.

God, who bore our weaknesses and healed our sicknesses,
have mercy on us.

God, who became obedient unto death, even death on a
cross,
have mercy on us.

God, who at the beginning breathed into us life, and
appointed the hour of our death,
have mercy on us.

Hear our prayers, good Jesus, and grant that, dying to sin
here, we may live for you in heaven:
Good Jesus, hear us.

May we, remaining your faithful soldiers and servants here, receive hereafter the crown of glory:
Good Jesus, hear us.

May we accept with joy all the suffering of sickness and death as no more than we deserve:
Good Jesus, hear us.

Be with us in the valley of the shadow of death:
Good Jesus, hear us.

Let us not, at our last hour, fall away from you:
Good Jesus, hear us.

Forgive us our sins, and strengthen us with the Bread of Life:
Good Jesus, hear us.

Let us die in your faith and fear, in sure and certain hope of the resurrection to eternal life:
Good Jesus, hear us.

Deliver us, Lord, at our last hour; as you delivered Enoch and Elijah from the death which must come to all,
Save and deliver us.

As you delivered Noah from the flood,
Save and deliver us.

As you delivered Job from his affliction,
Save and deliver us.

As you delivered Isaac from the knife,
Save and deliver us.

As you delivered Lot from Sodom,
Save and deliver us.

As you delivered Daniel from the lions' den,
Save and deliver us.

As you delivered the three young men from the fiery furnace,
Save and deliver us.

As you delivered Esther and her people from the power of Haman,
Save and deliver us.

As you delivered Susanna from false condemnation and
stoning,
Save and deliver us.

As you have always delivered from evil those who put
their trust in you,
Save and deliver us.

Deliver us, Lord, on that fearful day, when the heavens
and the earth shall pass away, when you shall come to
judge the world by fire:
Save and deliver us.

In the day of judgement, when the books are opened, and
the dead, great and small, shall stand before you:
Save and deliver us.

Holy God, holy and strong, holy and immortal:
have mercy on us.

Jesus, Lamb of God:
have mercy on us.

Jesus, bearer of our sins:
have mercy on us.

Jesus, redeemer of the world:
give us your peace.

Let us pray with confidence to the Father in the words our
Saviour gave us:

**Our Father in heaven,
hallowed be your name,
your kingdom come,
your will be done,
on earth as in heaven.
Give us today our daily bread.
Forgive us our sins
as we forgive those who sin against us.
Lead us not into temptation
but deliver us from evil.**

Deliver us, Lord, from every evil,
and grant us peace in our day.
In your mercy keep us free from sin
and protect us from all anxiety
as we wait in joyful hope
for the coming of our Saviour Jesus Christ.

**For the kingdom, the power, and the glory are yours,
now and for ever.   Amen.**

Happy are the dead:
who die in the faith of Christ.

Father, you made us in your image
and your Son accepted death for our salvation.
Help us to keep watch in prayer at all times.
May we be free from all sin
when we leave this world,
and rejoice in peace with you for ever;
through Jesus Christ our Lord.   **Amen.**

2. The Great 'O's
A Service of Hope and Expectation

The Advent Antiphons, sung originally as antiphons to the
Magnificat at the Evening Office from 17 to 23 December, have
provided a rich source of devotional imagery in Advent, and are well
known through the hymn 'O come, O come, Emmanuel'.

While the Antiphons may be used in their traditional context as
antiphons to the Magnificat at Evening Prayer, they may also be used
as opening Sentences, or as an Advent Litany (see D.3b (p. 130)). In
this service they become the framework for a rite of expectation and
preparation, appropriate for the second part of Advent.

This celebration looks not to the past but to the future, and its main
emphasis is not on contrition for personal shortcoming, but on the
proclamation of God's universal judgement.

THE ENTRANCE

1   At the Entrance, the Advent Prose is sung.

> **Pour down, O heavens, from above,**
> **And let the skies rain down righteousness.**

> Turn your fierce anger from us, O Lord,
> and remember not our sins for ever.
> Your holy cities have become a desert,
> Zion a wilderness, Jerusalem a desolation;
> our holy and beautiful house,
> where our fathers† praised you.

> **Pour down, O heavens, from above,**
> **and let the skies rain down righteousness.**

> We have sinned and become like one who is unclean;
> we have all withered like a leaf,
> and our iniquities like the wind have swept us away.
> You have hidden your face from us,
> and abandoned us to our iniquities.

> **Pour down, O heavens, from above,**
> **and let the skies rain down righteousness.**

† or forebears if preferred

You are my witnesses, says the Lord,
and my servant whom I have chosen,
that you may know me and believe me.
I myself am the Lord, and none but I can deliver;
what my hand holds, none can snatch away.

Pour down, O heavens, from above,
and let the skies rain down righteousness.

Comfort my people, comfort them;
my salvation shall not be delayed.
I have swept your offences away like a cloud;
fear not, for I will save you.
I am the Lord your God, the Holy One of Israel,
your Redeemer.

Pour down, O heavens, from above,
and let the skies rain down righteousness.

2   The president welcomes the people.

Grace, mercy, and peace from God our Father and the
Lord Jesus Christ be with you.
The Lord bless you.

There may follow an introduction or bidding, after which the
president says

3   THE COLLECT

Either this Collect following

Almighty God,
before the judgement seat of whose Son,
the Lord Christ, we must all appear;
keep us steadfast and faithful in his service,
and enable us so to judge ourselves in this life,
that we may not be condemned
    on the day of his appearing;
for his tender mercy's sake.   **Amen.**   *4*

or the Collect for Advent Sunday (27, p.345)

4 **THE MINISTRY OF THE WORD**

Before each Reading an 'O' Antiphon is said or sung; after
each Reading a verse of the hymn 'O come, O come,
Emmanuel' is sung by all.

O wisdom, coming forth from the Most High, filling all
creation and reigning to the ends of the earth; come and
teach us the way of truth.

If the Antiphon is spoken, then this response may be used by
all.

Amen. Come, Lord Jesus.

READING   *Ecclesiasticus 24. 3-9*

> O come, thou wisdom from on high
> who madest all in earth and sky,
> creating man from dust and clay:
> to us reveal salvation's way.
> > **Rejoice! Rejoice! Emmanuel**
> > **shall come to thee, O Israel.**   18

O Lord of Lords, and ruler of the House of Israel, you
appeared to Moses in the fire of the burning bush, and
gave him the law on Sinai: come with your outstretched
arm and ransom us.   19

Amen. Come, Lord Jesus.

READING   *Exodus 3. 1-6*

> O come, O come, Adonai,
> who in thy glorious majesty
> from Sinai's mountain, clothed in awe,
> gavest thy folk the ancient law.
> > **Rejoice! Rejoice! Emmanuel**
> > **shall come to thee, O Israel.**

O root of Jesse, standing as a sign among the nations;
kings will keep silence before you for whom the nations
long; come and save us and delay no longer.

Amen. Come, Lord Jesus.

READING   *Isaiah 11. 1-4a*

> O come, thou root of Jesse! Draw
> the quarry from the lion's claw;
> from those dread caverns of the grave,
> from nether hell thy people save.
> **Rejoice! Rejoice! Emmanuel**
> **shall come to thee, O Israel.**

O key of David and sceptre of the House of Israel; you
open and none can shut; you shut and none can open:
come and free the captives from prison, and break down
the walls of death.

Amen. Come, Lord Jesus.

READING   *Isaiah 22. 21-23*

> O come, thou Lord of David's key!
> The royal door fling wide and free;
> safeguard for us the heavenward road,
> and bar the way to death's abode.
> **Rejoice! Rejoice! Emmanuel**
> **shall come to thee, O Israel.**

O morning star, splendour of the light eternal and bright
sun of righteousness: come and bring light to those who
dwell in darkness and walk in the shadow of death.

Amen. Come, Lord Jesus.

READING   *Numbers 24. 15b-17*

> O come, O come, thou dayspring bright!
> Pour on our souls thy healing light;
> dispel the long night's lingering gloom,
> and pierce the shadows of the tomb.
> **Rejoice! Rejoice! Emmanuel**
> **shall come to thee, O Israel.**

O king of the nations, you alone can fulfil their desires: cornerstone, binding all together: come and save the creature you fashioned from the dust of the earth.

Amen. Come, Lord Jesus.

READING   *Jeremiah 30. 7-11a*

> O come, desire of nations! Show
> thy kingly reign on earth below;
> thou cornerstone, uniting all,
> restore the ruin of our fall.
> **Rejoice! Rejoice! Emmanuel**
> **shall come to thee, O Israel.**

O Emmanuel, our King and Lawgiver, hope of the nations and their saviour: come and save us, O Lord our God.

Amen. Come, Lord Jesus.

Stand

THE GOSPEL READING   *Matthew 1. 18-23*

A reading from the Holy Gospel according to Matthew.
Glory to Christ our Saviour.

At the end the reader says

This is the Gospel of Christ.
Praise to Christ our Lord.

> O come, O come, Emmanuel!
> Redeem thy captive Israel,
> that into exile drear is gone
> far from the face of God's dear Son.
> **Rejoice! Rejoice! Emmanuel**
> **shall come to thee, O Israel.**

5   AN ADDRESS may be given.

THE CELEBRATION OF PENITENCE AND RECONCILIATION

6   The Act of Penitence and Reconciliation has four parts:
(1) Examination of conscience, (2) prayer for God's mercy,
(3) act of penitence and contrition, (4) declaration of
absolution. They may take the following forms or be drawn
from Appendix B.

(1) EXAMINATION OF CONSCIENCE

A minister leads the examination of conscience, concluding
each section with

Have mercy on us, Lord, for we have sinned.

Lord, have mercy.
(Christ, have mercy.
Lord, have mercy.)

During the examination of conscience, psalms, canticles, or
hymns of penitence may be sung.

(2) PRAYER FOR GOD'S MERCY

At the end of the examination of conscience may be said

Holy God,
Holy and mighty,
Holy and immortal,
have mercy on us.

Have mercy on your servants, Lord.
Have mercy on us, Lord, in your kingdom
and grant us your salvation,
now and at the hour of our death.   Amen.

(3) ACT OF PENITENCE AND CONTRITION

Almighty God,
long-suffering and of great goodness:
I confess to you with my whole heart
my neglect and forgetfulness of your commandments,

my wrong doing, thinking, and speaking;
the hurts I have done to others;
and the good I have left undone.
O God, forgive me, for I have sinned against you;
and raise me to newness of life;
through Jesus Christ our Lord.   Amen.   20

(4) ACT OF ABSOLUTION

The president stands, and says with outstretched arms

God, the Father of mercies,
has reconciled the world to himself
through the death and resurrection
    of his Son Jesus Christ,
not counting our trespasses against us,
but sending his Holy Spirit
to shed abroad his love among us.
By the ministry of reconciliation
entrusted by Christ to his Church,
receive his pardon and peace
to stand before him in his strength alone,
this day and evermore.   **Amen.**

Let us pray for the coming of the kingdom, saying:

Our Father in heaven, *or*	Our Father, who art in heaven,
hallowed be your name,	hallowed be thy name;
your kingdom come,	thy kingdom come;
your will be done,	thy will be done;
on earth as in heaven.	on earth as it is in heaven.
Give us today our daily bread.	Give us this day our daily bread.
Forgive us our sins	And forgive us our trespasses,
as we forgive those	as we forgive those
who sin against us.	who trespass against us.
Lead us not into temptation	And lead us not into temptation;
but deliver us from evil.	but deliver us from evil.
For the kingdom, the power,	For thine is the kingdom,
and the glory are yours	the power, and the glory,
now and for ever. Amen.	for ever and ever. Amen.

THE CONCLUSION

7   The president says this prayer of thanksgiving.

Lord our God,
on the first day of creation
you made the light that scatters all darkness.
Let Christ, the light of lights,
hidden from all eternity,
shine at last on your people
and free us from the darkness of sin.
Fill our lives with good works
as we go out to meet your Son,
so that we may rejoice to welcome him at his coming.
We ask this in the name of Jesus the Lord.   **Amen.**

A HYMN or SONG of thanksgiving may be sung.

8   THE DISMISSAL

The president blesses the people.

May God the Father, judge all-merciful,
make us worthy of a place in his kingdom.   **Amen.**

May God the Son, coming among us in power,
reveal in our midst the promise of his glory.   **Amen.**

May God the Holy Spirit make us steadfast in faith,
joyful in hope and constant in love.   **Amen.**

And the blessing of God almighty,
the Father, the Son, and the Holy Spirit,
be upon you and remain with you always.   **Amen.**

Minister   Go in the peace of Christ.
           Thanks be to God.

3. Appendix to Penitential Rites

A. SONGS

1 THE ADVENT PROSE

**Pour down, O heavens, from above,
and let the skies rain down righteousness.**

Turn your fierce anger from us, O Lord,
and remember not our sins for ever.
Your holy cities have become a desert,
Zion a wilderness, Jerusalem a desolation;
our holy and beautiful house,
where our fathers† praised you.

**Pour down, O heavens, from above,
and let the skies rain down righteousness.**

We have sinned and become like one who is unclean;
we have all withered like a leaf,
and our iniquities like the wind have swept us away.
You have hidden your face from us,
and abandoned us to our iniquities.

**Pour down, O heavens, from above,
and let the skies rain down righteousness.**

You are my witnesses, says the Lord,
and my servant whom I have chosen,
that you may know me and believe me.
I myself am the Lord, and none but I can deliver;
what my hand holds, none can snatch away.

**Pour down, O heavens, from above,
and let the skies rain down righteousness.**

Comfort my people, comfort them;
my salvation shall not be delayed.
I have swept your offences away like a cloud;
fear not, for I will save you.

† or forebears if preferred

I am the Lord your God, the Holy One of Israel,
your redeemer.

**Pour down, O heavens, from above,
and let the skies rain down righteousness.**

2 DIES IRAE

This hymn is particularly suitable for use as an office hymn
during the week or weeks before Advent. If so used at Morning
and Evening Prayer it may be divided into two parts: verses 1-8
and 9-18. If used also at Night Prayer it may be divided into
three parts: verses 1-6, 7-12 and 13-18. An alternative version
is to be found in *AMR* (no. 466).

1 Day of wrath and doom impending,
   David's word with Sibyl's blending!†
   Heaven and earth in ashes ending!

2 O what fear man's bosom rendeth,
   When from heaven the Judge descendeth,
   On whose sentence all dependeth!

3 Wondrous sound the trumpet flingeth,
   Through earth's sepulchres it ringeth,
   All before the throne it bringeth.

4 Death is struck, and nature quaking,
   All creation is awaking,
   To its Judge an answer making.

5 Lo! the book exactly worded,
   Wherein all hath been recorded;
   Thence shall judgement be awarded.

6 When the Judge his seat attaineth,
   And each hidden deed arraigneth,
   Nothing unavenged remaineth.

7 What shall I, frail man, be pleading?
   Who for me be interceding,
   When the just are mercy needing?

† Note: The reference in verse 1 to the Sibyl, the oracular voice of the pagan
classical world, indicates the universal expectation of a Day of Judgement
at the end of all things.

8 King of majesty tremendous,
   Who dost free salvation send us,
   Fount of pity, then befriend us!

9 Think, kind Jesus! – my salvation
   Caused thy wondrous incarnation;
   Leave me not to reprobation.

10 Faint and weary thou hast sought me,
   On the Cross of suffering bought me;
   Shall such grace be vainly brought me?

11 Righteous Judge! for sin's pollution
   Grant thy gift of absolution,
   Ere that day of retribution.

12 Guilty, now I pour my moaning,
   All my shame with anguish owning;
   Spare, O God, thy suppliant groaning!

13 Through the sinful woman shriven,
   Through the dying thief forgiven,
   Thou to me a hope hast given.

14 Worthless are my prayers and sighing,
   Yet, good Lord, in grace complying,
   Rescue me from night undying.

15 With thy sheep a place provide me,
   From the goats afar divide me,
   To thy right hand do thou guide me.

16 When the wicked are confounded,
   Doomed to shame and woe unbounded,
   Call me, with thy Saints surrounded.

17 Low I kneel, with heart's submission;
   See, like ashes my contrition!
   Help me in my last condition!

18 Ah! that day of tears and mourning!
   From the dust of earth returning,
   Man for judgement must prepare him;
   Spare, O God, in mercy spare him!

or

1   That day of wrath, that dreadful day,
When heaven and earth shall pass away,
What power shall be the sinner's stay?
How shall he meet that dreadful day?

2   When, shrivelling like a parched scroll,
The flaming heavens together roll;
When louder yet, and yet more dread,
Swells the high trump that wakes the dead:

3   O, on that day, that wrathful day,
When man to judgement wakes from clay,
Be thou, O Christ, the sinner's stay,
Though heaven and earth shall pass away.
Sir Walter Scott

or

1   Hear'st thou, my soul, what serious things
Both the Psalm and Sibyl sings
Of a sure Judge, from whose sharp ray
The world in flames shall fly away?

2   O that Trump, whose blast shall run
An even round with the circling sun,
And urge the murmuring graves to bring
Pale mankind forth to meet his King!

4   Shall all that labour, all that cost
Of love, and even that loss, be lost;
And this loved soul, judged worth no less
Than all that way and weariness?

5   Those mercies which thy Mary found,
And who thy Cross confessed and crowned,
Hope tells my heart, the same loves be
Still alive, and still for me.

6   Though both my prayers and tears combine,
Both worthless are, for they are mine;
But thou thy bounteous self still be,
and show thou art, by saving me.
Richard Crashaw   21

B. ACTS OF PENITENCE

1 A PENITENTIAL LITANY

You know, O Lord, the vigilance of my spiritual enemies, and the weakness of my humanity.

Lord Jesus Christ, Son of God,
have mercy on me, a sinner.

Cover me with the wings of your loving mercy, that I may sleep not in death.

Lord Jesus Christ, Son of God,
have mercy on me, a sinner.

Enlighten the eyes of my mind, that I may delight in your word, and glorify you in praise, O lover of souls.

Lord Jesus Christ, Son of God,
have mercy on me, a sinner.

How awesome is your judgement, O Lord, when we shall stand before you, the books are opened, deeds are put to the test, and thoughts are searched out.

Lord Jesus Christ, Son of God,
have mercy on me, a sinner.

Quench the flames of your anger, lighten my darkness, and show mercy on me for the sake of your tender love.

Lord Jesus Christ, Son of God,
have mercy on me, a sinner.

Grant me, O God, the tears of the sinful woman, and let me wash your feet, for they have led me from the broad path of destruction.

Lord Jesus Christ, Son of God,
have mercy on me, a sinner.

Let me offer you the sweet sacrifice of a pure life, fashioned by my repentance.

Lord Jesus Christ, Son of God,
have mercy on me, a sinner.

Let me hear that voice of yours for which I long, saying,
Your faith has saved you; go in peace.

Lord Jesus Christ, Son of God,
have mercy on me, a sinner.

For you are the lover of souls, and to you is glory, praise,
dominion and power, now and to the ages of ages.
Amen. *Byzantine*

2 AN ACT OF PENITENCE

PREPARATION

Lord my God, I call for help:
Let my prayer come into your presence.

Lord God, we come to you
with sorrow for our sins,
and we ask for your help and strength.
Help us to know ourselves
and to accept our weakness.
Strengthen us with your forgiving love,
so that we may more courageously
    follow and obey your Son,
whose birth we are soon to celebrate.   **Amen.**

Lord, let me hear the call of your prophet
    John the Baptist,
that I may truly repent and be converted.
Let what is crooked in me become straight,
let what is rough become smooth,
and what is empty be filled;
through Jesus Christ our Lord.   Amen.

One of the following, or some other suitable passage of
scripture is read.

Romans 13. 11-14; Philippians 4. 4-7

An address or conducted meditation follows, with a period of
silence for self-examination.

CONFESSION

Almighty God,
long-suffering and of great goodness:
I confess to you,
I confess with my whole heart
my neglect and forgetfulness of your commandments,
my wrong doing, thinking, and speaking;
the hurts I have done to others;
and the good I have left undone.
O God, forgive me, for I have sinned against you;
and raise me to newness of life;
through Jesus Christ our Lord.   Amen.   *20*

or

My God, for love of you
I desire to hate and forsake all sins
by which I have ever displeased you;
and I resolve by the help of your grace
to commit them no more;
and to avoid all the opportunities of sin.
Help me to do this,
through Jesus Christ our Lord.   Amen.   *20*

ABSOLUTION

The almighty and merciful Lord
grant you pardon and forgiveness of all your sins,
time for amendment of life,
and the grace and strength of the Holy Spirit.   **Amen.**

(or when water is used)

The president prays over a vessel of water

Lord God almighty,
creator of all life,
of body and soul,
accept this water;
as we use it in faith,
recalling our baptism,
forgive our sins
and save us from the power of evil.

Lord, in your mercy
give us living water,
always springing up
as a fountain of salvation:
free us, body and soul,
from all that may harm us,
and welcome us into your presence
in purity of heart.
Grant this through Christ our Lord.　**Amen.**　　　*20*

The president and people are sprinkled with the water.
Meanwhile suitable anthems (especially the Advent Prose)
may be sung.

The president concludes

May almighty God cleanse us from sin
and make us worthy of the kingdom of his glory.　**Amen.**

20

D. SENTENCES AND PRAYERS FOR USE BETWEEN ALL SAINTS' DAY AND CHRISTMAS

1 INVITATION TO CONFESSION

a   When the Lord comes, he will bring to light things now hidden in darkness, and will disclose the purposes of the heart. In that light we confess our sins.

b   Jesus says, Repent, for the kingdom of heaven is close at hand. So let us turn away from sin and turn to him, confessing our sins in penitence and faith.

2 PENITENCE

a   Lord Jesus, you came to gather the nations
into the peace of your kingdom.
Lord, have mercy.
Lord, have mercy.

You come in word and sacrament
to strengthen us in holiness.
Christ, have mercy.
Christ, have mercy.

You will come in glory
with salvation for your people.
Lord, have mercy.
Lord, have mercy.   *10*

b   Turn to us again, O God our Saviour,
and let your anger cease from us.
Lord, have mercy.
Lord, have mercy.

Show us your mercy, O Lord,
and grant us your salvation.
Christ, have mercy.
Christ, have mercy.

Your salvation is near for those that fear you,
that glory may dwell in our land.
Lord, have mercy.
Lord, have mercy.   *3*

3   **INTERCESSION**

a   In joyful expectation of his coming to our aid
     we pray to Jesus, saying,
     Maranatha
     Come, Lord Jesus.

     Come to your Church as Lord and Judge.
     We pray for . . .
     Help us to live in the light of your coming
     and give us a longing for your rule.
     Maranatha
     Come, Lord Jesus.

     Come to your world as King of the nations.
     We pray for . . .
     Before you rulers will stand in silence.
     Maranatha
     Come, Lord Jesus.

     Come to your people with a message of victory and peace.
     We pray for . . .
     Give us the victory over death, temptation, and evil.
     Maranatha
     Come, Lord Jesus.

     Come to us as Saviour and Comforter.
     We pray for . . .
     Break in to those areas of our lives
     where we live with failure and distress,
     and set us free to serve you for ever.
     Maranatha
     Come, Lord Jesus.

Come to us from heaven with power and great glory,
to lift us up to meet you,
with all your saints and angels,
to live with you for ever.
Maranatha
Come, Lord Jesus.

b   This litany is based on the Advent Antiphons, and thus may appropriately be used from 17 December onwards. It may be used as it stands, or biddings may be inserted before each section.   4

Our Lord says, 'Surely I am coming quickly'. Even so, come, Lord Jesus!

O Wisdom, Breath of the Most High, pervading and permeating all creation; come and make us friends of God.

Maranatha. Come, Lord Jesus.†

O Lord of lords and Leader of the house of Israel, who appeared to Moses in the burning bush and gave him your law on Sinai; come and save us with your mighty arm.

Maranatha. Come, Lord Jesus.

O Root of Jesse, standing as a signal to the nations, before you all kings are silent, to you the nations will do homage; come and save us, delay no longer.

Maranatha. Come, Lord Jesus.

O Key of David and Ruler of the house of Israel, when you open no one can close, when you close no one can open; come and proclaim liberty to the captives and set free the oppressed.

Maranatha. Come, Lord Jesus.

† or **Amen. Come, Lord Jesus.**

O Rising Sun, Splendour of eternal light and Sun of justice; come and give light to those who live in darkness and the shadow of death.

Maranatha. Come, Lord Jesus.

O King of the nations, the Ruler they long for, the Cornerstone binding all together; come and save the people you fashioned from the dust of the earth.

Maranatha. Come, Lord Jesus.

O Emmanuel, our King and our Lawgiver, the Anointed of the nations and their Saviour; come and save us, O Lord our God.

Maranatha. Come, Lord Jesus.

The Spirit and the Bride say, 'Come!'

Maranatha. Come, Lord Jesus.

Lord, you are the one who is to come.

Maranatha. Come, Lord Jesus.

Come, O Lord, and visit us in peace:
that we may rejoice before you with a perfect heart.

Come, Lord Jesus, do not delay;
give new courage to your people
who trust in your love.
By your coming, raise us
to the joy of your kingdom,
where you live and reign
with the Father and the Spirit,
one God for ever and ever.   **Amen.**

May the Lord when he comes find us watching and waiting.   **Amen.**

4   INTRODUCTION TO THE PEACE

a   In the tender compassion of our God
    the dawn from on high shall break upon us,
    to shine on those who dwell in darkness
        and the shadow of death,
    and to guide our feet into the way of peace.

b   The God of peace make us holy in all things
    that we may be ready at the coming of our Lord
        Jesus Christ.

5   PROPER PREFACES

a   And now we give you thanks
    because you sent him to redeem us from sin and death,
    and to make us heirs of everlasting life;
    that when he shall come again in power and great triumph
        to judge the world,
    we may with joy behold his appearing,
    and in confidence may stand before him.   12

b   And now we give you thanks
    because he is the Saviour.
    In your mercy and faithfulness
    you have promised to us after the fall
    that his truth might instruct the ignorant,
    his holiness purify sinners,
    and his strength sustain the weak.
    Since the time is at hand when
        the one whom you sent should come,
    since the day of our deliverance has begun to dawn,
    full of confidence in your promises, we exult with joy.

c   And now we give you thanks
    because you anointed Jesus Christ,
    your only Son, as priest and king.
    Crowned with thorns, he offered his life upon the cross,
    that he might draw all people
    into that kingdom where now he reigns in glory.

d   And now we give you thanks
      because you anointed Jesus Christ, your only Son,
      as the eternal priest and king of all.
      As a priest he offered up his life on the cross,
      that by his one sacrifice
      he might present to you an eternal kingdom;
      a kingdom of truth and life;
      a kingdom of justice, love, and peace.   *11*

e   And now we give you thanks
      because when he humbled himself
      to come among us as a man,
      he fulfilled the plan you formed long ago
      and opened for us the way of salvation.
      So now we watch for the day,
      knowing that the salvation promised us will be ours
      when Christ our Lord will come again in glory.   *10*

f   And now we give you thanks
      because his future coming was proclaimed
         by all the prophets.
      The virgin mother bore him in her womb
         with love beyond all telling.
      John the Baptist was his herald
      and made him known when at last he came.
      In his love Christ has filled us with joy
      as we prepared to celebrate his birth,
      so that when he comes he may find us watching in prayer,
      our hearts filled with wonder and praise.

g   And now we give you thanks
      because your Son our Lord was awaited by the prophets,
      announced by an angel,
      conceived by a virgin,
      and proclaimed at last to men and women of every race.

6 POST-COMMUNION PRAYERS

a   Almighty God, by your gift
    the tree of life was set at the heart of the earthly paradise,
    and the bread of life was set at the heart of your Church.
    Let this divine nourishment bring us,
    not to judgement, but to life eternal;
    through Jesus Christ our Lord.   4

b   Generous God,
    you have fed us at your heavenly table.
    Kindle us with the fire of your Spirit
    that when Christ comes again
    we may shine like lights before his face;
    who is alive and reigns with you and the Holy Spirit,
    one God, now and for ever.   22

c   Loving Father,
    your Son Jesus Christ has come to us
    in word and Spirit, in bread and cup.
    Preserve us from condemnation in body and soul
    when he comes to judge the living and the dead.
    through Jesus Christ our Lord.   22

d   Gracious Lord,
    in this holy sacrament
    you give substance to our hope.
    Bring us at the last
    to that pure life for which we long;
    through Jesus Christ our Lord.   23

e   God our Father,
    whose Son was born into the world
    to free us from sin and death,
    and to bring us to everlasting life:
    purify us by his perfect sacrifice,
    that, when he comes in power and glory,
    we may greet without shame or fear;
    through Jesus Christ our Lord.   4

The Book of Common Prayer orders the use of the Collect for
Advent Sunday throughout the season, but more recent
provision allows only one Collect at the beginning of the
Eucharist. Those who value the tradition of the Advent Collect
throughout the season may appropriately use it as a Post-
Communion prayer.

7   BLESSINGS

a   May God the Father,
 who loved the world so much that he sent his only Son,
 give you grace to prepare for life eternal.   **Amen.**

 May God the Son,
 who comes to us as Redeemer and Judge,
 reveal to you the path from darkness to light.   **Amen.**

 May God the Holy Spirit,
 by whose working the Virgin Mary conceived the Christ,
 help you bear the fruits of holiness.   **Amen.**

 And the blessing of God almighty,
 the Father, the Son, and the Holy Spirit,
 be upon you and remain with you always.   **Amen.**   *13*

b   May God the Father, judge all-merciful,
 make us worthy of a place in his kingdom.   **Amen.**

 May God the Son, coming among us in power,
 reveal in our midst the promise of his glory.   **Amen.**

 May God the Holy Spirit make us steadfast in faith,
 joyful in hope and constant in love.   **Amen.**

 And the blessing . . .

c   Christ the Sun of Righteousness shine upon you,
 scatter the darkness from your path,
 and make you ready to meet him when he comes in glory;
 and the blessing . . .   *8**

d   May God himself, the God of peace,
 make you perfect and holy;
 and keep you safe and blameless, in spirit, soul, and body,
 for the coming of our Lord Jesus Christ;
 and the blessing . . .

E. FOR CHURCH AND HOME

Prayer in the home has played an important part in both Jewish and Christian tradition and can deeply enrich our grasp of the grace of God made known to us in Jesus Christ. Imaginative patterns of domestic prayer need not be limited to homes with young children.

Much of the material in this book can be used or adapted for use in the home. It may also be suitable for use in schools.

1 THE ADVENT WREATH

The Advent Wreath has four red or blue candles in a ring around a white or gold candle. The first candle is lit on Advent Sunday; additional ones are lit, one on each Sunday, and the white or gold one on Christmas Day.

The new candle each week may appropriately be lit after the Gospel Reading, before the Peace, or after Communion. At the latter point, the prayer(s) used at the lighting become a natural Post-Communion prayer. All five candles may appropriately be alight during services through the Christmas season.

There are several traditions about the meaning or theme of each candle. The scheme that accords best with the proposed Lectionary is:

Advent 1	The Patriarchs
Advent 2	The Prophets
Advent 3	John the Baptist
Advent 4	The Virgin Mary
Christmas Day	The Christ

Each of the four Sundays then reminds us of those who prepared for the coming of Christ. 'The Patriarchs' can naturally focus on Abraham, our father in faith, and David, Jesus' ancestor in whose city he was born. 'The Prophets' gives an opportunity to reflect on the way the birth of the Messiah was 'foretold'. John, who proclaimed the Saviour, and Mary, who bore him in her womb, complete the picture.

The prayers below reflect these four themes. The second and third prayer in each case are written with children in mind, and the third is to be said by the congregation together. Only one prayer need be used on any occasion, though the second and third fit well together in each case.

ADVENT 1

1 Blessed are you, Sovereign Lord, God of our ancestors:
to you be praise and glory for ever!
You called the patriarchs to live by the light of faith
and to journey in the hope of your promised fulfilment.
May we be obedient to your call
and be ready and watchful to receive your Christ,
a lamp to our feet and a light to our path;
for you are our light and our salvation.
Blessed be God for ever.

2 God of Abraham and Sarah,
and all the patriarchs of old,
you are our Father too.
Your love is revealed to us in Jesus Christ,
Son of God and Son of David.
Help us in preparing to celebrate his birth
to make our hearts ready for your Holy Spirit
to make his home among us.
We ask this through Jesus Christ,
the Light who is coming into the world. *17*

3 **Lord Jesus, Light of the world,**
born in David's city of Bethlehem,
born like him to be a king:
Be born in our hearts this Christmastide,
be king of our lives today. *17*

ADVENT 2

1 Blessed are you, Sovereign Lord, just and true,
to you be praise and glory for ever!
Of old you spoke by the mouth of your prophets
but in our days you speak through your Son
whom you have appointed the heir of all things.
Grant us, your people, to walk in his light
that we may be found ready and watching
when he comes again in glory and judgement;
for you are our light and our salvation.
Blessed be God for ever.

2   God our Father,
     you spoke to the prophets of old
     of a Saviour who would bring peace.
     You helped them to spread the joyful message
     of his coming kingdom.
     Help us, as we prepare to celebrate his birth,
     to share with those around us
     the good news of your power and love.
     We ask this through Jesus Christ,
     the Light who is coming into the world.   *17*

3   **Lord Jesus, Light of the world,**
     the prophets said you would bring peace
     and save your people in trouble.
     Give peace in our hearts at Christmastide
     and show all the world God's love.   *17*

ADVENT 3

1   Blessed are you, Sovereign Lord, just and true:
     to you be praise and glory for ever!
     Your prophet John the Baptist was witness to the truth
     as a burning and shining light.
     May we your servants rejoice in his light,
     and so be led to witness to him
     who is the Lord of our coming Kingdom,
     Jesus our Saviour and King of the ages.
     Blessed be God for ever.

2   God our Father,
     you gave to Zechariah and Elisabeth in their old age
     a son called John.
     He grew up strong in spirit,
     prepared the people for the coming of the Lord,
     and baptized them in the Jordan to wash away their sins.
     Help us, who have been baptized into Christ,
     to be ready to welcome him into our hearts,
     and to grow strong in faith by the power of the Spirit.
     We ask this through Jesus Christ,
     the Light who is coming into the world.   *17*

3 **Lord Jesus, Light of the world,**
John told the people to prepare,
for you were very near.
As Christmas grows closer day by day,
help us to be ready to welcome you now.   *17*

ADVENT 4

1 Blessed are you, Sovereign Lord, merciful and gentle:
to you be praise and glory for ever!
Your light has shone in our darkened world
through the child-bearing of blessed Mary;
grant that we who have seen your glory
may daily be renewed in your image
and prepared like her for the coming of your Son,
who is the Lord and Saviour of all.
Blessed be God for ever.

2 God our Father,
the angel Gabriel told the Virgin Mary
that she was to be the mother of your Son.
Though Mary was afraid,
she responded to your call with joy.
Help us, whom you call to serve you,
to share like her in your great work
of bringing to our world your love and healing.
We ask this through Jesus Christ,
the Light who is coming into the world.   *17*

3 **Lord Jesus, Light of the world,**
blessed is Gabriel who brought good news;
blessed is Mary your mother and ours.
Bless your Church preparing for Christmas;
and bless us your children who long for your coming.   *17*

CHRISTMAS DAY

1 Blessed are you, Sovereign Lord, King of Peace:
   to you be praise and glory for ever!
   The new light of your incarnate word
   gives gladness in our sorrow,
   and a presence in our isolation.
   Fill our lives with your light,
   until they overflow with gladness and praise.
   Blessed be God for ever.

2 God our Father,
   today the Saviour is born
   and those who live in darkness are seeing a great light.
   Help us, who greet the birth of Christ with joy,
   to live in the light of your Son,
   and to share the good news of your love.
   We ask this through Jesus Christ,
   the Light who has come into the world.   *17*

3 **Lord Jesus, Light of Light,**
   you have come among us.
   Help us who live by your light
   to shine as lights in your world.
   Glory to God in the highest!   *17*

2 THE JESSE TREE

The Christmas tree can have a liturgical character if it is decorated to take the form of a Jesse Tree. Jesse Trees exist in the form of stone carvings, stained glass windows, and elaborate candelabra, and were designed to show the genealogy of Christ in the form of a tree.

When this idea is adapted for the decoration of the Christmas tree, the decorations are symbolic of events or people in the history of salvation. The sun, moon, or stars can represent the creation, an apple stands for the fall, an ark or dove for the flood, the burning bush for Moses, a harp for King David, a temple for King Solomon, and so on. There can be an angel of the annunciation, a rose or lily for the Blessed Virgin, and various symbols for Christ, such as a fish or a star. The coloured balls which customarily hang on the tree can be painted with monograms symbolizing Christ, such as XP or IHS. A small loaf together with a miniature chalice made of metal foil can be hung on the tree to represent the Eucharist.

The easiest way to make most of the figures is to use cardboard, cut to outline, and then covered with metal foil in different colours. Another source of material is postcards and old Christmas cards. The process of making these designs will give parents an opportunity to talk with children about the themes which lie behind them.

On the evening of Christmas Eve the Tree and Crib may be blessed, while the main candle of the Advent Wreath is lit. This is a good opportunity for family prayers, or a simple part of a Crib service in church.

One or more of these prayers may be used.

1   In the beginning you gave us the tree of life;
we come to you, **Lord Jesus Christ.**

On the tree of the cross you took away our sins;
we come to you, **Lord Jesus Christ.**

You are the new branch of the tree of David,
bringing hope to all peoples;
we come to you, **Lord Jesus Christ.**

2   Loving God, may your gift to us of Jesus Christ
set us free to love and serve others
and to worship you with joy.   **Amen.**

3 Lord Jesus Christ,
  you shared human suffering
  to reveal your Father's love:
  draw near to those for whom Christmas brings little joy –
  the hungry, the suffering, the lonely, and the bereaved;
  may they find joy and hope in you.   **Amen.**

4 O God, you desire to enfold
  both heaven and earth in a single peace.
  Let the design of your great love
  lighten upon the waste of our angers and sorrows;
  and give peace to your church,
  peace among nations,
  peace in our homes,
  and peace in our hearts;
  through Jesus Christ our Lord.   **Amen.**   32

3 TABLE PRAYERS

Before each of these prayers the following introduction may be used.

Let us give thanks to the Lord our God.
It is right to give him thanks and praise.

Advent

We thank you, Father, maker of heaven and earth,
for the food and shelter of this home,
for the hope you give us in the scriptures,
and for the light you bring us in Jesus Christ.   **Amen.**

Christmas

We thank you, Father, giver of all good things,
for the joy of this season of Christmas,
for the good news of a Saviour,
and for the wonder of the Word made flesh,
your Son, Jesus Christ, our Lord.   **Amen.**

New Year

We thank you, Father, Lord of all time,
for the gifts of food, warmth, and company,
for your love and protection of this home,
and, in all that this year may hold,
for the friendship of Jesus Christ, our Lord.   **Amen.**

Epiphany

We thank you, Father, God of love,
for the signs of your love on this table,
for your love made known through all the world
and shining on us in the face of Jesus Christ, our Lord.
Amen.

The prayers of Part 1 (The Advent Wreath) may also be used as
Table Prayers, and the introduction given above may be used.

4 SATURDAY EVENING

Prayer in the home on Saturday evening may form part of preparation for Sunday worship.

As suggested in the Introduction to the Service of Light (Chapter I), p.10, one of the readings for the next day can be read; a song can be sung; a responsory can be used; there can be a time of prayer, either silent, led by one person, or with all participating; a collect can be used.

One of the following may be suitable as a concluding prayer.

Father of mercy,
continue, we pray, your loving kindness to us all.
May we walk in the way of righteousness before you,
loyal to your law and clinging to good deeds.
Keep far from us all manner of shame, grief, and care;
and grant that peace, light, and joy
may ever abide in our home;
for with you is the fountain of life,
and in your light we see light. **Amen.**

God in the night
God at my right
God all the day
God with me stay
God in my heart
Never depart
God with thy might
Keep us in light
Through this dark night. **Amen.**

As watchmen look for the morning
so do we look for you, O Christ.
Come with the dawning of the day
and make yourself known to us in the breaking of bread;
for you are our God for ever and ever. **Amen.** 19

Yours is the day, O Lord, and yours is the night.
Let Christ the Sun of Righteousness abide in our hearts
to drive away the darkness of evil thoughts:
for he is Lord for ever and ever. **Amen.**

IV

CHRISTMAS

A. INTRODUCTION

In this chapter we have provided for the twelve days from Christmas to the Epiphany. We have also made provision for those services in late Advent that have, to a great extent, left behind the Advent emphasis on the Kingly Coming, and are preparing people to celebrate once again the birth at Bethlehem that Christ may be born again in them at the Christmas festival.

The heart of the Christmas celebration of the Incarnation is the Eucharist of Christmas Day. The provision for that service allows for its use at different times of day and night, and much of the material provided can be used at every celebration, whether at midnight or at any stage in the day. In structure the service departs from the Rite A shape only in the position of the Prayers of Penitence. It envisages the dedication of the crib at the beginning of the principal liturgy of Christmas (in most, but not all, churches this will probably be at the midnight celebration) and sees the penitence at the crib as response to the love of God revealed in the child in the manger. Thus the penitential material becomes part of the preparation while the president is still, so to speak, on his way to the celebration.

But before Christmas night and morning comes – in many churches – the Carol Service. Here we have not given one set form, but provided rich resources. A Carol Service can be built on the Light Service plus Vigil pattern already described. There are several sets of lections provided, and a number of forms of Introduction and concluding Collects. One of the Solemn Blessings for Advent or Christmas would also appropriately be used. For those seeking a less formal service than one modelled on the Festival of Nine Lessons and Carols, this material will enable them to devise something tailored to their needs and opportunities.

There are three forms of service that have been devised with families and children very much in mind.

The first is a Christingle Service, for use at any time during the Advent/Christmas/Epiphany cycle, and the rationale of this service is described in its own introduction.

The second is a Crib Service. In the form we have provided, it is a Christmas Eve Service, and responds to the need in many parishes to hold a late afternoon or early evening non-sacramental service. It can be a very simple child-oriented service or can be extended to be a longer or more adult service more in line with the other Vigil Services in the book. Material from it can, with sensitive editing, also be used for a Crib Service or Family Service on an earlier date, such as the Fourth Sunday in Advent, or on Christmas Day itself.

At the heart of it, however and whenever it is celebrated, is the building-up of the crib with the telling of the story. It is a teaching service, but one that naturally leads into prayer and praise.

The third is a form for Christmas morning. This is supplementary to the Eucharist. In many churches the Eucharist for Christmas Night or Morning will provide all that is needed. In other churches this additional service will either provide for a separate service or allow for some variations in the morning Eucharist from the one celebrated in the night. This latter form, for instance, provides a shorter form of Christmas Intercession.

The chapter ends with provision of prayer material for use at the crib and more generally, and with eucharistic Prefaces and Post-Communion prayers for the holy days after Christmas. It is also intended that material provided for Christmas Eve and Christmas Day should be used at the Eucharist through the days until Epiphany.

The Sundays after Christmas provide particular difficulties, and in the Lectionary we have given maximum freedom to those who minister to provide what is appropriate in their communities. We have provided Propers for the First Sunday after Christmas, which give a Holy Family theme, but have also allowed for the celebration of St Stephen, St John, The Holy Innocents, or The

Naming of Jesus, if one of these falls on the Sunday. We also allow the minister to continue a much more straightforwardly incarnational theme by using 'spare' lections from the provision for Christmas Day itself. Indeed, we also allow the Readings and Psalms for Christmas 1 (The Holy Family) to be transferred to Christmas 2 (when there is such a Sunday) if this is pastorally desirable. The aim is to give priority to the most important material at times when people will be present, and to provide flexibility so that suitable complementary material can be used at other times.

B. CAROL SERVICES IN CHRISTMASTIDE

1 THE SERVICE OF LIGHT

In the Service of Light in Christmastide (section 1) the choice of John 1. 1-5 is particularly suitable, unless it is to be used as the Gospel. In Section 4, options d and e are particularly suitable, as are j (For the Blessed Virgin Mary) and f (For the New Year).

2 BIDDING PRAYERS AND INTRODUCTIONS

1   The Service of Nine Lessons with Carols was first drawn up by Edward Benson when Bishop of Truro for use in that cathedral, and was later simplified and adapted for use in the Chapel of King's College, Cambridge, in 1918 by the then Dean, Eric Milner-White, who wrote the Bidding Prayer which follows. The Pattern of Readings, together with the Bidding Prayer, the concluding Collect and the Blessing, is to be found in Chapter I, C.8 (pp.28-30).   5†

Beloved in Christ, be it this Christmastide our care and delight to hear again the message of the angels, and in heart and mind to go even unto Bethlehem and see this thing which is come to pass, and the Babe lying in a manger.

Therefore let us read and mark in Holy Scripture the tale of the loving purposes of God from the first days of our disobedience unto the glorious Redemption brought us by this Holy Child.

But first, let us pray for the needs of the whole world; for peace on earth and goodwill among all his people; for unity and brotherhood within the Church he came to build, and especially in this city (town, village) of . . . and diocese of . . .

And because this of all things would rejoice his heart, let us remember, in his name, the poor and helpless, the cold, the hungry, and the oppressed; the sick and them that mourn,

† Numbers in right-hand margin refer to Sources and Acknowledgements (pp.416-419).

the lonely and the unloved, the aged and the little children; all those who know not the Lord Jesus, or who love him not, or who by sin have grieved his heart of love.

Lastly, let us remember before God all those who rejoice with us, but upon another shore, and in a greater light, that multitude which no man can number, whose hope was in the Word made flesh, and with whom in the Lord Jesus we are for ever one.

These prayers and praises let us humbly offer up to the Throne of Heaven, in the words which Christ himself hath taught us:

> Our Father,
> which art in heaven,
> hallowed be thy name;
> thy kingdom come;
> thy will be done;
> in earth as it is in heaven.
> Give us this day our daily bread.
> And forgive us our trespasses,
> as we forgive them that trespass against us.
> And lead us not into temptation;
> but deliver us from evil;
> for thine is the kingdom,
> the power and the glory,
> for ever and ever.   Amen.

May the Almighty God bless us with his grace; Christ give us the joys of everlasting life, and unto the fellowship of the citizens above may the King of Angels bring us all.   **Amen.**

2   In the name of Christ and his Church I bid you welcome to . . . today.   4

We have come together as the family of God in our Father's presence to celebrate the festival of Christmas. In this service we hear and receive the good news of the birth of Christ, and we offer to God our thanksgiving in the joyful singing of carols.

But first we pray:

For all Christian people, that by this festival they may be renewed to fulfil Christ's work in this world; and especially for . . . our Bishop and the clergy and people of this diocese;

For the world, which is already Christ's, that those who bear responsibility for its future, in politics, in industry, in commerce, and in education and communication, may be inspired by the message of Christmas to work together for the establishment of justice, freedom and peace everywhere;

For all in special need, the sick, the anxious, the lonely, the fearful, and the bereaved.

We commend all whom we love, or who have asked for our prayers, to the unfailing mercy of our heavenly Father, and say together, as Christ himself taught us,

Our Father in heaven,   *or*
hallowed be your name,
your kingdom come,
your will be done,
on earth as in heaven.
Give us today our daily bread.
Forgive us our sins
as we forgive those
   who sin against us.
Lead us not into temptation
but deliver us from evil.
	Our Father, who art in heaven,
	hallowed be thy name;
	thy kingdom come;
	thy will be done;
	on earth as it is in heaven.
	Give us this day our daily bread.
	And forgive us our trespasses,
	as we forgive those
	   who trespass against us.
	And lead us not into temptation;
	but deliver us from evil.

For the kingdom, the power,
   and the glory are yours
now and for ever.   Amen.
	For thine is the kingdom,
	   the power, and the glory,
	for ever and ever. Amen.

May the humility of the shepherds, the faith of the wise men, the joy of the angels, and the peace of the Christ Child, be God's gift to us and to all men, this Christmas and always.   **Amen.**

3   My friends, let us love one another, for love is of God.
And whoever loves is born of God and knows God.

Whoever does not love, does not know God
for God is love.

In this was the love of God made manifest among us
that God sent his only Son into the world,
so that we might live through him.

In this is love, not that we loved God
but that he loved us.

My friends, if God so loved us,
we also ought to love one another.

4   The people who walked in darkness
have seen a great light.

For to us a child is born
to us a Son is given.

His name will be called
wonderful, counsellor, mighty God,
the everlasting Father,
the Prince of Peace.

Glory to God in the highest
and peace to his people on earth.

3 PATTERNS OF READINGS

The following Patterns of Readings from Chapter I, C are suitable in
Christmastide.

(3) The King and his Kingdom (Matthean)
(6) Good News for the Poor (Lukan)
(7) The Gospel of Luke
(8) Festival of Nine Lessons and Carols
(9) The New Creation (Johannine)

All these Patterns of Readings are suitable for carol services as well as
for Vigils in Christmastide.

Patterns 3, 6, and 9 take a central theme of each of the Gospels of
Matthew, Luke and John, and provide a Pattern of Readings which is
congruent with the basic theological thrust of each Gospel.

The Festival of Nine Lessons and Carols is traditionally introduced by
the Bidding Prayer (2 (1)), and concluded by the Collect for Christmas
Eve and the Blessing. These are printed in the traditional form, together
with the Readings, in Chapter I, C.8.

In addition to these provisions, 7 (The Gospel of Luke) presents the Lukan birth narrative arranged sequentially in seven sections.

Other patterns of readings may be contrived, but they should respect the integrity of the individual Gospel around which they are grouped.

4 CONCLUSIONS

1   Blessed be the Lord, the God of Israel,
    he has come to his people and set them free.

    Light has sprung up for the righteous
    and joyful gladness for those who are true-hearted.

    Glory to God in the highest
    and peace to his people on earth.   *11*

2   The Word of Life which was from the beginning
    we proclaim to you.

    The darkness is passing away
    and the true light is already shining,
    the Word of Life which was from the beginning.

    That which we heard, which we saw with our eyes,
    and touched with our own hands,
    we proclaim to you.

    For our fellowship is with the Father,
    and with his Son Jesus Christ our Lord:
    the Word of Life which was from the beginning
    we proclaim to you.   *24*

3   See what love the Father has given us
    that we should be called the children of God.

    You are my sons and daughters:
    this day have I begotten you.
    See what love the Father has given us.

    As many as received him,
    to them he gave power to become the children of God.
    See what love the Father has given us.

Glory to the Father, and to the Son,
and to the Holy Spirit.
**See what love the Father has given us
that we should be called the children of God.**   24

4   Let us bless the living God:

He was born of the Virgin Mary,
Revealed in his glory,

Worshipped by angels,
Proclaimed among the nations,

Believed in throughout the world,
Exalted to the highest heavens.

Glory to God in the highest
and peace to his people on earth.

5   The Lord be with you
and also with you.

Let us bless the Lord.
Thanks be to God.

May he who by his incarnation gathered into one
things earthly and heavenly,
bestow upon you the fullness of inward peace and goodwill;
and the blessing of God almighty,
the Father, the Son, and the Holy Spirit,
be upon you and remain with you always.   **Amen.**   8*

C. THE CHRISTINGLE SERVICE

INTRODUCTION

The Christingle Service is a relatively recent development in Britain of the Moravian custom of distributing lighted candles to children on Christmas Eve. In the Moravian Church the candles are usually surrounded by a white ruff of paper strips.

In Britain the distribution of candles has been replaced by the distribution of Christingles. A Christingle 'consists of an orange, in the top of which a small hole has been bored. A cleansed goose quill, from which the feathered portion has been removed, is wrapped in a white paper frill and inserted in the hole. The protruding end of the quill is cut into half a dozen sharp "points", to which are affixed blanched almonds, raisins and small jellied sweets of different colours. A small Christmas tree candle is pushed down into the heart of the goose quill to complete the Christingle' (J H Foy). In addition, many Christingles have a length of red ribbon tied around the circumference of the orange, and nowadays cocktail sticks usually replace the goose quill.

The origin and derivation of the Christingle is uncertain. The word 'Christingle' means 'Christ-Light'. The orange is said to represent the world, the candle Christ as the light of the world, the white frill purity, and the nuts, raisins, and sweets the fruits of the earth, God's good gifts to his children. The red ribbon is a reminder of the incarnation and passion of Jesus, in which all Christians share.

In the light of their association in the Moravian Church with Christmas Eve, Christingle services have normally been celebrated in Britain during the period between Advent and Epiphany. The image of Christ as our light is predominant in the celebration, suggesting the revelation of God, judgement, glory, and Christian witness as appropriate themes for the service. Yet Jesus does not describe himself simply as 'the light' but as 'the light of the world'. For this reason, the needs of the world are also at the forefront of Christingle celebrations, in prayer and in the offering of gifts for the needy.

It was The Children's Society who, in 1968, popularized the Christingle service, and many are now held in support of its work. The present service does not preclude this association, but encourages a flexible treatment of its rich traditional imagery.

PREPARATION

1   The minister greets the people using these or other appropriate words.

Christ has brought us out of darkness:
to live in his marvellous light.

2   There follows an INTRODUCTION or BIDDING.
The BIDDING may take this form.

Brothers and sisters in Christ, welcome to . . . today. We have come together in the presence of God our Father to rejoice in the gift of Jesus to us as the light of the world. In this service we hear and receive the story and message of the coming of Christ, and we offer to God our thanksgiving in prayer and song.

The Christingle speaks of the world in which we live, and we pray today

> for all Christians, that we may be mirrors of the light of Christ in the world;
> for those who do not know the light of Christ in their lives;
> for those who bear responsibility in our world for government, education, commerce, and communication;
> for all children and for young people who lack the basic necessities of food, shelter, and clothing;
> for those who are in special need, the sick and anxious, the lonely and fearful, and for those who are bereaved.

We commend all whom we love, or who have asked for our prayers, to the unfailing love of God, and say together, as Christ taught us

Our Father in heaven,	*or*	Our Father, who art in heaven,
hallowed be your name,		hallowed be thy name;
your kingdom come,		thy kingdom come;
your will be done,		thy will be done;
on earth as in heaven.		on earth as it is in heaven.
Give us today our daily bread.		Give us this day our daily bread.

Forgive us our sins
as we forgive those
  who sin against us.
Lead us not into temptation
but deliver us from evil.
	And forgive us our trespasses,
	as we forgive those
	  who trespass against us.
	And lead us not into temptation;
	but deliver us from evil.

For the kingdom, the power,
  and the glory are yours
now and for ever. **Amen.**
	For thine is the kingdom,
	  the power, and the glory,
	for ever and ever. **Amen.**

May God our Father grant us the light of Christ, that we may shine with his love, be prompt to serve, and ever eager to follow in his steps, who is the true light and source of life. **Amen.**

3 A SONG, CAROL, or HYMN may be sung. Suitable Christingle and seasonal hymns of light are listed in the Appendix to this service (p.162).

THANKSGIVING

This act of thanksgiving may be used when the distribution of the Christingles (or candles) is to take place at section 11. Section 4 should normally be omitted if the distribution of Christingles (or candles) takes place at section 6.

One prominently placed Christingle may be lit. Alternatively, during Advent, the candles of an Advent wreath may be lit; during Christmastide or Epiphany, another candle may be lit.

4 An act of THANKSGIVING may be made, all standing, in one of these forms, or in other suitable words.

a Gracious God, we give you thanks and praise
for Jesus Christ our Lord:
for he was the word before all creation.
Through him all things come to be,
not one thing has its being but through him.

Jesus, light of the world,
we worship and adore you.

His life is the light that shines in the dark,
a light that darkness cannot overpower.

156

Jesus, light of the world,
we worship and adore you.

The Word was the true light coming into the world.
He was in the world
that had its being through him,
and the world did not know him.

Jesus, light of the world,
we worship and adore you.

He came to his own, and they did not accept him.
But to all who accept him
he gives power to become children of God.

Jesus, light of the world,
we worship and adore you.

The Word was made flesh and lived among us,
and we have seen his glory,
as the only Son of the Father,
full of grace and truth.

Jesus, light of the world,
we worship and adore you.

To God our creator,
born as one of us,
be all praise and glory.
With all the company of heaven, we worship, saying:

Holy, holy, holy is the Lord God almighty,
who was, and is, and is to come;
to him be glory and honour for ever and ever.   Amen.

b   Glory to Christ, Son of Mary;
born a child,
you share our humanity:
Glory to God in the highest.

Glory to Christ, Son of David;
born to rule,
you receive gifts from the wise:
Glory to God in the highest.

Glory to Christ, Son of Man;
born our Saviour,
you are the light of the world:
Glory to God in the highest.

We celebrate the coming of our God
with all the voices of heaven:

**Holy, holy, holy Lord,
God of power and might,
Heaven and earth are full of your glory.
Hosanna in the highest.**

**Blessed is he who comes in the name of the Lord.
Hosanna in the highest.**

5   A SONG, CAROL, or HYMN may be sung.

6   THE LIGHTING AND PRESENTATION OF THE CHRISTINGLES, or of
     CANDLES, may take place here or at section 11. The text is
     printed at section 11. After the distribution a SONG, CAROL, or
     HYMN may be sung, and the minister and people may process
     within or around the church.

THE MINISTRY OF THE WORD

7   One or more READINGS follow. Suggested readings are listed in
     the Appendix to this service. These may be interspersed with
     one or more SONGS, CAROLS, or HYMNS.

     At the beginning or end of each reading the reader may say

     God's word is a lantern to our feet:
     and a light to our path.

8   SERMON or TALK

9   A SONG, CAROL, or HYMN is sung, during which Christingle gifts
     and offerings of money may be collected and presented.
     Offerings may be presented by groups and by individuals.

     These words may be used.

Blessed are you, Lord our God, King of the universe!
From your hands we receive these gifts of your creation.
Bless us who bless your holy name,
and grant that we may be used
in the service of your kingdom.

PRAYERS

10 Prayers are said for the Church, the world, and for those in
special need. The prayers may take any suitable form, and may
include the response.

We pray to the Father
in Christ our Lord.

and end with

Lord of the Church,
hear our prayer,
and make us one in heart and mind
to serve you in Christ our Lord.   Amen.

For an alternative form of prayer see the Appendix to this
service.

If it has not been said earlier in the service, THE LORD'S PRAYER
may follow.

As Christ has taught us, so we pray

Our Father in heaven, *or*	Our Father, who art in heaven,
hallowed be your name,	hallowed be thy name;
your kingdom come,	thy kingdom come;
your will be done,	thy will be done;
on earth as in heaven.	on earth as it is in heaven.
Give us today our daily bread.	Give us this day our daily bread.
Forgive us our sins	And forgive us our trespasses,
as we forgive those	as we forgive those
who sin against us.	who trespass against us.
Lead us not into temptation	And lead us not into temptation;
but deliver us from evil.	but deliver us from evil.
For the kingdom, the power,	For thine is the kingdom,
and the glory are yours	the power, and the glory,
now and for ever. Amen.	for ever and ever. Amen.

THE LIGHTING AND PRESENTATION OF THE CHRISTINGLES OR OF CANDLES

11   The Christingles (or candles) are lit and are presented to members of the congregation, if this has not already taken place at section 6.

12   Before or after the distribution, THIS COLLECT may be said by the minister.

Father of lights,
from whom comes every good and perfect gift:
keep us in the light of Christ,
to shine in your world,
that all may believe in you
through Jesus Christ our Lord.   **Amen.**

13   During the distribution of the Christingles (or candles) A SONG, CAROL, or HYMN may be sung, and/or the following ACCLAMATIONS may be used.

By the shedding of Christ's blood we are redeemed:
Praise to Christ our Saviour!

In Christ's death is our life:
Praise to Christ our Saviour!

CONCLUSION

14   THE BLESSING may be given.

Christ the Sun of Righteousness shine upon you
and make you ready to meet him when he comes in glory;
and the blessing of God almighty,
the Father, the Son, and the Holy Spirit,
be upon you and remain with you always.   **Amen.**

15   THE DISMISSAL

God shines in your hearts:
Praise to Christ our light!

Christ is the light of the world!
Praise to Christ our light!

Go, in the power of the Spirit, to bring light to others:
Praise to Christ our light!

16   A SONG, CAROL, or HYMN may be sung, and the minister and
people process out of the church.

APPENDIX TO CHRISTINGLE SERVICE

A. HYMNS

A CHRISTINGLE HYMN

Tune: Falling Fifths 7775 775 by Noel Tredinnick

God whose love is everywhere
made our earth and all things fair,
ever keeps them in his care:
praise the God of love!
He who hung the stars in space
holds the spinning world in place;
praise the God of love!

Come with thankful songs to sing
of the gifts the seasons bring,
summer, winter, autumn, spring;
praise the God of love!
He who gives us breath and birth
gives us all the fruitful earth;
praise the God of love!

Mark what love the Lord displayed,
all our sins upon him laid,
by his blood our ransom paid;
praise the God of love!
Circled by that scarlet band
all the world is in his hand;
praise the God of love!

See the sign of love appear,
flame of glory, bright and clear,
light for all the world is here;
praise the God of love!
Gloom and darkness, get you gone!
Christ the Light of life has shone;
praise the God of love!

© Timothy Dudley-Smith 1988. USA © Hope Publishing Company

Suitable hymns of light include:

General

All the earth was dark	MP2 288
Come let us worship vv.1,4,5	MP2 329
Lord, make me a mountain	MP2 483
O gladsome light, O grace	NEH 247
or	
Hail, gladdening light	AMNS 58
O Christ, who art the light and day	NEH 61
O Lord, you are my light	MP2 513
Be thou my vision, O Lord of my heart	NEH 339, AMNS 343
The Spirit lives to set us free	MP2 588

In Advent

Creator of the stars of night	NEH 1. AMNS 23
Lord, the light of your love is shining	Make Way 6
O come thou dayspring bright	NEH 11
or	
O splendour of God's glory bright	EH 52
Christ, whose glory fills the skies	NEH 234, AMNS 4

At Christmas

God of God, light of light	NEH 30, AMNS 34
Come thou redeemer of the earth	NEH 19
O Trinity of blessed light	NEH 54
The light of Christ	Fresh Sounds 98
The race that long in darkness pined	NEH 57, AMNS 52
Brightest and best of the sons of the morning	NEH 49, AMNS 47

Key

| EH | English Hymnal | AMNS | Hymns Ancient and Modern New Standard |
| NEH | New English Hymnal | MP2 | Mission Praise 2 |

B. READINGS

Suitable readings include:

Advent
Isaiah 51. 4-6 (or 4-11)
Isaiah 60. 1-3; 17-20
Romans 13. 11-14 (or 8-14)

Christmastide
Isaiah 9. 2, 6-7
Luke 2. 8-14
John 1. 1-5
John 1. 9-14 (or 6-14)

Epiphany
Isaiah 60. 1-3; 17-20
Acts 13. 44-49
2 Corinthians 4. 5-6 (or 2-6)
Revelation 21. 22-26
Revelation 22. 1-5

General
Psalm 139. 1-2, 7-12 (or 1-12)
Matthew 5. 14-16
Luke 11. 33-36
John 3. 16-21
John 8. 12 (or 12-20)
Ephesians 5. 8-14 (or 6-14)
Colossians 1. 11-14 (or 9-14)
Timothy 1. 8-10 (or 8-14)
1 Peter 2. 9-10 (or 4-10)
1 John 1. 5-7 (or 5-10)
1 John 4. 7-12 (or 7-19)
1 John 4. 13-19 (or 7-19)

C. LITANY

The following LITANY may be used for the Prayers.

In faith we pray:
We pray to you, our God.

Silence

For all people in their daily life and work:
For our families, friends and neighbours, and for all those who are alone.
For the just and responsible use of your creation:
For the victims of hunger, fear and injustice.
For those in danger, sorrow, or any kind of trouble:
For those who minister to the sick, the lonely, and the needy.
For the peace and unity of the Church of God:
For our own needs and for the needs of others.

Silence. The minister or people may add their own requests.

In faith we pray,
We pray to you, our God.
We thank you, Lord, for the blessings of this life.

Silence. The minister or people may add their own thanksgivings.

We give you thanks:
And praise your holy name.

God our Saviour,
**you know us and love us
and hear our prayer:
keep us in the eternal fellowship
of Jesus Christ our Lord. Amen.**

When the Christingle Service includes the giving of gifts for the work of The Children's Society, prayers for the work of the Society are appropriate.

A PRAYER FOR THE CHILDREN'S SOCIETY

O Lord Jesus Christ, who said to your disciples, 'You are the light of the world': grant that The Children's Society may bring light, hope and happiness to children, young people, and families who face particular darkness or need; help all staff members and volunteers to be inspired by your understanding and strengthened by your grace, that the care they give may be both a special support and a sign of your kingdom, where you live and reign with the Father and the Holy Spirit, one God now and for ever. **Amen.** 26

D. SERVICES FOR CHRISTMAS

1. A Crib Service
or a Vigil Service for Christmas Eve

Note: In a Crib Service or a meditative vigil for Christmas Eve some of
the following material may be useful. Whatever structure is adopted,
the telling of the story should lead to praise and thanksgiving, and be
concluded by prayer.

1 The minister introduces the service in these or similar words.

We meet to celebrate the coming of Christ into the world.

The Word was made flesh, and dwelt among us
and we beheld his glory.

or

The glory of the Lord has been revealed
and all flesh shall see it together.

2 Candles may be lit, with these or other words.

Jesus Christ is the light of the world,
a light no darkness can quench.

The shepherds kept watch by night,
and your glory shone round about them.

The darkness is not dark to you,
the night is as bright as the day.

Let your light scatter the darkness
and illumine your Church with your glory.

3 These PRAYERS OF PENITENCE may be used.

Christ the light of the world has come to dispel the darkness
of our hearts. In his light let us examine ourselves and
confess our sins.

Silence is kept.

165

Lord of grace and truth,
we confess our unworthiness
to stand in your presence as your children.

We have sinned:
Forgive and heal us.

The Virgin Mary accepted your call
to be the mother of Jesus.
Forgive our disobedience to your will.

We have sinned:
Forgive and heal us.

Your Son our Saviour
was born in poverty in a manger.
Forgive our greed and rejection of your ways.

We have sinned:
Forgive and heal us.

The shepherds left their flocks
to go to Bethlehem.
Forgive our self-interest and lack of vision.

We have sinned:
Forgive and heal us.

The wise men followed the star
to find Jesus the king.
Forgive our reluctance to seek you.

We have sinned:
Forgive and heal us.

May the God of all healing and forgiveness
draw you to himself
that you may behold the glory of his Son,
the Word made flesh,
and be cleansed from all your sins,
through Jesus Christ our Lord.   **Amen.**

27

4   PSALM 113 is said or sung, or the Canticle 'Glory to God in the Highest'.

Praise the Lord!

Give praise, you servants of the Lord;
praise the name of the Lord.
Let the name of the Lord be blessed
from this time forth for evermore.

Praise the Lord!

From the rising of the sun to its setting
let the name of the Lord be praised.
The Lord is high above all nations,
and his glory above the heavens.

Praise the Lord!

Who is like the Lord our God,
who sits enthroned on high
but stoops to behold the heavens and the earth?
He takes up the weak from the dust
and lifts up the poor from the ashes.

Praise the Lord!

He sets them with the princes
with the princes of his people.
He makes the woman of a childless house
to be a joyful mother of children.

Praise the Lord!

5   THE COLLECT

Holy Jesus,
to deliver us from the power of darkness
you humbled yourself to be born among us
    and laid in a manger.
Let the light of your love always shine in our hearts,
and bring us at last
    to the joyful vision of your beauty,
for you are now alive and reign
    with the Father and the Holy Spirit,   *4*
God for ever and ever. **Amen.**   *57**

6 THE SERVICE OF THE WORD

One or more READINGS follow, with suitable HYMNS, CAROLS or SONGS.

This section may be expanded into a meditative vigil with a series of Readings, Canticles, and Collects drawn from the provision in Chapter I, The Service of Light.

Where a simpler, more narrative form is desired, Chapter I, C.7 (The Gospel of Luke) provides an appropriate form.

7 THANKSGIVING

Hymns or carols may be sung, and the figures may be brought in and placed in the Christmas Crib, where this part of the service may take place.

It is traditional for the figure of the Christ child to be placed in the Crib at the time of the First Eucharist of Christmas, either at midnight or on Christmas morning.

Blessed are you, God of all glory,
through your Son the Christ.
His name is Jesus
because he saves his people from their sin.

He will be called Emmanuel:
God is with us. Alleluia!

Let us praise the Lord, the God of Israel:
he has come to his people and set them free.

He gave up the glory of heaven
and took the form of a servant.

The Word was made flesh
and we beheld his glory.

In humility he walked the path of obedience
to die on the cross.

God raised him to the highest place above
and gave him the name above every name:
Jesus Christ is Lord!

So all beings in heaven and earth will fall at his feet,
and proclaim to the glory of God
Jesus Christ is Lord!

This night Christ is born:
Alleluia!

This night the Saviour comes:
Alleluia!

This night the angels sing on earth:
Alleluia! Glory to God in the Highest!   28

When this Thanksgiving is used at a service on Christmas
morning, the word 'Today' is substituted for the words 'This
night' in the final acclamations.

8   PRAYERS OF INTERCESSION

Christ, who was born in a stable,
give courage to all who are homeless.
In your mercy
hear our prayer.

Christ, who fled into Egypt,
give comfort to all refugees.
In your mercy
hear our prayer.

Christ, who fasted in the desert,
give relief to all who are starving.
In your mercy
hear our prayer.

Christ, who hung in agony on the cross,
give strength to all who suffer.
In your mercy
hear our prayer.

Christ, who died to save us,
give us your forgiveness.
In your mercy
hear our prayer.

**Save us today, and use us in your loving purpose,
to your glory.   Amen.**   29

9 United as members of his family,
  we pray with one heart and voice.

Our Father in heaven,	*or*	**Our Father, who art in heaven,**
hallowed be your name,		**hallowed be thy name;**
your kingdom come,		**thy kingdom come;**
your will be done,		**thy will be done;**
on earth as in heaven.		**on earth as it is in heaven.**
Give us today our daily bread.		**Give us this day our daily bread.**
Forgive us our sins		**And forgive us our trespasses,**
as we forgive those		**as we forgive those**
who sin against us.		**who trespass against us.**
Lead us not into temptation		**And lead us not into temptation;**
but deliver us from evil.		**but deliver us from evil.**

For the kingdom, the power,	**For thine is the kingdom,**
and the glory are yours	**the power, and the glory,**
now and for ever. Amen.	**for ever and ever. Amen.**

10 THE BLESSING

The service may end with this or another Blessing.

Let us bless the living God:

He was born of the Virgin Mary,
Revealed in his glory,

Worshipped by angels,
Proclaimed among the nations,

Believed in throughout the world,
Exalted to the highest heavens.

Blessed be God our strength and our salvation
Now and for ever. Amen.

And the blessing of God almighty,
the Father, the Son, and the Holy Spirit,
be upon you and remain with you always. **Amen.**

2. The Eucharist of Christmas Night or Morning

THE PREPARATION

1   A HYMN or CAROL may be sung, during which the president and other ministers go to the Crib. At the Crib these words may be used.

Welcome all wonders in one sight!
Eternity shut in a span.
Summer in winter, Day in night,
Heaven in earth, and God in man.

Great little one whose all-embracing birth
Brings earth to heaven, stoops heaven to earth.

or

Do I not fill heaven and earth? says the Lord.
Now he is made flesh and laid in a narrow manger.
From eternity to eternity you are God,
And now we see you as a new-born child.   *4*

2   THE DEDICATION OF THE CRIB

The president may say

Dear friends, as we meet to celebrate the birth of Christ, let us pray that God will bless this crib, that all who worship his Son, born of the Virgin Mary, may come to share his life in glory.

God our Father, on this night (day) your Son Jesus Christ was born of the Virgin Mary for us and for our salvation; bless this crib which we have prepared to celebrate that holy birth; may all who see it be strengthened in faith, and receive the fullness of life he came to bring; who is alive and reigns for ever.   **Amen.**   *30*

PRAYERS OF PENITENCE

3　These Prayers of Penitence are used at the Crib.

Minister
Christ the Light of the World has come to dispel the
darkness of our hearts. In his light let us examine
ourselves and confess our sins.

Silence is kept.

Lord of grace and truth,
we confess our unworthiness
to stand in your presence as your children.

We have sinned:
Forgive and heal us.

The Virgin Mary accepted your call
to be the mother of Jesus.
Forgive our disobedience to your will.

We have sinned:
Forgive and heal us.

Your Son our Saviour
was born in poverty in a manger.
Forgive our greed and rejection of your ways.

We have sinned:
Forgive and heal us.

The shepherds left their flocks
to go to Bethlehem.
Forgive our self-interest and lack of vision.

We have sinned:
Forgive and heal us.

The wise men followed the star
to find Jesus the King.
Forgive our reluctance to seek you.

We have sinned:
Forgive and heal us.

Almighty God,
who forgives all who truly repent,
have mercy upon us,
pardon and deliver us from all our sins,
confirm and strengthen us in all goodness,
and keep us in life eternal;
through Jesus Christ our Lord.   **Amen.**

The ministers move from the Crib to the place where the Ministry of the Word is celebrated. GLORIA IN EXCELSIS is used here or at section 6, or A HYMN is sung.

**Glory to God in the highest,
and peace to his people on earth.**

**Lord God, heavenly King,
almighty God and Father,
we worship you, we give you thanks,
we praise you for your glory.**

**Lord Jesus Christ, only Son of the Father,
Lord God, Lamb of God,
you take away the sin of the world:
have mercy on us;
you are seated at the right hand of the Father:
receive our prayer.**

**For you alone are the Holy One,
you alone are the Lord,
you alone are the Most High,
Jesus Christ,
with the Holy Spirit,
in the glory of God the Father.   Amen.**

5   The president greets the people.

**Grace and peace from God our Father
and the Lord Jesus Christ be with you.
And also with you.**

6   GLORIA IN EXCELSIS is used here if it has not been used before the Greeting.

7 THE COLLECT

President
Let us pray in the peace of this Christmas celebration that
our joy in the birth of Christ will last for ever.

Silence is kept.

At night
Eternal God,
who made this most holy night
to shine with the brightness of your one true light:
bring us, who have known the revelation
    of that light on earth,
to see the radiance of your heavenly glory;
through Jesus Christ your Son our Lord,
who is alive and reigns with you and the Holy Spirit,
one God, now and for ever.   **Amen.**   8

In daytime
All praise to you,
Almighty God and heavenly king,
who sent your Son into the world
to take our nature upon him
and to be born of a pure virgin.
Grant that, as we are born again in him,
so he may continually dwell in us
and reign on earth as he reigns in heaven
with you and the Holy Spirit,
now and for ever.   **Amen.**   8

THE MINISTRY OF THE WORD

8   Either two or three READINGS FROM SCRIPTURE follow, the last of
    which is the Gospel.

9 **Sit**

OLD TESTAMENT READING

At the end the reader may say

This is the word of the Lord.
Thanks be to God.

10 THIS CANTICLE, or A PSALM or A HYMN may be used.

Response **The Spirit of the Lord shall rest upon him.**

1 There shall come forth a shoot
from the stump of Jesse:
and a branch shall grow out of its roots,

2 And the Spirit of the Lord shall rest upon him:
the spirit of wisdom and understanding,

3 The spirit of counsel and might:
the spirit of knowledge and the fear of the Lord.

The Spirit of the Lord shall rest upon him.

4 He shall not judge by what his eyes see:
or decide by what his ears hear,

5 But with righteousness he shall judge the poor:
and decide with equity for the meek of the earth.

The Spirit of the Lord shall rest upon him.

6 The wolf shall dwell with the lamb:
and the leopard shall lie down with the kid,

7 The calf and the young lion together:
with a little child to lead them. *24*

The Spirit of the Lord shall rest upon him. *31*

11 **Sit**

NEW TESTAMENT READING (EPISTLE)

At the end the reader may say

This is the word of the Lord.
Thanks be to God.

12 A CANTICLE, A HYMN, or A PSALM may be used.

13 THIS ACCLAMATION or another short song may precede and/or follow the Gospel.

Today Christ is born:
Alleluia!
Today the Saviour has come:
Alleluia!
Today the angels sing on earth:
Alleluia! Glory to God in the highest!

14 **Stand**

THE GOSPEL

When it is announced

Glory to Christ our Saviour.

At the end the reader says

This is the Gospel of Christ.
Praise to Christ our Lord.

15 **Sit**

THE SERMON

16 **Stand**

THE NICENE CREED is said.

We believe in one God,
the Father, the almighty,
maker of heaven and earth,
of all that is,
seen and unseen.

We believe in one Lord, Jesus Christ,
the only Son of God,
eternally begotten of the Father,
God from God, Light from Light,
true God from true God,
begotten, not made,
of one Being with the Father.
Through him all things were made.

For us men and for our salvation
he came down from heaven;
by the power of the Holy Spirit
he became incarnate of the Virgin Mary,
    and was made man.
For our sake he was crucified under Pontius Pilate;
he suffered death and was buried.
On the third day he rose again
in accordance with the Scriptures;
he ascended into heaven
and is seated at the right hand of the Father.
He will come again in glory
to judge the living and the dead,
and his kingdom will have no end.

We believe in the Holy Spirit,
the Lord, the giver of life,
who proceeds from the Father and the Son.
With the Father and the Son he is worshipped
    and glorified.
He has spoken through the Prophets.

We believe in one holy catholic
    and apostolic Church.
We acknowledge one baptism for the
    forgiveness of sins.
We look for the resurrection of the dead,
and the life of the world to come.   Amen.

THE PRAYERS

17   PRAYERS OF INTERCESSION are said. This form may be used.

Insertions into this form should be very brief. When used during the day, the words 'on this holy day' are substituted for 'in this holy night'.

After each petition there is silence followed by

Lord, in your mercy
Hear our prayer.

Father, in this holy night your Son our Saviour was born in human form. Renew your Church as the body of Christ.

In this holy night Christians the world over are celebrating his birth. Open our hearts that he may be born in us today.

In this holy night there was no room for your Son in the inn. Protect with your love those who have no home and all who live in poverty.

In this holy night Mary in the pain of labour brought your Son to birth. Hold in your hand (. . . and) all who are in pain or distress today.

In this holy night your Christ came as a light shining in the darkness. Bring comfort to (. . . and) all who suffer in the sadness of our world.

In this holy night shepherds in the field heard good tidings of joy. Give us grace to preach the gospel of Christ's redemption.

In this holy night the angels sang 'Peace to God's people on earth'. Strengthen those who work for peace and justice in (. . . and in) all the world.

In this holy night strangers found the Holy Family, and saw the baby lying in the manger. Bless our homes and all whom we love.

In this holy night heaven is come down to earth, and earth is raised to heaven. Keep in safety (. . . and) all those who have gone through death in the hope of heaven.

In this holy night angels and shepherds worshipped at the manger throne. Receive the worship we offer in fellowship with Blessed Mary and all the saints.   13

Merciful Father,
accept these prayers
for the sake of your Son,
our Saviour Jesus Christ.   Amen.

18 All may say

> We do not presume
> to come to this your table, merciful Lord,
> trusting in our own righteousness,
> but in your manifold and great mercies.
> We are not worthy
> so much as to gather up the crumbs under your table.
> But you are the same Lord
> whose nature is always to have mercy.
> Grant us therefore, gracious Lord,
> so to eat the flesh of your dear Son Jesus Christ
> and to drink his blood,
> that we may evermore dwell in him
> and he in us.   Amen.

THE PEACE

19 **Stand**

> Unto us a child is born, unto us a son is given:
> and his name is called the Prince of Peace.

> The peace of the Lord be always with you
> **And also with you.**

A minister may say

> Let us offer one another a sign of peace.

and all may exchange a sign of peace.

THE PREPARATION OF THE GIFTS

20 The bread and wine are placed on the holy table.

21 The president may praise God for his gifts in appropriate
words to which all respond

> **Blessed be God for ever.**

22 The offerings of the people may be collected and presented. These words may be used.

Yours, Lord, is the greatness, the power,
the glory, the splendour, and the majesty;
for everything in heaven and on earth is yours.
All things come from you,
and of your own do we give you.

23 At the preparation of the gifts A HYMN may be sung.

THE EUCHARISTIC PRAYER

24 The president takes the bread and cup into his hands and replaces them on the holy table.

25 The president uses one of the authorized EUCHARISTIC PRAYERS. This or another authorized PROPER PREFACE is used.

And now we give you thanks
because in the incarnation of the Word
a new light has dawned upon the world;
you have become one with us
that we might become one with you
    in your glorious kingdom.   8

or

And now we give you thanks
because for love of our fallen race
he most wonderfully and humbly chose to be made man,
and to take our nature as nevermore to lay it by,
so that we might be born again by your Spirit
and restored in your image.   32

THE COMMUNION

26   THE LORD'S PRAYER is said in one of the following forms.

As our Saviour taught us, so we pray

Our Father in heaven,	*or*	Our Father, who art in heaven,
hallowed be your name,		hallowed be thy name;
your kingdom come,		thy kingdom come;
your will be done,		thy will be done;
on earth as in heaven.		on earth as it is in heaven.
Give us today our daily bread.		Give us this day our daily bread.
Forgive us our sins		And forgive us our trespasses,
as we forgive those		as we forgive those
who sin against us.		who trespass against us.
Lead us not into temptation		And lead us not into temptation;
but deliver us from evil.		but deliver us from evil.

For the kingdom, the power, For thine is the kingdom,
  and the glory are yours   the power, and the glory,
now and for ever.   Amen.   for ever and ever.   Amen.

27   The president breaks the consecrated bread, saying

We break this bread
to share in the body of Christ.
**Though we are many, we are one body,
because we all share in one bread.**

28   Either here or during the distribution one of the following
ANTHEMS may be said.

**Lamb of God, you take away the sins of the world:
have mercy on us.**

**Lamb of God, you take away the sins of the world:
have mercy on us.**

**Lamb of God, you take away the sins of the world:
grant us peace.**

or

**Jesus, Lamb of God: have mercy on us.
Jesus, bearer of our sins: have mercy on us.
Jesus, redeemer of the world: give us your peace.**

29 Before the distribution the president says

Christ is the bread which has come down from heaven.
Lord, give us this bread for ever.

Draw near with faith. Receive the body of our Lord Jesus
Christ which he gave for you, and his blood which he shed
for you.

Eat and drink in remembrance that he died for you, and
feed on him in your hearts by faith with thanksgiving.

30 The president and people receive the Communion. Any
authorized words of distribution may be used. During the
distribution HYMNS and ANTHEMS may be sung. The Alternative
Service Book provision is followed for consecration of
additional bread and wine and for disposing of what remains.

AFTER COMMUNION

31 The president may use one of these sentences.

The shepherds said, 'Let us go to Bethlehem, and see the
thing that the Lord has made known to us.'   *Luke 2. 15*

or

The Word was made flesh, and lived among us: and we
saw his glory.   *John 1. 14*

32 **Silence** may be kept and A HYMN may be sung.

33 One or more of the following prayers or other suitable prayers
are said.

34 *At night*

God our Father,
tonight you have made known to us again
the power and coming of our Lord Jesus Christ;
may our Christmas celebration
confirm our faith and fix our eyes on him
until the day dawns
and Christ the Morning Star
rises in our hearts.
To him be glory both now and for ever.   Amen.

Daytime

Gracious Father,
our eyes have seen the King in his beauty;
by this living bread and saving cup
let his likeness be formed in us
and grow until the end of time;
through Christ our Lord.   **Amen.**

35 **Almighty God,**
we thank you for feeding us
with the body and blood of your Son
Jesus Christ.
Through him we offer you our souls and bodies
to be a living sacrifice.
Send us out
in the power of your Spirit
to live and work
to your praise and glory.   Amen.

THE DISMISSAL

36 The president may say THIS BLESSING.

May the Father,
who has loved the eternal Son
from before the foundation of the world,
shed that love upon you his children.   **Amen.**

May Christ,
who by his incarnation gathered into one
things earthly and heavenly,
fill you with joy and peace.   **Amen.**

May the Holy Spirit,
by whose overshadowing Mary became the Godbearer,
give you grace to carry the good news of Christ.   **Amen.**

And the blessing of God almighty,
the Father, the Son, and the Holy Spirit,
be upon you and remain with you always.   **Amen.**

37 *Minister*   Go in peace to love and serve the Lord.
                 In the name of Christ.   **Amen.**

     or

     Minister   Go in the peace of Christ.
                 Thanks be to God.

3. A Service for Christmas Morning

In a service for Christmas morning some of the following material may be useful. Other material may be found in the Crib Service (pp. 165-170). Whatever structure is adopted, the telling of the story should lead to thanksgiving and self-offering, and be concluded in praise and prayer.

1   INTRODUCTION AND GREETING

I bring you good news of great joy:
a Saviour has been born to you. Alleluia!
Unto us a child is born, a son is given. Alleluia!

Hear the words of St Luke:
When the angels had gone from them into heaven, the shepherds said one to another, 'Let us go to Bethlehem and see this thing that has happened which the Lord has made known to us.' So they hastened, and found Mary and Joseph, and the baby lying in a manger.

He is Christ the Lord. Alleluia!
We worship and adore him. Alleluia!

2   PENITENCE

As we kneel with the shepherds before the newborn Christ child, we open our hearts in penitence and faith:

You, Lord, were born for our salvation.
Lord, have mercy.
Lord, have mercy.

You came as Saviour to bring wholeness and peace.
Christ, have mercy.
Christ, have mercy.

You came to bring light into the darkness of our lives.
Lord, have mercy.
Lord, have mercy.

May Almighty God, who sent his Son into the world to save sinners, bring you his pardon and peace, now and for ever.   **Amen.**

3   A CANTICLE, SONG, or HYMN may be sung.

4   THE COLLECT

THE MINISTRY OF THE WORD

5   READINGS and CAROLS may follow, with periods of silence.
AN ADDRESS may be given.

6   THE CREED may be said in this or any other authorized form.

We proclaim the Church's faith in Jesus Christ:

**We believe and declare that our Lord Jesus Christ,
the Son of God, is both divine and human;**

God, of the being of the Father,
the only Son from before time began;
human from the being of his mother, born in the world.

**Fully God and fully human;
one human person with mind and body.**

As God he is equal to the Father,
as human he is less than the Father.

**Although he is both divine and human
he is not two beings but one Christ.**

One, not by turning God into flesh,
but by taking humanity into God.

**Truly one, not by mixing humanity with Godhead,
but by being one person.**

For as mind and body form one human being,
so the one Christ is both divine and human.

**The Word became flesh and lived among us;
we have seen his glory,
the glory of the only Son from the Father,
full of grace and truth.**

7   Gifts and offerings may be presented and this form of
     THANKSGIVING used.

Blessed are you, Son of Mary;
born a child,
you share our humanity:
Heaven and earth shout their praise.

Blessed are you, Son of David;
born to rule,
you receive gifts from the wise:
Heaven and earth shout their praise.

Blessed are you, Son of Man;
born our Saviour,
you are the light of the world:
Heaven and earth shout their praise.

With all the voices of heaven
we celebrate the coming of our God:
Hosanna in the highest.

Glory to God in the highest,
and peace to his people on earth.

Blessed is he who comes in the name of the Lord.
Hosanna in the highest.   *11*

8   PRAYERS OF INTERCESSION

We bring before God our needs and the needs of his world.

Unto us a child is born, unto us a son is given.

Wonderful Counsellor,
give your wisdom to the rulers of the nations.
Lord, in your mercy
hear our prayer.

Mighty God,
make the whole world know
that the government is on your shoulders.
Lord, in your mercy
hear our prayer.

Everlasting Father,
establish your reign of justice and righteousness
for ever.
Lord, in your mercy
hear our prayer.

Prince of peace,
bring in the endless kingdom of your peace.
Lord, in your mercy
hear our prayer.

Almighty Lord,
Hear our prayer,
and fulfil your purposes in us,
as you accomplished your will
in our Lord Jesus Christ. Amen.

So, united as members of the Lord's family, we pray with
one heart and voice:

Our Father in heaven,	*or*	Our Father, who art in heaven,
hallowed be your name,		hallowed be thy name;
your kingdom come,		thy kingdom come;
your will be done,		thy will be done;
on earth as in heaven.		on earth as it is in heaven.
Give us today our daily bread.		Give us this day our daily bread.
Forgive us our sins		And forgive us our trespasses,
as we forgive those		as we forgive those
who sin against us.		who trespass against us.
Lead us not into temptation		And lead us not into temptation;
but deliver us from evil.		but deliver us from evil.
For the kingdom, the power,		For thine is the kingdom,
and the glory are yours		the power, and the glory,
now and for ever. Amen.		for ever and ever. Amen.

9　THE BLESSING

May the joy of the angels,
the eagerness of the shepherds,
the perseverance of the wise men,
the obedience of Joseph and Mary,
and the peace of the Christ child
be yours this Christmas.

And the blessing of God almighty,
the Father, the Son and the Holy Spirit,
be upon you and remain with you always.　**Amen.**

E. SENTENCES AND PRAYERS FOR USE AT CHRISTMASTIDE

1. Prayers at the Christmas Crib

It is traditional to decorate the Church with a crib from the Eve of Christmas Day until the end of the season.

For pastoral reasons it may be necessary for the crib to be placed in the church earlier in Advent. In particular the building of the crib, with the aid of children, provides a good teaching opportunity within a service on Advent 4 or Christmas Eve. Or it might be incorporated within a pre-Christmas Christingle Service. Dramatically it is preferable for the figures of the shepherds not to 'arrive' until Christmas Eve, nor the wise men until Epiphany – though they may be 'on the way' in some other part of the church. The figure of the Christ child should, if possible, be placed in the crib at the Midnight Eucharist or next morning.

The provision in this book for the principal Eucharist of Christmas Night or Day begins with the blessing of the crib. This is preferable to some of the earlier occasions that are chosen for the blessing of the crib. The placing of the figure of the Christ child in the crib on Christmas night, followed by the blessing of the crib, can be a dramatic declaration that Christmas is here. But the prayers of dedication at the crib can take place on one of several occasions, according to pastoral need, and a number of forms of prayer are provided here.

In churches where space and movements allow, it may be appropriate to stop at the crib for a prayer during the entrance procession at the main Eucharist on each Sunday and major feast day through the season. The material in the following chapter for the Feast of the Epiphany and the Feast of the Baptism of the Lord provides for parts of the liturgy to be celebrated at the crib and for the gifts of the Magi to be made.

Where churches are keeping the season of the Incarnation until 2 February, the Feast of the Presentation, along the lines advocated in this book, it is right to keep the crib for the forty days until the Presentation. At the Candlemas Liturgy, a 'station' may be made at the crib during the entrance procession, and after the service the crib is dismantled. This is preferable to moving the crib after the Feast of the Epiphany or the following Sunday.

Although the crib can be a focus of devotion during the liturgy in the Christmas and Epiphany season, people may also be encouraged to use the crib as a personal means of devotion outside the liturgy. Accordingly we offer a selection of prayers which may be used in a variety of ways.

a. THE DEDICATION OF THE CRIB

Before the Midnight Eucharist

Today you will know that the Lord is coming to save us:
and in the morning you will see his glory.

Hear the words of the prophet Isaiah:
The Lord himself will give you a sign. It is this: the maiden
is with child and will soon give birth to a son whom she
will call Emmanuel, a name which means 'God is with us'.

Thanks be to God.   4

After the Midnight Eucharist

A light will shine on us this day:
The Lord is born for us.

Hear the words of Saint Luke:
When the angels had gone from them into heaven, the
shepherds said one to another, 'Let us go to Bethlehem
and see this thing that has happened which the Lord has
made known to us.' So they hurried away, and found
Mary and Joseph, and the baby lying in a manger.

Thanks be to God.   4

On other occasions

A hallowed day has dawned upon us.
Come and worship the Lord:
for a great light has shone on the earth.

Hear the words of the Book of Wisdom:
When peaceful silence lay over all and night was in the
midst of her swift course, from your royal throne, O God,
down from the heavens, leapt your almighty Word.

Hear the words of Saint John:
God's love for us was revealed when God sent his only Son
into the world so that we could have life through him.

Thanks be to God.

Let us pray
that God our Father will bless this crib,
and that all who worship his Son,
born of the Virgin Mary,
may come to share his life in glory.   *30*

God our Father,
on this night (day) your Son Jesus Christ
was born of the Virgin Mary for us
and for our salvation.
Bless this crib,
which we have prepared to celebrate that holy birth;
may all who see it be strengthened in faith
and receive the fullness of life he came to bring,
who lives and reigns for ever and ever.   **Amen.**   *30*

In the faith of Christ,
and in your name, O God most holy,
we hallow this crib of Christmas,
to set before the eyes of your children
the great love and humility
of Jesus Christ your only Son;
who for us, and for our salvation,
came down as at this time from heaven,
and was incarnate by the Holy Spirit
of the Virgin Mary his mother,
and was made man;
to whom with you and the same Spirit
be all honour, majesty, glory, and worship,
now and to the ages of ages.   **Amen.**   *32**

May the grace of Christ our Saviour be with us
all.   **Amen.**

b. ADDITIONAL PRAYERS

1   To you, O Christ, Word of the Father,
    we offer our lowly prayers and humble thanks;
    for love of our human race
    you most wonderfully chose to be made man,
    and to take our nature as nevermore to lay it by;
    so that we might be born again by your Spirit
    and restored in the image of God;
    to whom, one blessed Trinity,
    be given all honour, might, majesty, and power,
    now and for ever.   **Amen.**   32*

2   Glory to God in the highest,
    and peace to his people on earth.

    Lord, God, heavenly King,
    almighty God and Father,
    we worship you, we give you thanks,
    we praise you for your glory.

    Today you fill our hearts with joy
    as we recognize in Christ the revelation of your love.
    No eye can see his glory as our God,
    yet now he is seen like one of us.

    Christ is your Son before all ages,
    yet now he is born in time.
    He has come to lift up all things to himself,
    to restore unity to creation,
    and to lead us from exile into your heavenly kingdom.

    To us a child is born, to us a Son is given;
    and he shall be called the Prince of Peace.

    He alone is the Holy One,
    he alone is the Lord,
    he alone is the Most High,
    Jesus Christ,
    with the Holy Spirit,
    in the glory of God the Father.   **Amen.**   10

3   O God the Son, highest and holiest,
    who humbled yourself to share our birth and our death:
    bring us with the shepherds and the wise men
    to kneel before your holy cradle,
    that we may come to sing with your angels
    your glorious praises in heaven;
    where with the Father and the Holy Spirit
    you live and reign, God, world without end.   32*

4   We pray you, Lord, to purify our hearts
    that they may be worthy to become your dwelling-place.
    Let us never fail to find room for you,
    but come and abide in us,
    that we also may abide in you,
    for as at this time you were born into the world for us,
    and live and reign, King of kings and Lord of lords,
    now and for ever.   33

5   Lord, by the song of the angels
    you disclosed your birth to your own people,
    and by the leading of a star
    you revealed your glory to strangers.
    Teach us to know you now,
    and to make you known to all.   30

6   The kings, Lord,
    brought myrrh, frankincense, and gold.
    Lord, we are nothing,
    we bring you what you have given,
    our lives for your life.   30

7   May the humility of the shepherds,
    the perseverance of the wise men,
    the joy of the angels,
    and the peace of the Christ child
    be God's gifts to us
    this Christmas time, and always.   30

2. Additional Prayers for the Eucharist in Christmastide

Much of the material in the services for Christmas Eve and Christmas Day is suitable for use at the Eucharist for the days until Epiphany.

PENITENCE

1   Lord Jesus, you are mighty God and Prince of Peace:
    Lord, have mercy.
    Lord, have mercy.

    Lord Jesus, you are Son of God and Son of Mary:
    Christ, have mercy.
    Christ, have mercy.

    Lord Jesus, you are Word made flesh
    and splendour of the Father:
    Lord, have mercy.
    Lord, have mercy.   *10*

2   God be gracious to us and bless us,
    and make your face shine upon us:
    Lord, have mercy.
    Lord, have mercy.

    May your ways be known on the earth,
    your saving power among the nations:
    Christ, have mercy.
    Christ, have mercy.

    You, Lord, have made known your salvation,
    and reveal your justice in the sight of nations:
    Lord, have mercy.
    Lord, have mercy.

    May the God of all healing and forgiveness
    draw you to himself,
    that you may behold the glory of his Son,
    the Word made flesh,
    and be cleansed from all your sins
    through Jesus Christ our Lord.   **Amen.**   *3*

PREFACE

And now we give you thanks
because in the wonder of the incarnation
your eternal Word has brought to the eyes of faith
a new and radiant vision of your glory.
In him we see our God made visible
and so are caught up in the love of God we cannot see.

POST-COMMUNION

Lord God, through the appearing of our Saviour
you have abolished death
and brought life and immortality to light;
let this living bread and saving cup
refresh and strengthen us
that with your saints
we may praise you for ever and ever.

ST STEPHEN FIRST MARTYR (26 December)

PREFACE

And now we give you thanks
for the example of your chosen servant Stephen;
as a deacon he preached the good news of your Kingdom;
he saw your glory, and as the first martyr
he committed his spirit to the Saviour.

or, for use with Eucharistic Prayer 2 or 4

. . . through Jesus Christ (your only Son) our Lord.

For love of us fallen sinners
he most wonderfully and humbly chose to be made
    human,
and to take our nature upon him,
so that we might be born again by your Spirit
and restored in your image;

The love that brought him down to earth
lifted your martyr Stephen from earth to heaven.

By that love he spoke your word
    with wisdom and the Spirit;
By that love he saw your glory
    and Jesus at your right hand;
By that love he overcame the anger of his accusers
    and forgave their cruelty;
By that love he committed his spirit into your hands
    and won the crown of righteousness.

POST-COMMUNION

Merciful Lord,
we thank you for the signs of your mercy
revealed in birth and death.
Save us by the coming of your Son,
and give us joy in honouring Stephen,
first martyr of the new Israel.

10

ST JOHN THE EVANGELIST (27 December)

PREFACE

And now we give you thanks
for the grace and truth shown forth
in John, your evangelist and apostle;
by the light of Christ's appearing
we behold your glory
and are born again to life eternal.

POST-COMMUNION

Eternal God,
your apostle and evangelist John
proclaimed your word made flesh among us.
May we who have shared the bread of life
remain for ever your children,
born according to your will,
and lifted up to behold the glory
of your Son Jesus Christ.   *11*

THE HOLY INNOCENTS (28 December)

PREFACE

And now we give you thanks
for the witness of the infants
who died cruelly, not yet knowing the new-born Christ,
that your grace might be made perfect in human weakness,
and the way of salvation prepared in our sinful world.

POST-COMMUNION

God almighty,
in your greatness you stooped to share human life
with the most defenceless of your creatures.
May we who have received these gifts of your passion
rejoice in celebrating the wordless witness
of the holy innocents to your Son our Lord.

3. Prayers at the New Year

The material in this section may be suitable for use at or near New Year's Day.

Suitable material for a Vigil for the New Year will be found in The Service of Light (Chapter I, B, Acclamations e and f, and C, Patterns 9 and 10), and in the Appendix, Lectionary 1, under 1 January.

SENTENCES

You crown the year with your goodness.   *Psalm 65. 11*

Many are the plans in the human heart,
but it is the purpose of the Lord that will be established.
                                                Proverbs 19. 21

The Lord knows the path I take:
when he has tried me I shall come forth as gold.   *Job 23. 10*

Seek first the kingdom of God and his righteousness
and all these things will be yours as well.   *Matthew 6. 33*

Do not worry about tomorrow:
tomorrow will take care of itself.
Each day has trouble enough of its own.   *Matthew 6. 34*

Do not be anxious:
in everything make your requests known to God
in prayer and petition with thanksgiving.   *Philippians 4. 7*

I am the Alpha and the Omega. The first and the last,
the beginning and the end.   *Revelation 22. 13*

COLLECTS

God and Father of our Lord Jesus Christ,
whose years never fail
and whose mercies are new each returning day:
let the radiance of your Spirit renew our lives,
warming our hearts and giving light to our minds;
that we may pass the coming year
in joyful obedience and firm faith;
through him who is the beginning and the end,
your Son Christ our Lord.   4

O God, by whose command
the order of time runs its course:
forgive our impatience, perfect our faith,
and, while we wait for the fulfilment of your promises,
grant us to have a good hope because of your word;
through Jesus Christ our Lord.   4

Eternal Lord God,
we give you thanks for bringing us
    through the changes of time
to the beginning of another year.
Forgive us the wrong we have done
    in the year that is past,
and help us to spend the rest of our days
to your honour and glory;
through Jesus Christ our Lord.

INTERCESSIONS

In a world of change and hope,
of fear and adventure,
faithful God,
glorify your name.

In human rebellion and obedience,
in our seeking and our finding,
faithful God,
glorify your name.

In the common life of our society,
in prosperity and need,
faithful God,
glorify your name.

As your Church proclaims your goodness
in words and action,
faithful God,
glorify your name.

Among our friends
and in our homes,
faithful God,
glorify your name.

In our times of joy,
in our days of sorrow,
faithful God,
glorify your name.

In our strengths and triumphs,
in our weakness and at our death,
faithful God,
glorify your name.

In your saints in glory
and on the day of Christ's coming,
faithful God,
glorify your name.

BLESSING

The Lord bless you and watch over you,
the Lord make his face shine upon you
and be gracious to you,
the Lord look kindly on you
and give you peace;
and the blessing of God almighty,
the Father, the Son, and the Holy Spirit,
be upon you and remain with you always.   **Amen.**   8

or

May God keep you in all your days.

May Christ shield you in all your ways.

May the Spirit bring you healing and peace.

May God the Holy Trinity drive all darkness from you
and pour upon you blessing and light.   **Amen.**

V

EPIPHANYTIDE

A. INTRODUCTION

The Epiphany, or the Manifestation of Christ, has been celebrated in the Christian tradition in a variety of ways. The Feast celebrated on 6 January has been exclusively focused on the Visit of the Magi only in the Western Church. In other Christian traditions, the Manifestation of Christ, the revealing of his true nature, has been focused on the Declaration made at his baptism in the Jordan, as in St Mark's Gospel, and the revelation made at Cana in Galilee.

In the acts of worship for Epiphanytide, therefore, provision is made for celebrating not only the Visit of the Magi but also the Baptism of the Lord, kept as a major festival on the first Sunday after the Epiphany. In addition there are suggestions for keeping Epiphanytide until the Presentation of Christ on 2 February as a season giving prominence to the mission of the Church, the true 'making manifest' of Christ.

Full provision is made here for a service for the Feast of the Baptism of the Lord in two forms: either as a tripartite Ministry of the Word culminating in a Prayer of Thanksgiving over Water and the renewal of the baptismal covenant; or in a form of the service which makes provision for the administration of Holy Baptism. With appropriate hymns and carols, these forms of service are complete liturgies on their own, and may form suitable Epiphany Carol Services or Epiphany Processions.

While these orders may also be used as the Service of the Word to be followed by the celebration of the Eucharist, further provision is made to mark the season with a Thanksgiving for Water followed by Prayers of Penitence and Renewal when it is desired to insert such a commemoration into a regular eucharistic order. This provision gives expression to the tradition which speaks of baptism as a new birth by water and the Spirit (John 3) – a sign of the New Creation; and this distinctive Epiphanytide emphasis complements the Paschal stress on Baptism as dying and rising with Christ (Romans 6).

Together with these provisions are Bidding Prayers and Conclusions for Vigils and Carol Services, based on the Patterns of Readings set out in the Service of Light, and also Prayers and Readings for the Mission of the Church, and for use in the week of Prayer for Christian Unity.

Lectionary 2 in the Appendix allows for a very brief Epiphany season, simply up to and including the Feast of the Baptism of the Lord on Epiphany 1, and thereafter the return to locally devised themes, not necessarily incarnational in character. But the main thrust of our Calendar, and of the provision in Lectionary 1, is an Epiphany season that carries forward the incarnation and revelation themes through a longer festal period until the Feast of the Presentation, Candlemas, on 2 February (or the nearest Sunday to it). We have therefore provided material for use throughout this season, with particular emphasis on the mission of the Church.

These forty days from Christmas to Candlemas constitute a period parallel to the fifty days from Easter to Pentecost. The appropriate liturgical colour is white throughout; and the Sundays between 6 January and 2 February are Sundays of Epiphany, rather than after Epiphany.

In making the whole season from Christmas to Candlemas a reflection on the incarnation and its revealing, we have simply returned to the old Sarum rite which did the same.

B. CAROL SERVICES AND VIGIL SERVICES IN EPIPHANYTIDE

1 THE SERVICE OF LIGHT

In the Service of Light (see Chapter 1, B), any of the options in section 1 are suitable, and in section 4, among the Acclamations of the Light, d, e, f, g, and h are particularly suitable. In section 5, Psalm 141 is particularly suitable.

2 BIDDING PRAYERS AND INTRODUCTIONS

1   Three wonders mark this Holy Day,
as the Church is joined to a heavenly bridegroom.

This day a star leads the wise men to the manger.
Alleluia!

This day water is made wine at the wedding feast.
Alleluia!

This day Jesus is revealed as the Christ
in the waters of baptism.
Alleluia! Praise to you, Lord Jesus Christ.   *19*†

2   In the name of Christ, who called us out of darkness into his own marvellous light, to be a kingdom of priests to our God, we welcome you.
Grace to you and peace.

As we rejoice in the Word made flesh, who comes among us to reveal God's glory, so we pray that his kingly reign may be acknowledged throughout the world.

And so we pray for the unity and mission of Christ's Church, for the ministers of the gospel of Christ, and for all for whom we bear witness.

---

† Numbers in the right-hand margin refer to Sources and Acknowledgements (pp.416-419).

We pray for this world, which is already Christ's, that we may have reverence for the natural order and respect for every person, made in the image and likeness of God.

And we pray for those who stand in need, for the lonely, the fearful, and the anxious, for the sick and the bereaved, and for all who have no one to pray for them.

May God our Father take us and use us in his service; may he open our eyes to see his glory, and equip us to bless his people, now and at all times.   **Amen.**   *3*

3   Give praise, you servants of the Lord:
O praise the name of the Lord.

Let the name of the Lord be blessed:
from the rising of the sun to its setting.

Light has sprung up for the righteous:
And joyful gladness for those who are true-hearted.

Rejoice in the Lord, you righteous:
Sing to the Lord and praise his name.

from Psalms 113 and 97

4   Let us give thanks to the God of our Lord Jesus Christ,
who has blessed us in Christ with every spiritual blessing.

Before the world was made, God chose us in Christ
that we might be holy and blameless before him.

Let us praise God for the glory of his grace,
for the free gift he gave us in his dear Son.

To Father, Son, and Holy Spirit
**give praise and dominion, honour and might,
for ever and ever.   Amen.**

Ephesians 1. 3-6

3 PATTERNS OF READINGS

The following patterns of Readings from Chapter I, C are suitable in
Epiphanytide:

(9)   The New Creation
(11)   A Light to the Nations: for the Vigil of Epiphany
(12)   The Anointed Lord: for the Vigil of the Baptism
(14)   For Apostles and Evangelists.

This last pattern is particularly suitable for Vigils of Prayer for the
Mission of the Church, or for Vigils of Prayer for vocation and
discipleship. The other three patterns are suitable not only for Carol
Services, or Vigils of the Feast of the Epiphany and the Baptism of the
Lord, but also for Services of Prayer and Praise in Epiphanytide.

4 CONCLUSIONS

1   God be gracious to us and bless us:
      And make your face shine upon us.

      May your ways be known on the earth:
      Your saving power among all nations.

      You, Lord, have made known your salvation
      And reveal your justice in the sight of the nations.

2   **Glory to God, whose power at work among us
      can do infinitely more than all we can ask or conceive;
      to him be glory in the Church and in Christ Jesus,
      for ever and ever.   Amen.**

3   Let us bless the living God:

      He was born of the Virgin Mary,
      Revealed in his glory,

      Worshipped by angels,
      Proclaimed among the nations,

      Believed in throughout the world,
      Exalted to the highest heavens.

      Blessed be God, our strength and our salvation,
      Now and for ever.   Amen.

C. THE EPIPHANY OF CHRIST

A SERVICE FOR THE FEAST OF THE BAPTISM OF THE LORD

NOTES

1 This service is most appropriately used on the first Sunday after the Epiphany, the Feast of the Baptism of Christ. It may also be used on the Feast of the Epiphany, or its Vigil, or at any suitable time within Epiphanytide.

2 With suitable hymns and carols this service forms an Epiphany Procession or Epiphany Carol Service, at the climax of which is the Renewal of the Covenant or of Baptismal vows. Places are indicated for hymns and carols, but they may be omitted or inserted in other places.

3 If it is desired to combine this service with the Holy Communion, the Our Father (section 26), the final hymn (section 29), and the Blessing (section 30), are omitted, and the Holy Communion begins, after the Renewal of the Covenant, with the Peace. In this case, sections 10-14, 'The New Creation is Revealed in the Water made Wine', may be more appropriately used after section 25.

4 Any movement through the church will depend on the position of the Crib, the Font, and the Holy Table, and whether or not the service is combined with the Eucharist. If the Font is not easily accessible, or too close to the Crib, a large vessel can be set on a table in the middle of the church for the Prayer over the Water, to be carried from there to the Font at the end of the service.

5 The gifts in section 6 may be any one or all three of the traditional gifts. The Christmas Collections may appropriately be offered at this point. At section 11, the wine may appropriately be the wine for use in the Service of Holy Communion during the year.

6 The Acclamations may appropriately be made by a deacon. The President of the Rite should normally be a bishop or a priest.

7 The Canticles from Isaiah (section 5), Revelation (section 10) and Ezekiel (section 15), set as Responses, may be said or sung in any suitable form.

8 Intercession. A Bidding may precede the Prayer in section 4, or appropriate Biddings may be introduced before the Gospel Collects. Alternatively, provision is made for intercessory prayer at section 26.

INTRODUCTION

1   Three wonders mark this holy day,
    as the Church is joined to her heavenly Bridegroom.

    This day a star leads the wise men to the manger.
    Alleluia!

    This day water is made wine at the wedding feast.
    Alleluia!

    This day Jesus is revealed as the Christ
    in the waters of baptism.
    Alleluia! Praise to you, Lord Jesus Christ!   *19*

2   A HYMN may be sung here or after section 4.

3   The president welcomes the people.

    Grace and peace from God our Father
    and the Lord Jesus Christ be with you.
    And also with you.

4   There may follow an Introduction or Bidding, after which the
    president prays

    Grant us, Lord, who behold your glory,
    to drink from the waters of the new creation
    flowing from the river of life at your baptism.
    Give us the wings of the Spirit
    that we may hasten to meet you at your coming,
    and praise you, with the Father and the Holy Spirit,
    now and for ever.   **Amen.**

THE KING OF ALL THE WORLD
IS REVEALED TO THE MAGI

5   This day a star leads the wise men to the manger.

    Arise, shine; for your light has come
    And the glory of the Lord has risen upon you.

    Nations shall come to your light
    And Kings to the brightness of your rising.

They shall bring gold and frankincense
And proclaim the praise of the Lord.

Your gates will lie open continually
Shut neither by day nor by night.

No more will the sun give you daylight
Nor moonlight shine upon you.

But the Lord will be your everlasting light
Your God will be your splendour.

from Isaiah 60

6   As the gifts are brought, THIS ACCLAMATION is made.

Blessed are you, Lord our God, King of the universe:
you receive our sacrifice of praise and thanksgiving.
May our prayer be set forth in your sight as incense,
And the lifting up of our hands be an evening sacrifice.
Blessed be God for ever.

3

Or, if preferred, the following acclamation may be used.

Blessed are you, Lord our God, King of the Universe:
your word has gone forth to the ends of the world.
May the whole creation be filled with your glory,
and all nations do you service.
Blessed be God for ever.

7   The Procession, with the gifts, moves to the Crib, as a Hymn is
sung or music is played. The congregation may follow.

8   A Reading from the Gospel according to Matthew.
Glory to Christ our Saviour.

Matthew 2. 1-2, 8-11

At the end the reader says

This is the Gospel of Christ.
Praise to Christ our Lord.

The gifts may be placed before the Crib.

212

9   *President*   Let us pray.

Eternal God,
who by the shining of a star
led the wise men to the worship of your Son:
guide by his light the nations of the earth,
that the whole world may behold your glory;
through Jesus Christ our Lord.   **Amen.**   8

Before the Reading and after the Collect, suitable Hymns or
Carols may be sung.

THE NEW CREATION IS REVEALED
IN THE WATER MADE WINE

10   This day water is made wine at the wedding feast.

I saw the holy city, New Jerusalem,
coming down out of heaven from God
Prepared as a bride adorned for her husband.

And I heard a great voice from the Throne, saying:
Behold, the dwelling of God is with his people.

He will dwell with them and they shall be his own:
And God himself shall be with them.

Behold, I make all things new:
I am Alpha and Omega, the beginning and the end.

To the thirsty I will give water without price:
From the fountain of the water of life.

from Revelation 21

11   As a chalice or a flagon of wine is brought, THIS ACCLAMATION is
made.

Blessed are you, Lord our God, King of the universe:
for the marriage of the Lamb has come.
Make your Church ready, and clothe her
with the righteous deeds of the saints,
to join the praises of your new creation.
Blessed be God for ever.   3

12   The Procession, with the chalice or flagon of wine, moves to the holy table as a Hymn is sung or music is played. The congregation may follow.

13   A Reading from the Gospel according to John.
Glory to Christ our Saviour.

John 2. 1-11

At the end the reader says

This is the Gospel of Christ.
Praise to Christ our Lord.

The chalice or flagon of wine may be placed on the holy table.

14   *President*   Let us pray.

Almighty God,
in Christ you make all things new.
Transform the poverty of our nature
by the riches of your grace,
and in the renewal of our lives
make known your heavenly glory;
through Jesus Christ our Lord.   **Amen.**   8

Before the Reading and after the Collect suitable Hymns and Carols may be sung.

THE CHRIST IS REVEALED
IN THE WATERS OF BAPTISM

15   This day Jesus is revealed as the Christ
in the waters of baptism.

I will take you from the nations:
and gather you from all countries.

I will sprinkle clean water upon you:
and purify you from all defilement.

A new heart I will give you:
and put a new spirit within you.

You shall be my people:
and I shall be your God.

from Ezekiel 36

16   As water is brought, THIS ACCLAMATION is made.

Blessed are you,
Lord our God, King of the universe:
you bring waters out of the stony rock.
For with you is the well of life,
and in your light shall we see light.
Blessed be God for ever.   3

17   The Procession with the water moves to the Font, as a Hymn is
       sung or music is played. The congregation may follow.

18   A Reading from the Gospel according to Mark.
       Glory to Christ our Saviour.

Mark 1. 1-11 (or 1. 4-5, 7-11)

At the end the reader says

This is the Gospel of Christ.
Praise to Christ our Lord.

19   *President*   Let us pray.

Almighty God,
who anointed Jesus at his Baptism with the Holy Spirit
and revealed him as your beloved Son:
give to us who are born of water and the Spirit,
the will to surrender ourselves to your service,
that we may rejoice to be called your children;
through Jesus Christ our Lord.   **Amen.**   8

Before the Reading, suitable Hymns or Carols may be sung.

20   After the Collect, the water is poured out with these or other
suitable words.

The springs of water were made holy
when Christ appeared on earth.
Draw water from the wells of salvation;
for, by his baptism, Christ our God
has made the whole creation one.   *19*

or

God in Christ gives us the water welling up for eternal life.
With joy you will draw water from the wells of salvation.
Lord, give us this water, and we shall thirst no more.

Then the president stands before the water, and says

21   *Either*

The Lord be with you.
And also with you.

Lift up your hearts.
We lift them to the Lord.

Let us give thanks to the Lord our God.
It is right to give him thanks and praise.

It is indeed right, it is our duty and our joy
at all times to give you thanks and praise,
for today the grace of the Holy Spirit
in the form of a dove descended upon the waters.   *3*

[Today the sun that never sets has risen
and the world is filled with splendour
by the light of the Lord.
Today the clouds drop down upon mankind
the dew of righteousness from on high.
Today the Uncreated of his own will
accepts the laying on of hands from his own creature.
Today the waters of the Jordan
are transformed for healing by the coming of the Lord.

Today our transgressions are washed away
by the waters of the river.
Today the blinding mist of the world is dispersed
by the Epiphany of our God.
Today things above keep feast with things below,
and things below commune with things above.]   *34*

Therefore, heavenly Father,
accept our sacrifice of praise,
and by the power of your life-giving Spirit
sanctify these waters of your new creation,
that we, with all who have been born anew
by water and the Spirit,
may be renewed in your image,
walk by the light of faith,
and serve you in newness of life.
Through your anointed Son, Jesus Christ our Lord,
to whom with you and the Holy Spirit
we lift our voices of praise:
Blessed be God, our strength and our salvation,
now and for ever.   Amen.   *3*

or

22   Let us give thanks to the Lord our God.
It is right to give him thanks and praise.

Father, for your gift of water in creation
We give you thanks and praise.

For your Spirit, sweeping over the waters,
bringing light and life
We give you thanks and praise.

For your son Jesus Christ our Lord,
baptized in the river Jordan
We give you thanks and praise.

For your new creation,
brought to birth by water and the Spirit
We give you thanks and praise.

For your grace bestowed upon us your children,
washing away our sins
We give you thanks and praise.

So, Father, accept our sacrifice of praise;
By the power of your life-giving Spirit
bless these waters of your new creation.
Lord, receive our prayer.

May we your servants who have been washed in them
be made one with your Son,
who took the form of a servant.
Lord, receive our prayer.

May your Holy Spirit, who has brought us to new birth
in the family of your Church,
raise us in Christ, our anointed Lord,
to full and eternal life.
Lord, receive our prayer.

For all might, majesty and dominion are yours,
now and for ever.
Alleluia! Amen.

23 The Prayer over the Water may be followed by a suitable chant
or acclamation.

THE RENEWAL OF THE COVENANT

24 The congregation remains standing.

25 *Either*

President
At your baptism you turned to Christ, repented of your sins,
and renounced evil. Do you now renew your allegiance to
Christ?

**I do, and with God's grace I will follow him as my Saviour
and Lord.**

Do you believe in God the Father?

**I believe in God, the Father almighty,
creator of heaven and earth.**

Do you believe in Jesus Christ, the Son of God?

**I believe in Jesus Christ, his only Son, our Lord.
He was conceived by the Holy Spirit,
born of the Virgin Mary,
suffered under Pontius Pilate,
was crucified, died, and was buried.
He descended to the dead.
On the third day he rose again.
He ascended into heaven,
and is seated at the right hand of the Father.
And will come again to judge the living and the dead.**

Do you believe in God the Holy Spirit?

**I believe in the Holy Spirit,
the holy catholic Church,
the communion of saints,
the forgiveness of sins,
the resurrection of the body,
and the life everlasting.   Amen.**

Will you continue in the apostles' teaching and fellowship, in the breaking of bread, and in the prayers?
With the help of God, I will.

Will you persevere in resisting evil, and whenever you fall into sin, repent and return to the Lord?
With the help of God, I will.

Will you proclaim by word and example the Good News of God in Christ?
With the help of God, I will.

Will you seek and serve Christ in all people, loving your neighbour as yourself?
With the help of God, I will.

Will you recognize Christ's authority over human society, by prayer for the world and its leaders, by defending the weak, and by seeking peace and justice?
With the help of God, I will.   *12*

26   *or*

President

In the Old Covenant, God chose Israel to be his people and to obey his laws. Our Lord Jesus Christ, by his death and resurrection, has given a New Covenant to all who trust in him. We stand within this Covenant and we bear his name.

On the one side, God promises to give us new life in Christ. On the other side, we are pledged to live no more for ourselves but for him.

Let us now renew our part in this Covenant which God has made with his people, and take the yoke of Christ upon us.

Christ has many services to be done; some are easy, others are difficult; some bring honour, others bring reproach; some are suitable to our natural inclinations and material interests, others are contrary to both. In some we may please Christ and please ourselves, in others we cannot please Christ except by denying ourselves. Yet the power to do all these things is given us in Christ who strengthens us.

Lord God,
in our baptism you called us and brought us into your Church, commissioning us to witness to the faith of the crucified Christ and to be his faithful disciples to the end of our lives; so now with joy we take upon ourselves the yoke of obedience and for love of you engage ourselves to seek and do your perfect will.
We are no longer our own, but yours.

We are no longer our own, but yours.
Put us to what you will, rank us with whom you will;
put us to doing, put us to suffering;
let us be employed for you or laid aside for you,
exalted for you or brought low for you;
let us be full, let us be empty;
let us have all things, let us have nothing;
We freely and wholeheartedly yield all things to your
pleasure and disposal.

And now, glorious and blessed God,
Father, Son, and Holy Spirit,
you are ours and we are yours.
So be it.
And the covenant which we have made on earth,
let it be ratified in heaven.   9

THE PRAYERS

27   Prayers may be offered here for the ministry and mission of the
Church, and for the world which the Church is called to serve.
Suitable material will be found in D.3 below, section 2.

28   As we look for the coming of the Kingdom, let us pray
together in the words our Saviour has taught us:

Our Father in heaven,	*or*	Our Father, who art in heaven,
hallowed be your name,		hallowed be thy name;
your kingdom come,		thy kingdom come;
your will be done,		thy will be done;
on earth as in heaven.		on earth as it is in heaven.
Give us today our daily bread.		Give us this day our daily bread.
Forgive us our sins		And forgive us our trespasses,
as we forgive those		as we forgive those
who sin against us.		who trespass against us.
Lead us not into temptation		And lead us not into temptation;
but deliver us from evil.		but deliver us from evil.

For the kingdom, the power,   For thine is the kingdom,
  and the glory are yours   the power, and the glory,
now and for ever.   **Amen.**   for ever and ever.   **Amen.**

29   *President*
May God the Creator, the rock of our salvation,
who has given us new birth by water and the Holy Spirit
and forgiven all our sins
through our Lord Jesus Christ,
keep us faithful to our calling, now and for ever.   **Amen.**

30   The water may be sprinkled over the people, or placed in vessels
by the door for them to make the Sign of the Cross as they
leave, or poured out over the threshold.

These words may be used.

Remember your baptism into Christ Jesus.
Thanks be to God.

A Hymn or other chant may be sung.

THE BLESSING AND DISMISSAL

31   The Blessing follows in either of these forms.

President
May God, who in Christ gives us a spring of water
welling up to eternal life,
perfect in you the image of his glory;
and the blessing of God almighty,
the Father, the Son and the Holy Spirit,
be upon you and remain with you always.   **Amen.**   *3*

or

May God the Father,
who led the Wise Men by the shining of a star
to find the Christ, the Light from Light,
lead you also in your pilgrimage to find the Lord.   **Amen.**

May God the Son,
who turned water into wine at the Wedding Feast at Cana,
transform your lives and make glad your hearts.   **Amen.**

May God the Holy Spirit,
who came upon the beloved Son
at his baptism in the River Jordan,
pour out his gifts on you
who have come to the waters of new birth.   **Amen.**

And the blessing of God almighty,
the Father, the Son, and the Holy Spirit,
be upon you and remain with you always.   **Amen.**

32   *Minister*   Go in peace to love and serve the Lord.
                In the name of Christ.   Amen.

D. SENTENCES AND PRAYERS FOR USE FROM THE EPIPHANY TO CANDLEMAS

1. On the Feast of the Epiphany

1　GREETING

Blessed are you, Lord our God, King of the universe!
**From the rising of the sun to its setting
your name is proclaimed in all the world.**

The Lord of glory be with you.
The Lord bless you.

2　INVITATION TO CONFESSION

The grace of God has dawned upon the world with healing
for all. Though we have grieved him, yet he will heal us if
we confess our sins in penitence and faith.　　　*20*

3　THE GOSPEL

The Gospel may be read from the Crib. After the Gospel, the
traditional gifts of gold, frankincense, and myrrh may be
offered at the Crib. Alternatively, the three figures of the Wise
Men may be placed in the Crib.

4　THESE ACCLAMATIONS may be made.

At the offering of Gold

Blessed are you, Lord our God, King of the Universe:
to you be praise and glory for ever!
As gold in the furnace is tried
and purified seven times in the fire,
so purify our hearts and minds
that we may be a royal priesthood
acceptable in the service of your kingdom.

Blessed be God for ever!

At the offering of Incense

Blessed are you, Lord our God, King of the Universe:
to you be praise and glory for ever!
As our prayer rises up in your presence as incense,
so may we be presented before you
with penitent hearts and uplifted hands
to offer ourselves in your priestly service.

Blessed be God for ever!

At the offering of Myrrh

Blessed are you, Lord our God, King of the Universe:
to you be praise and glory for ever!
As you give medicine to heal our sickness
and the leaves of the tree of life
for the healing of the nations,
so anoint us with your healing power
that we may be the first-fruits of your new creation.

Blessed be God for ever! 3

5   After the gifts have been offered, A SERMON may be preached.

6   INTERCESSION

This form may be used.

Today the Wise Men knelt before our Saviour. Let us also
kneel to worship him with great joy, and to make our
prayer to his heavenly Father.

Father, the wise men came from the east
to worship your Son:
grant to Christians everywhere a true spirit of adoration.

Lord, in your mercy
Hear our prayer.

Father, you are the King of Kings and Lord of Lords:
grant an abundance of peace to your world.

Lord, in your mercy
Hear our prayer.

Father, the Holy Family shared the life of the people of Nazareth:
protect in your mercy our neighbours and our families,
together with the whole community of which we are part.

Lord, in your mercy
Hear our prayer.

Father, though you were rich, for our sake you became poor:
show your love for the poor and powerless, and strengthen
(. . . and all) those who suffer.

Lord, in your mercy
Hear our prayer.

Father, the wise men presented to your Son gold, incense, and myrrh:
accept the gifts we bring, and the offering of our hearts at
the beginning of this new year.

Lord, in your mercy
Hear our prayer.

Father, you are the King of Heaven, the hope of all who trust in you:
give to (. . . and all) the faithful departed the wonders of
your salvation.

Lord, in your mercy
Hear our prayer.

Rejoicing in the fellowship of wise men, shepherds, and
angels, and of the Blessed Virgin Mary and Saint Joseph,
we commend ourselves and all Christian people to your
unfailing love.

Merciful Father,
Accept these prayers
for the sake of your Son,
our Saviour Jesus Christ.   Amen.   *13*

7 THE PEACE

Let the peace of Christ rule in your hearts
to which you are called as members of one body.

or

Our Saviour Christ is the Prince of Peace.
Of the increase of his government and of peace
there shall be no end.

8 PROPER PREFACE

Either

And now we give you thanks
because in coming to dwell among us as man,
he revealed the radiance of your glory,
and brought us out of darkness
into your own marvellous light.   *8*

or

And now we give you thanks
because you have brought us from darkness to light
and made your light shine in our hearts
to bring us the knowledge of your glory
in the face of Jesus Christ, our Lord.

9 AT THE BREAKING OF THE BREAD

We break the bread of life,
and that life is the light of the world.
**God here among us,
light in the midst of us,
bring us to light and life.**   *11*

10 POST-COMMUNION PRAYER

Lord God,
the bright splendour of all the nations:
may we who with the Wise Men
have beheld the glory of your presence
discern the radiance of your Son
even Jesus Christ our Lord.   **Amen.**

11   THE BLESSING

a   May God the Father,
     who led the Wise Men by the shining of a star
     to find the Christ, the Light from Light,
     lead you in your pilgrimage to find the Lord.   **Amen.**

     May God who has delivered us from the dominion of
         darkness
     give us a place with the saints in light
     in the kingdom of his beloved Son.   **Amen.**

     May the light of the glorious gospel of Christ
     shine in your hearts and fill your lives
     with his joy and peace.   **Amen.**

     And the blessing of God almighty,
     the Father, the Son, and the Holy Spirit,
     be upon you and remain with you always.   **Amen.**

b   Christ our Lord, to whom kings bowed down in worship
     and offered gifts, reveal to you his glory
     and pour upon you the riches of his grace;
     and the blessing . . .

c   May God the Father,
     who led the Wise Men by the shining of a star
     to find the Christ, the Light from Light,
     lead you also in your pilgrimage to find the Lord.   **Amen.**

     May God the Son,
     who turned water into wine at the Wedding Feast at Cana,
     transform your lives and make glad your hearts.   **Amen.**

     May God the Holy Spirit,
     who came upon the beloved Son
     at his baptism in the River Jordan,
     pour out his gifts on you
     who have come to the waters of new birth.   **Amen.**

     And the blessing of God almighty,
     the Father, the Son, and the Holy Spirit,
     be upon you and remain with you always.   **Amen.**

2. On the Feast of the Baptism of the Lord

1   After the Gospel, or after the Sermon, water is poured into the Font with these words.

The springs of water were made holy
when Christ appeared on earth.
Draw water from the wells of salvation;
for by his baptism
Christ our God
has made the whole creation one.   19

or

God in Christ gives us water welling up for eternal life.
With joy you will draw water from the wells of salvation.
Lord, give us this water, and we shall thirst no more.

2   The president stands before the water, and says

Let us give thanks to the Lord our God.
He is worthy of all thanksgiving and praise.

Blessed are you, Lord our God, King of the universe:
You are our light and our salvation!
For today the grace of the Holy Spirit
in the form of a dove descended upon the waters.
Therefore, heavenly Father, accept our sacrifice of praise,
and by the power of that same life-giving Spirit
sanctify these waters of your new creation;
that we, with all who have been born anew
by water and the Spirit,
may be renewed in your image,
walk by the light of faith,
and serve you in newness of life;
through your anointed Son, Jesus Christ our Lord,
to whom with you and the Holy Spirit
we lift our voices of praise:

Blessed be God, our strength and our salvation,
now and for ever.   Amen.   3

3   This or other suitable CHANTS or ACCLAMATIONS may be sung.

I saw water flowing
from the threshold of the Temple.
Wherever the river flows
everything will spring to life. Alleluia!

On the banks of the river grow trees
bearing every kind of fruit.
Their leaves will not wither
nor their fruit fail.

Their fruit will serve for food,
their leaves for the healing of the nations.
For the river of the water of life
flows from the throne of God and of the Lamb.

4   The Thanksgiving over Water may be followed by this act of
penitence and dedication.

God of truth,
you are faithful to the covenant you have made with us;
look in mercy on your people.

Cleanse us, Lord, from all our sins:
Wash us, and we shall be whiter than snow.

We have broken the pledges of our baptism,
and failed to be your disciples.

Cleanse us, Lord, from all our sins:
Wash us, and we shall be whiter than snow.

Though we are saved by Christ
and dead to sin through the deep waters of death,
we have not witnessed to his grace by our manner of life.

Cleanse us, Lord, from all our sins:
Wash us, and we shall be whiter than snow.

We have shown indifference to those in need
and have been afraid to stand up for justice and truth.

Cleanse us, Lord, from all our sins:
Wash us, and we shall be whiter than snow.

We have been slow to forgive, and have failed to
    remember
your repeated forgiveness of our sins.

Cleanse us, Lord, from all our sins:
Wash us, and we shall be whiter than snow.

Today we rejoice and give thanks
because your Son humbled himself to be baptized in the
    Jordan.
Through the waters you have given us the mystery of
    baptism
for the remission of our sins.

Cleanse us, Lord, from all our sins:
Wash us, and we shall be whiter than snow.

Through water and Spirit
you give us new life as the people of God,
and pour out upon us the gifts of your new covenant.

Cleanse us, Lord, from all our sins:
Wash us, and we shall be whiter than snow.

President
Almighty God,
in Christ you make all things new.
Transform the poverty of our nature
by the riches of your grace,
and in the renewal of our lives
make known your heavenly glory;
through Jesus Christ our Lord.   **Amen.**   8

or

Almighty God,
in our baptism you have consecrated us
to be temples of your Holy Spirit.
May we, whom you have counted worthy,
nurture your indwelling Spirit with a lively faith,
and worship you with upright lives;
through Jesus Christ.   **Amen.**

5   The water may be sprinkled over the people, or they may
come and sign themselves with the Cross in it as the president
says

'Come', say the Spirit and the Bride,
'Come forward, you who are thirsty,
receive the water of life,
free gift to all who desire it.'

6   THE PEACE

God has made us one in Christ.
He has set his seal upon us,
and as a pledge of what is to come
has given the Spirit to dwell in our hearts.   *3*

The peace of the Lord be always with you
and also with you.

7   PROPER PREFACE

And now we give you thanks
because you celebrated your new gift of Baptism
by signs and wonders at the Jordan.
Your voice was heard from heaven
to awaken faith in the presence among us
of your Word made flesh.
Your Spirit was seen as a dove,
revealing Jesus as your servant,
and anointing him with joy as the Christ,
sent to bring to the poor the good news of salvation.
Therefore, as we celebrate the union of earth and heaven,
we rejoice to echo songs of the angels in heaven
for ever praising you and saying: *10*

8   AT THE BREAKING OF THE BREAD

We break the bread of life,
and that life is the light of the world:
**God here among us,
light in the midst of us,
bring us to light and life.**   *11*

9   A PRAYER AFTER COMMUNION

Father, in baptism we die to sin,
rise again to new life,
and find our true place in Christ's living body.
Send us out sealed in the blood of the New Covenant,
to bring your reconciliation to this wounded world;
through Jesus Christ our Lord.   **Amen.**

10   THE BLESSING

President
God, who in his Christ gives us a spring of water
welling up to eternal life,
perfect in you the image of his glory;
and the blessing of God Almighty,
the Father, the Son, and the Holy Spirit,
be upon you and remain with you always.   **Amen.**   *3*

or

May God the Father,
who led the Wise Men by the shining of a star
to find the Christ, the Light from Light,
lead you also in your pilgrimage to find the Lord.   **Amen.**

May God the Son,
who turned water into wine at the Wedding Feast at Cana,
transform your lives and make glad your hearts.   **Amen.**

May God the Holy Spirit,
who came upon the beloved Son
at his baptism in the River Jordan,
pour out his gifts on you
who have come to the waters of new birth.   **Amen.**

And the blessing of God almighty,
the Father, the Son, and the Holy Spirit,
be upon you and remain with you always.   **Amen.**

3. In Epiphanytide

1 PENITENCE

a God be gracious to us and bless us,
and make your face shine upon us:
Lord, have mercy.
Lord, have mercy.

May your ways be known on the earth,
your saving power among the nations:
Christ, have mercy.
Christ, have mercy.

You, Lord, have made known your salvation,
and reveal your justice in the sight of the nations:
Lord, have mercy.
Lord, have mercy. *3*

b Lord Jesus, you are mighty God and Prince of Peace:
Lord, have mercy.
Lord, have mercy.

Lord Jesus, you are Son of God and Son of Mary:
Christ, have mercy.
Christ, have mercy.

Lord Jesus, you are Word made flesh
and splendour of the Father:
Lord, have mercy.
Lord, have mercy. *10*

c You raise the dead to life in the Spirit:
Lord, have mercy.
Lord, have mercy.

You bring pardon and peace to the broken in heart:
Christ, have mercy.
Christ, have mercy.

You make one by your Spirit the torn and divided:
Lord, have mercy.
Lord, have mercy. *10*

2   INTERCESSION

a   *For the Epiphany*

Today the Wise Men knelt before our Saviour. Let us also kneel to worship him with great joy, and to make our prayer to his heavenly Father.

Father, the wise men came from the east
to worship your Son:
grant to Christians everywhere a true spirit of adoration.

Lord, in your mercy
hear our prayer.

Father, you are the King of Kings and Lord of Lords:
grant an abundance of peace to your world.

Lord, in your mercy
hear our prayer.

Father, the Holy Family shared the life of the people of Nazareth:
protect in your mercy our neighbours and our families, together with the whole community of which we are part.

Lord, in your mercy
hear our prayer.

Father, though you were rich, for our sake you became poor:
show your love for the poor and powerless, and strengthen (. . . and all) who suffer.

Lord, in your mercy
hear our prayer.

Father, the wise men presented to your Son gold, incense, and myrrh:
accept the gifts we bring, and the offering of our hearts at the beginning of this new year.

Lord, in your mercy
hear our prayer.

Father, you are the King of Heaven, the hope of all who
trust in you:
give to (. . . and all) the faithful departed the wonders of
your salvation.

Lord, in your mercy
hear our prayer.

Rejoicing in the fellowship of wise men, shepherds, and
angels, and of the Blessed Virgin Mary and Saint Joseph,
we commend ourselves and all Christian people to your
unfailing love.

Merciful Father,
**accept these prayers
for the sake of your Son,
our Saviour Jesus Christ.   Amen.**   13

b   *For the Right Use of Gifts*

We pray that Christ may be seen in the life of the Church,
saying,
Jesus, Lord of the Church
in your mercy hear us.

You have called us into the family
of those who are the children of God.
May our love for our brothers and sisters in Christ
be strengthened by your grace.

Jesus, Lord of the Church
in your mercy hear us.

You have called us to be a temple
where the Holy Spirit can dwell.
Give us clean hands and pure hearts
so that our lives will reflect your holiness.

Jesus, Lord of the Church
in your mercy hear us.

You have called us to be a light to the world
so that those in darkness come to you.
May our lives shine as a witness
to the saving grace you have given for all.

Jesus, Lord of the Church
in your mercy hear us.

You have called us members of the body of Christ,
so when one suffers all suffer together.
We ask for your comfort and healing power
to bring hope to those in distress.

Jesus, Lord of the Church
in your mercy hear us.

You have called us to be the Bride
where Christ the Lord is the Bridegroom.
Prepare us for the wedding feast
where we will be united with him for ever.

Lord of the Church
**hear our prayer,
and make us one in heart and mind
to serve you with joy for ever. Amen.**

29*

c *For the Ministry and Mission of the Church*

We pray for the coming of God's kingdom, saying,
Father, by your Spirit
bring in your kingdom.

You came in Jesus to bring good news to the poor,
sight to the blind, freedom to the captives,
and salvation to your people:
anoint us with your Spirit;
rouse us to work in his name.
Father, by your Spirit
bring in your kingdom.

Send us to bring help to the poor
and freedom to the oppressed.
Father, by your Spirit
bring in your kingdom.

236

Send us to tell the world
the good news of your healing love.
Father, by your Spirit
bring in your kingdom.

Send us to those who mourn,
to bring joy and gladness instead of grief.
Father, by your Spirit
bring in your kingdom.

Send us to proclaim that the time is here
for you to save your people.
Father, by your Spirit
bring in your kingdom.

Lord of the Church
hear our prayer,
and make us one in heart and mind
to serve you with joy for ever.   Amen.

3   AT THE PEACE

a   Christ is our peace.
If anyone is in Christ, there is a new creation.
The old has passed away: behold, the new has come.

2 Corinthians 5. 17

b   God has made us one in Christ.
He has set his seal upon us,
and as a pledge of what is to come
has given the Spirit to dwell in our hearts.

2 Corinthians 1. 22

c   We are all one in Christ Jesus.
We belong to him through faith,
heirs of the promise of the Spirit of Peace.

Galatians 3. 28

4   PROPER PREFACES

a   And now we give you thanks
      because by water and the Holy Spirit
      you have made us a holy people
      in Jesus Christ our Lord;
      you renew that mystery in bread and wine
      to show forth your glory in all the world.   *11**

b   And now we give you thanks
      because you have revealed your eternal plan of salvation,
      and have shown your Son Jesus Christ
      to be the light to the nations.   *11**

c   And now we give you thanks
      because, in the mystery of the Word made flesh,
      you have caused a new light to shine in our hearts
      to give the knowledge of your glory
      in the face of Jesus Christ our Lord.   *11**

d   Today we give you thanks
      because you have anointed your Son as the Messiah,
      the light of the nations,
      and revealed him as the hope
      of all who thirst for righteousness and peace.

5   POST-COMMUNION PRAYERS

a   God of truth,
      we have seen with our eyes
      and touched with our hands
      the bread of life.
      Strengthen our faith
      that we may grow in love for you
      and for each other;
      through Jesus Christ our risen Lord.   *11*

b   God of glory, you nourish us with your Word
which is the bread of life.
Fill us with your Holy Spirit,
that through us the light of your glory
may shine in all the world.
We ask this in the name of Jesus Christ.   *31*

c   Eternal Father,
we thank you for refreshing us
with these heavenly gifts.
May our communion
strengthen us in faith,
build us up in hope,
and make us grow in love,
for the sake of Jesus Christ our Lord.

d   Lord,
by your mercy we have feasted upon the bread of life,
and have shared the cup of salvation.
Help us so to live out our days
that our lives may proclaim your wonders;
through Jesus Christ our Lord.

e   Father in heaven,
we pray that the joy of this celebration
may fill our hearts
with a new and deeper sense of your love
for us and for your world,
and that we may reflect your love
by lives of service;
through Christ our Lord.

6   BLESSINGS

a   Christ our Lord,
    to whom kings bowed down in worship and offered gifts,
    reveal to you his glory
    and pour down upon you the riches of his grace;
    and the blessing . . .

b   Christ, who by his incarnation
    gathered into one things earthly and heavenly,
    fill you with his joy and peace;
    and the blessing . . .   8*

c   Christ the Son of God gladden your hearts
    with the good news of his kingdom;
    and the blessing . . .   8

4. For the Mission of the Church

1   INTRODUCTORY SENTENCES

The grace of God has dawned upon the world with healing for the human race.

Titus 2. 11

The love of Christ leaves us no choice because we are convinced that one man has died for all.

2 Corinthians 5. 14

What we preach is not ourselves, but Jesus Christ as Lord with ourselves as your servants for Jesus' sake.

2 Corinthians 4. 5

The secret is revealed: Christ in you, the hope of glory.

Colossians 1. 27

The spirit of truth will bear witness to me; and you also are witnesses.

John 16. 26-27

2   INVITATIONS TO PENITENCE

a   If anyone sins, we have an advocate with the Father, Jesus Christ the righteous; and he is the propitiation for our sins, and not for ours only, but also for the sins of the whole world.

b   I set no store by life: I only want to finish the race and complete the task which the Lord Jesus assigned to me, of bearing witness to the gospel of God's grace.

c   Do not be anxious about your life, what you shall eat or what you shall drink. Seek first God's kingdom and his righteousness.

3   PENITENCE

a   'I was hungry and you gave me no food,
     I was thirsty and you gave me no drink.'
     Lord, have mercy.
     Lord, have mercy.

     'I was a stranger and you did not welcome me,
     naked and you did not clothe me.'
     Christ, have mercy.
     Christ, have mercy.

     'I was sick and you did not visit me,
     in prison and you did not come to me.'
     Lord, have mercy.
     Lord, have mercy.

b   We have not held out the word of life
     in a dark and twisted world:
     Lord, have mercy.
     Lord, have mercy.

     We have failed to share our bread with the hungry:
     Christ, have mercy.
     Christ, have mercy.

     We have closed our hearts to the love of God:
     Lord, have mercy.
     Lord, have mercy.

4   INTERCESSION

     All or some of these petitions may be used.

     God of our salvation,
     hope of all the ends of the earth,
     we pray
     Your kingdom come.

     That the world may know Jesus Christ
     as the Prince of Peace,
     we pray
     Your kingdom come.

That all who are estranged and without hope
may be brought near in the blood of Christ,
we pray
Your kingdom come.

That the Church may be one in serving
and proclaiming the gospel,
we pray
Your kingdom come.

That we may be bold to speak the word of God
while you stretch out your hand to save,
we pray
Your kingdom come.

That the Church may be generous in giving,
faithful in serving, bold in proclaiming,
we pray
Your kingdom come.

That the Church may welcome and support
all whom God calls to faith,
we pray
Your kingdom come.

That all who serve the gospel may be kept in safety
while your Word accomplishes its purpose,
we pray
Your kingdom come.

That all who suffer for the gospel
may know the comfort and glory of Christ,
we pray
Your kingdom come.

That the day may come when every knee shall bow
and every tongue confess that Jesus Christ is Lord,
we pray
Your kingdom come.

5   INTRODUCTIONS TO THE PEACE

a   God has entrusted to us the message of reconciliation.
    First be reconciled to one another.

b   Welcome one another as Christ has welcomed you
    for the glory of God.

c   Christ came and proclaimed the gospel:
    peace to those who are far off
    and peace to those who are near.

6   PROPER PREFACE

    And now we give you thanks,
    for you are the hope of the nations,
    the builder of the city that is to come.
    Your love is made visible in Jesus Christ,
    you bring home the lost, restore the sinner
    and give dignity to the despised.
    In the face of Jesus Christ
    your light shines out,
    flooding lives with goodness and truth,
    gathering into one a divided and broken humanity.

7   IN PLACE OF THE BLESSING AND DISMISSAL

    The congregation turns to face the door.

a   To a troubled world
    Peace from Christ.

    To a searching world
    Love from Christ.

    To a dying world
    Hope from Christ.

b   We proclaim Jesus as Lord
    and ourselves as your servants for Jesus' sake.

    Arise, shine out, for your light has come;
    the glory of the Lord is rising upon you.

c   The Cross   **We shall take it**
    The Bread   **We shall break it**
    The pain   **We shall bear it**
    The joy   **We shall share it**
    The Gospel   **We shall live it**
    The Love   **We shall give it**
    The Light   **We shall cherish it**
    The darkness   **God shall perish it.**

Iona Community   34a

d   I set before you an open door,
    A door which no one can shut.

    Grace from the Father of light,
    Life from the Lamb of God.

5. For Christian Unity

The Week of Prayer for Christian Unity begins on 18 January (The Confession of Saint Peter) and ends on 25 January (The Conversion of Saint Paul). It is observed universally throughout the Church, and is increasingly given prominence in the statutory services which occur during the week as well as being a theme for special services.

The Unity Candle is a large candle, set up in a prominent place in church, rather like the Paschal Candle, and is lit during the week, at special services, and, because of one of the particular themes of Maundy Thursday, on Thursdays during the year.

The British Council of Churches, now succeeded by the Council of Churches for Britain and Ireland (CCBI) and Churches Together in England (CTE), has for many years published orders of service for the observance of the week. We provide here material which may be used in the construction of such services.

Although it is a fundamental principle that, as far as possible, nothing should replace the celebration of the Lord's resurrection as the main theme of a Sunday, there may be good pastoral cause to choose readings appropriate to Christian unity for one or more of the main Sunday services during the week.

1   PENITENCE

BIDDING

a   We have come together as God's family
to offer him our penitence and praise,
and to pray for the recovery of the unity of
    Christ's Church
and for the renewal of our common life.
The Lord is full of gentleness and compassion.
Let us then ask his forgiveness of our sins.

or

b   Our Lord Jesus Christ says,
A new commandment I give you,
that you love one another,
as I have loved you.

Let us confess to almighty God
our failure to accept his love,
and to share it with others.

or

c   In the presence of the God and Father of us all,
we meet together with one accord
from our various churches.
We give thanks for the spiritual unity
which is already ours as members of the Body of Christ.
We pray that this unity
may, by God's grace, become a visible unity,
so that his Church in every place
may demonstrate the healing power of the Gospel,
and be an instrument of his peace
in the life of the world.

CONFESSION

a   **Most merciful God,
we confess that we have sinned against you
and against one another,
in thought, and word, and deed.
We are truly sorry for our pride,
and for our lack of faith,
of understanding, and of love;
We repent of our narrow-mindedness,
of our bitterness and our prejudices;
Pardon and forgive us,
save us and renew us,
that we may delight in your will
and walk in your ways;
through Jesus Christ our Lord.**   4

or

b   Lord Jesus, you came to reconcile us
to one another and to the Father:
Lord, have mercy.
Christ, have mercy.

Lord Jesus, you heal the wounds of sin and division:
Lord, have mercy.
Christ, have mercy.

Lord Jesus, you intercede for us with your Father:
Lord, have mercy.
Christ, have mercy.

or

c   Let us ask God's forgiveness for the sins by which we have
hindered the recovery of unity and caused the name of
Christ to be blasphemed.

Lord, have mercy upon us.
Christ, have mercy upon us.

For the sins of thought; for ignorance of the faith by which
our fellow-Christians live; for intellectual pride and
isolation; and for the rejection of truth which we have
never tried to understand.

Lord, have mercy upon us.
Christ, have mercy upon us.

For the sins of temper; for apathy and complacency, for
prejudice and party spirit; for hasty judgement and
embittered controversy.

Lord, have mercy upon us.
Christ, have mercy upon us.

Pardon, O Lord, the sins
of our past ignorance and wilfulness;
uplift our hearts in love and energy and devotion,
that, being made clean from guilt and shame,
we may go forward
to serve you and your Church
in newness of life;
through Jesus Christ our Lord.   **Amen.**   37

ABSOLUTION

a   May the almighty and merciful Lord
grant us pardon and peace
through Jesus Christ our Lord.   **Amen.**

or, when water is used:

b   The president prays over a vessel of water

God our Father,
your gift of water
brings life and freshness to the earth;
in baptism it is a sign
of the washing away of our sins
and the gift of life eternal.

Accept this water, we pray:
renew the living spring of your life within us,
that we may be free from sin
and filled with your saving health;
through Christ our Lord.   **Amen.**   *20*

The president and people are sprinkled.
Meanwhile suitable anthems may be sung; see Canticles 4,
15, 26, 34 (Chapter VII).

The president concludes

May almighty God cleanse us from sin and make us
worthy of the kingdom of his glory.   **Amen.**

2   INTERCESSION

Either

a   Let us pray to the Lord, saying,
Lord, have mercy.

For the peace that comes from God alone, for the unity of
all peoples, and for the salvation of our souls, let us pray
to the Lord.
Lord, have mercy.

For the Church of Christ, for *N* our Bishop, (for . . .), and
for the whole people of God, let us pray to the Lord.
Lord, have mercy.

For the nations of the world, (for . . .), for Elizabeth our Queen and for all in authority, let us pray to the Lord.
Lord, have mercy.

For this city (or town or village or community), (for . . .), for our neighbours and our friends, let us pray to the Lord.
Lord, have mercy.

For the good earth which God has given us, and for the wisdom and will to conserve it, let us pray to the Lord.
Lord, have mercy.

For the aged and infirm, for the widowed and orphans, for the sick and suffering, (for . . .), and for all in need, let us pray to the Lord.
Lord, have mercy.

For the poor and the oppressed, for the unemployed and the destitute, for prisoners and captives, and for all who remember and care for them, let us pray to the Lord.
Lord, have mercy.

For . . . let us pray to the Lord.
Lord, have mercy.

For the dying and for those who mourn (the death of . . .), and for the faithful whom we entrust to God in the hope of the resurrection, let us pray to the Lord.
Lord, have mercy.

Rejoicing in the communion of (. . . and of all) the saints, let us commend ourselves, and one another, and all our life, to God.
To you, O Lord our God.

Silence

For yours is the majesty, O Father, Son, and Holy Spirit; yours is the kingdom and the power and the glory, now and for ever.   **Amen.**   12*

or

250

b   In faith let us pray to God our Father,
     his Son Jesus Christ,
     and the Holy Spirit.
     Kyrie eleison.

     For the Church of God throughout the world,
     let us invoke the Spirit.
     Kyrie eleison.

     For the leaders of the nations,
     that they may establish and defend justice and peace,
     let us pray for the wisdom of God.
     Kyrie eleison.

     For those who suffer oppression or violence,
     let us invoke the power of the Deliverer.
     Kyrie eleison.

     That the churches may discover again their visible unity
     in the one baptism which incorporates them in Christ,
     let us pray for the love of Christ.
     Kyrie eleison.

     That the churches may attain communion
     in the eucharist around one table,
     let us pray for the strength of Christ.
     Kyrie eleison.

     That the churches may recognize each other's ministries
     in the service of their one Lord,
     let us pray for the peace of Christ.
     Kyrie eleison.

     Free prayer of the congregation may follow.

     Into your hands, O Lord,
     we commend all for whom we pray,
     trusting in your mercy;
     through your Son, Jesus Christ, our Lord.   **Amen.**   *38*

3   THANKSGIVING

     Either

a   It is indeed right,
it is our duty and our joy,
at all times and in all places
to give you thanks and praise,
holy Father, heavenly King,
almighty and eternal God,
through Jesus Christ our Lord.

Who on the eve of his passion
prayed for the unity of all faithful people,
in him and in you,
by the Holy Spirit in the Church;
we believe that you will hear his prayer.

We give you thanks
for the unity of the Body of Christ,
and we await with joy
the day when we shall perfectly be one,
that the world may know that you have sent your Son
and that he loved us as you loved him.

Through him, and with him, and in him
by the power of the Holy Spirit,
with all who stand before you in earth and heaven,
we worship you, Father Almighty,
in songs of everlasting praise:

**Blessing and honour and glory and power
be yours for ever and ever.   Amen.**

or

b   Father, all-powerful and everliving God,
we do well always and everywhere to give you thanks
through Jesus Christ our Lord.

By him, your only Son,
who restored to us peace
at the price of the blood of his Cross,
you willed to reconcile all creatures.
By him you have led us to the knowledge of your truth,
so that by the bond of the one faith
and the one baptism
we might become his body.

By him you have given to all peoples your Holy Spirit
who works marvels by innumerable gifts,
distributes an abundant variety of graces,
gives us to announce the Word in various tongues,
gathers us together in unity,
remains in all the believers,
and fills and governs the entire Church.

Therefore with angels and archangels,
and with all the company of heaven,
we proclaim your great and glorious name,
for ever praising you and saying:

Holy, holy, holy Lord,
God of power and might,
heaven and earth are full of your glory.
Hosanna in the highest.   Amen.   39

4   PRAYERS OF COMMITMENT

Suitable when a service is held to mark the inauguration of a
local covenant as well as on more general occasions.

a   **God our Father,**
in the name of Christ
and in the power of the Spirit,
we commit ourselves
to you and to one another,
to live, work, and pray
as one body in Christ;
to do apart
nothing which we can do together,
and to do together
what we cannot do apart;
Give us vision,
give us courage,
and give us joy,
that the world may believe
that Jesus is Lord
to your eternal glory.   Amen.

or

b   **God our Father,**
    it is your purpose
    to bring your whole creation
    into full unity in Christ.
    We commit ourselves to you.
    Help us to live for others
    even as your love includes all;
    to seek out from others
    the truth they have grasped;
    to trust each other
    as fellow-workers
    in the one community you have given us;
    to obey your call
    to make visible
    the unity of your Church.
    Come, Holy Spirit, help us.   Amen.

5   A COMMEMORATION
    FOR USE AT MORNING AND EVENING PRAYER

a   This is the message that we have heard from the
        beginning:
    that we should love one another.

    Christ is our peace, who has made us one:
    he has broken down the barriers which divided us.

    Father,
    we pray for your Church throughout the world,
    that it may share to the full
    in the work of your Son,
    revealing you to men and women,
    and reconciling them to you
    and to one another;
    that Christians may learn to love one another
    and their neighbours, as you have loved us;
    that your Church
    may more and more reflect the unity
    which is your will and your gift;
    we pray through Jesus Christ our Lord.   **Amen.**

254

or

b   O God the Father of our Lord Jesus Christ,
our only Saviour, the Prince of Peace:
Give us grace seriously to lay to heart
the great dangers we are in by our unhappy divisions.
Take away all hatred and prejudice,
and whatever else may hinder us
from godly union and concord:
that, as there is but one Body and one Spirit,
one hope of our calling,
one Lord, one faith, one baptism,
one God and Father of us all;
so we may henceforth be all of one heart, and of one soul,
united in one holy bond of peace, of faith and charity
and may with one mind and one mouth glorify you;
through Jesus Christ our Lord.   **Amen.**   *41**

6   AT THE EUCHARIST

THE PEACE

a   If our life in Christ means anything,
if love can persuade at all,
or the Spirit that we have in common,
or any tenderness and sympathy,
then be united in your conviction
and united in your love,
with a common purpose and a common mind.

or

b   Our Lord Jesus Christ says,
If, when you are bringing your gift to the altar,
you remember your brother or sister
has a grievance against you,
leave your gift where it lies before the altar.
Go, make peace;
and only then come and offer your gift.

or

c   Christ is our hope;
we give him glory for the great grace
by which upon the cross
he stretched out his hands in love to us all.
By that same grace may he come, our risen Saviour,
into every gesture of unity and fellowship
which we make toward one another,
and make the peace we share his peace.

THE PREPARATION OF THE GIFTS AT THE EUCHARIST

a   Blessed are you, Lord God of the universe:
you are the giver of this bread,
fruit of the earth and of human labour.
Let it be for us the bread of life.
Blessed be God, now and for ever.

Blessed are you, Lord God of the universe:
you are the giver of this wine,
fruit of the vine and of human labour.
Let it be for us the wine of the eternal kingdom.
Blessed be God, now and for ever.

As the grain once scattered in the fields
and the grapes once dispersed on the hillside
are now reunited on this table
in bread and wine,
so, Lord, may your whole Church
soon be gathered together
from the corners of the earth into your kingdom.
Maranatha! Come, Lord Jesus!

b   The eyes of all wait upon you, O Lord,
And you give them their food in due season.
I will offer in your dwelling
an oblation with great gladness:
I will sing and speak praises to the Lord.

Lord, you have rescued my life from death:
and I will walk in your presence.

I will lift up the cup of salvation:
and call upon the name of the Lord.

c   As this bread was scattered
and then gathered and made one;
so may your Church be gathered into your Kingdom.
Glory to you, O God, for ever.

Wisdom has built her a house;
she has mixed her wine; she has set her table.
Glory to you, O God, for ever.

PROPER PREFACE

And now we give you thanks
because through Christ you bring us
to the knowledge of your truth,
that we may be united by one faith and one baptism
to become his body.
Through Christ you have given the Holy Spirit
to all peoples.
How wonderful are the works of the Spirit,
revealed in so many gifts!
Yet how marvellous is the unity
the Spirit creates from their diversity,
as he dwells in the hearts of your children,
filling the whole Church with his presence
and guiding it with his wisdom!

In our joy we sing to your glory
with all the choirs of angels:

Holy, holy, holy Lord,
God of power and might,
heaven and earth are full of your glory.
Hosanna in the highest.   Amen.

AFTER COMMUNION

a   God our Father,
whose Son at table offered himself
as the innocent Lamb,
and gave us this memorial of his passion
until the end of time;
for ever nourish your people
with his living bread and saving cup,
and strengthen them in holiness,
that the family of mankind may live
in the light of one faith
in one communion of love;
through the same Christ our Lord.   *10*

b   Eternal God and Father,
whose Son at supper
prayed that his disciples might be one,
as he is one with you;
draw us closer to him,
that in common love and obedience to you
we may be united to one another
in the fellowship of the one Spirit,
that the world may believe that he is Lord,
to your eternal glory;
through the same Christ our Lord.   *33**

7   AT THE END OF ANY SERVICE

Lord Jesus Christ,
Son of the living God,
teach us to walk in your way more trustfully,
to accept your truth more faithfully,
to share your life more lovingly;
so that we may come
by the power of the Holy Spirit
as one family to the kingdom of the Father,
where you live for ever and ever.   **Amen.**

VI
CANDLEMAS

A. INTRODUCTION

The Calendar and Lectionary 1 in the Appendix to *The Promise of His Glory* allow the feast on 2 February to be seen as an important and fully integrated festival of the Christmas cycle. It is not some optional extra, but the natural climax, after forty days, of the Christmas/Epiphany season. Although they allow an approach that ends the annual celebration of the Incarnation after twelve days, they encourage an imaginative use of the weeks of January as an exploration of the Epiphany themes, and see Candlemas as a fitting end to it and an important turning point in the Christian year.

This is a feast rich in meaning, with several related themes running through it – presentation, purification, meeting, light for the world. The several names by which it has been known in Christian history illustrate just how much it has to teach and to celebrate.

But the strongest attraction of Candlemas is the 'bitter-sweet' nature of what it celebrates. It is a feast day, and the revelation of the child Jesus in the Temple, greeted by Simeon and Anna, calls for rejoicing. Nevertheless, the prophetic words of Simeon, which speak of the falling and rising of many and the sword that will pierce, lead on to the passion and to Easter. The scriptures and the liturgy of the Christmas season have several pointers to the suffering of the Lord, but none more potent than the words of Simeon. Coming as they do at the very end of the Christmas celebration and with Lent nearly always very close, they make Candlemas a kind of pivot in the Christian year. It is as if we say, on 2 February, 'One last look back to Christmas, and now, turn towards the cross!' On such a reckoning, the liturgical colour changes after the Eucharist at Candlemas from the white of Epiphanytide to a more penitential colour as Lent approaches.

Where Candlemas is given this pivotal place, Sundays up to Candlemas need to be 'of Epiphany', and Sundays after Candlemas 'before Lent'. We also give encouragement for this feast to be celebrated on the nearest Sunday to 2 February, to enable it to make its impact.

In the old liturgies some of the 'bitter-sweet' flavour of the day was sometimes expressed through a striking change of liturgical colour, the procession in purple vestments and the Eucharist in white. In origin this probably reflects little more than the habitually penitential nature of Processional rites, even when associated with a feast. It is this tradition that we have tried to use creatively in the Eucharist of Candlemas. We have moved the procession to the end of the Eucharist, where Nunc Dimittis in any case seems more appropriate, given it a penitential feel and made it, especially by the Responsory that follows it, the point of transition from Christmas to Easter. As such it is a very powerful ending to all that *The Promise of His Glory* celebrates.

For those for whom a procession at the end seems impractical, we have provided an alternative structure with the procession at the beginning. But something important about the place of Candlemas as the hinge point in the Christian cycle is lost where a procession does not conclude the liturgy. Some of the subtleties of the day are missing.

In addition to the Eucharist, a Vigil Service for Candlemas is provided. This is on the same model as the other Vigil Services in this book but, in some ways, is the greatest of them, building as it does on the light theme that belongs to this festival. Instead of psalmody, biblical chants, mainly from the Byzantine rite, have been used between the readings, and, as at the Eucharist, a procession with lighted candles may be made at the end, as Nunc Dimittis is sung.

B. A VIGIL SERVICE FOR CANDLEMAS

NOTES

1 This Vigil Service for Candlemas may be used either as a service of preparation for the Feast, or, when the Feast is transferred to the following Sunday as suggested in the Calendar, on the Feast itself.

2 It is appropriate for a Deacon to bring in the light and sing the Acclamation, to proclaim the Gospel, and to lead the Prayers of Intercession.

3 **Readings** The number of Readings may be varied according to circumstances, but at least three are used before the Gospel Reading.

4 **Hymns** Places are indicated for these but they may be sung at other points or substituted for the Chants after the Readings.

5 When a procession is made at the end of the service, the candles should be carried to the door and then extinguished.

THE SERVICE OF LIGHT

1 In the darkness, the president introduces the service.

The Lord is my light and my salvation.
The Lord is my light and my salvation.

The Lord is the strength of my life.
The Lord is my light and my salvation.

Glory to the Father, and to the Son,
and to the Holy Spirit.
The Lord is my light and my salvation.

2 A minister brings in the light, and says

Jesus Christ is the light of the world,
A light no darkness can quench.

3 While the candles are lit and the light is shared, THIS HYMN is
   sung.

O gladsome light of the holy glory of the immortal Father,
heavenly, holy, blessed Jesus Christ.

Now that we have come to the setting of the sun
and behold the light of evening,
we praise you, Father, Son, and Holy Spirit.

For it is right at all times to worship you
    with voices of praise,
O Son of God and giver of life.
Therefore all the world glorifies you.   1†

or

O gladsome light, O grace
Of God the Father's face,
The eternal splendour wearing;
Celestial, holy, blest,
Our Saviour Jesus Christ,
Joyful in thine appearing.

Now, ere day fadeth quite,
We see the evening light,
Our wonted hymn outpouring;
Father of might unknown,
Thee, his incarnate Son,
And Holy Spirit adoring.

To thee of right belongs
All praise of holy songs,
O Son of God, lifegiver;
Thee, therefore, O Most High,
The world doth glorify,
And shall exalt for ever.   42

† Numbers in right-hand margin refer to Sources and Acknowledgements
(pp.416-419).

4   When the lights are lit, THIS ACCLAMATION is made.

Let us give thanks to the Lord our God.
He is worthy of all thanksgiving and praise.

Blessed are you, Lord our God, King of the universe:
To you be glory and praise for ever!
For you are our light and our salvation
and we your children wait for your loving kindness
in the midst of your temple.
In your Christ, born of the Virgin Mary,
there has sprung up a light for the righteous
and joyful gladness for those who are faithful.
As we, like Simeon and Anna, welcome him with joy,
presented before us as light of all the world,
may we be filled with his Spirit and made a living temple
to the praise and glory of your holy name.
And, as we join our praises with theirs,
grant us a quiet night and a perfect end
now and for ever.   **Amen.**

5   THIS PSALM may be sung.

I call to you, O Lord; come to me quickly:
hear my voice when I cry to you.

Let my prayer rise before you as incense:
the lifting up of my hands as the evening sacrifice.

Set a guard over my mouth, O Lord:
keep watch over the door of my lips.

Let not my heart be turned towards evil:
to busy myself with those who do wickedly.

Let my prayer rise before you as incense.

To you, Lord God, I turn my eyes:
I take refuge in you; do not leave me defenceless.

Glory to the Father, and to the Son,
and to the Holy Spirit:
as it was in the beginning, is now,
and shall be for ever.   Amen.

Let my prayer rise before you as incense.

6   *President*
     Eternal Light, shine into our hearts;
     eternal Goodness, deliver us from evil;
     eternal Power, be our support;
     eternal Wisdom, scatter the darkness of our ignorance;
     eternal Pity, have mercy on us;
     that with all our heart and mind and strength
         we may seek your face
     and be brought by your infinite mercy
         to your holy presence;
     through Jesus Christ our Lord.   **Amen.**   4

THE SERVICE OF THE WORD

7   READING i *Exodus 12. 51; 13. 2, 11-16*
              Consecrate to me all the first born.

CHANT

Search the Scriptures, as Christ told us in the gospels.
We find him born in our midst.
Born as a child and bound in swaddling clothes.
We find him born in our midst.
Laid in a manger and fed upon a mother's milk.
We find him born in our midst.
Presented in the temple and carried by Simeon.
We find him born in our midst.
In truth he has appeared in the world.
We find him born in our midst.   34

COLLECT

O Lord, you have given us your word
for a light to shine upon our path.
Grant us so to meditate on that word,
and to follow its teaching,
that we may find in it the light
that shines more and more
until the perfect day;
through Jesus Christ our Lord.   **Amen.**   4

8 READING 2 *Leviticus 12. 6-8*
The Law of Purification

CHANT

From the Virgin Mary shines forth Jesus, our Saviour.
Sun of Righteousness, our God for ever.
He gives light to those in darkness.
Sun of Righteousness, our God for ever.
Simeon rejoices, in old age carrying
the Redeemer of the world.
Sun of Righteousness, our God for ever.
Anna prophesies in the temple of our God.
Sun of Righteousness, our God for ever.
He is the one who offers and is offered for us.
Sun of Righteousness, our God for ever.
He bestows on us his risen power.
Sun of Righteousness, our God for ever.   34

COLLECT

Almighty and everlasting God,
you have stooped to raise fallen humanity
by the child-bearing of blessed Mary.
Grant that we who have seen your glory
revealed in our human nature,
and your love made perfect in our weakness,
may daily be renewed in your image,
and conformed to the pattern of your Son,
Jesus Christ our Lord.   **Amen.**   20

9 READING 3 *Isaiah 6. 1-8*
I saw the Lord, and his train filled the temple.

CANTICLE   A Song of Redemption
Colossians 1. 13-20

1   The Father has delivered us from
the dominion of darkness:
and transferred us to the Kingdom of his beloved Son.

2   In whom we have redemption:
the forgiveness of our sins.

265

3 He is the image of the invisible God:
  the first-born of all creation.

4 For in him all things were created:
  in heaven and on earth, visible and invisible.

5 All things were created through him and for him:
  he is before all things
    and in him all things hold together.

6 He is the head of the body, the Church:
  he is the beginning, the firstborn from the dead.

7 For it pleased God that in him all fullness
    should dwell:
  and through him all things be reconciled to himself. *24**

Glory to the Father, and to the Son,
and to the Holy Spirit:
as it was in the beginning, is now,
and shall be for ever.   Amen.

COLLECT

Lord God almighty,
you have given us the vision of your holiness,
and thereby of our own unworthiness to be your witnesses.
Touch, we pray, our lips with your cleansing fire;
that so cleansed and hallowed,
we may go out into the world
with the authority of your commission;
for Jesus Christ's sake.   **Amen.**   *54*

10 READING 4 *Isaiah 19. 1-4, 19-21*
              In that day the Egyptians will worship.

CHANT

Simeon takes in his arms the Lord of glory.
Now am I set free, for I have beheld my Saviour.
The heavenly God in mortal flesh.
Now am I set free, for I have beheld my Saviour.
He who speaks through the prophets.
Now am I set free, for I have beheld my Saviour.

Offering himself for us, in his own dwelling place.
Now am I set free, for I have beheld my Saviour.
He is fearful to all, yet his mercy knows no bounds.
Now am I set free, for I have beheld my Saviour. 27

COLLECT

O God,
by whose command the order of time runs its course:
forgive our impatience, perfect our faith,
and, while we wait for the fulfilment of your promises,
grant us to have a good hope because of your word;
through Jesus Christ our Lord.   **Amen.** 4

11   READING 5 *Haggai 2. 1-9*
           I will fill this house with splendour.

CHANT

Zion, adorn the bridal chamber.
Welcome Christ the King of glory.
Mary, the Virgin mother, has borne in the flesh
the king of eternity.
Welcome Christ the King of glory.
He comes to earth and appears in the temple.
Welcome Christ the King of glory.
As a sword, his words are sharp with judgement.
Welcome Christ the King of glory.
Praise to the Lord Christ Jesus, giver of life.
Welcome Christ the King of glory. 34

COLLECT

O God, who in the work of creation
commanded the light to shine out of darkness:
we pray that the light of the glorious gospel of Christ
may shine into the hearts of all your people,
dispelling the darkness of ignorance and unbelief,
and revealing to them the knowledge of your glory
in the face of Jesus Christ our Lord.   **Amen.** 4

12 READING 6 *Hebrews 10. 1-10*

We have been sanctified through the offering of the body of Jesus Christ.

Psalm 40. 8-13

1 Sacrifice and offering you do not desire:
   but my ears you have marked for obedience.

2 Burnt offering and sin-offering you have not required:
   then said I, lo I come.

3 In the scroll of the book it is written of me
       that I should do your will:
   O my God, I long to do it, your law delights my heart.

4 I have declared your righteousness
       in the great congregation:
   I have not restrained my lips, O Lord,
       and that you know.

5 I have not hidden your righteousness in my heart:
   I have spoken of your faithfulness and of your
       salvation.

6 I have not kept back your loving-kindness
       and your truth:
   from the great congregation.

13 The Gospel Reading is introduced by the minister with this Acclamation.

We proclaim not ourselves, but Christ Jesus as Lord,
and ourselves as your servants for Jesus' sake.

For the God who said 'Let light shine out of darkness'
has caused his light to shine within us

To give the light of the knowledge of the Glory of God
in the face of Jesus Christ.

Hear the words of the Gospel according to Luke.
Glory to Christ our Saviour.

THE GOSPEL READING *Luke 2. 22-40*
The Presentation in the Temple

After the Gospel the reader says

This is the Gospel of Christ.
Praise to Christ our Lord.

14   AN ADDRESS or HOMILY may be given.

THE PRAYERS

15   Prayers of penitence and intercession may be offered in this or
any suitable form. Any Biddings should precede this litany,
which is then said without interpolation.

In peace let us pray to the Lord.

By the mystery of the Word made flesh
Good Lord, deliver us.

By the birth in time of the timeless Son of God
Good Lord, deliver us.

By the baptism of the Son of God in the river Jordan
Good Lord, deliver us.

For the kingdoms of this world,
that they may become the Kingdom of our Lord
    and Christ,
We pray to you, O Lord.

For your holy, catholic and apostolic Church,
that it may be one,
We pray to you, O Lord.

For the witness of your faithful people,
that they may be lights in the world,
We pray to you, O Lord.

For the poor, the persecuted, the sick, and all who suffer;
that they may be relieved and protected,
We pray to you, O Lord.

For the aged, for refugees and all in danger,
that they may be strengthened and defended,
We pray to you, O Lord.

For those who walk in darkness and in the shadow
   of death,
that they may come to your eternal light,
We pray to you, O Lord.

President   Father, source of light and life,
              grant the prayers of your faithful people,
              and fill the world with your glory,
              through Christ our Lord.   **Amen.**

THE CONCLUSION

16   THE CANTICLE

During this Canticle a procession may be made to the doors of
the church.

THE SONG OF SIMEON: *Nunc Dimittis*

Luke 2. 29-32

**A light to lighten the nations
and the glory of your people Israel.**

Now, Lord, you let your servant go in peace:
your word has been fulfilled.

**A light to lighten the nations
and the glory of your people Israel.**

My own eyes have seen the salvation:
which you have prepared in the sight of every people.

**A light to lighten the nations
and the glory of your people Israel.**

A light to reveal you to the nations:
and the glory of your people Israel.

44

**A light to lighten the nations
and the glory of your people Israel.**

Glory to the Father, and to the Son,
and to the Holy Spirit:
as it was in the beginning, is now,
and shall be for ever.   Amen.

**A light to lighten the nations
and the glory of your people Israel.**

or

Lord, now lettest thou thy servant depart in peace:
according to thy word.

For mine eyes have seen thy salvation:
which thou hast prepared before the face of all people;

To be a light to lighten the Gentiles:
and to be the glory of thy people Israel.

Glory be to the Father, and to the Son,
and to the Holy Ghost:
as it was in the beginning, is now, and ever shall be,
world without end.   **Amen.**   *41*

17   THE COLLECT

President
Almighty Father,
whose Son Jesus Christ was presented in the Temple
and acclaimed the glory of Israel
and the light of the nations:
grant that in him we may be presented to you
and in the world may reflect his glory;
through Jesus Christ our Lord.   **Amen.**   *8*

18   THE BLESSING AND DISMISSAL

Let us bless the living God.

He was born of the Virgin Mary,
Revealed in his glory,
Worshipped by angels,
Proclaimed among the nations,
Believed in throughout the world,
Exalted to the highest heavens.
Blessed be God, our strength and our salvation,
Now and for ever.   Amen.

C. THE EUCHARIST OF CANDLEMAS

1   The Procession with lighted candles is the distinctive feature
of the Eucharist of Candlemas. This Order provides for the
Procession at the end of the Service. However, the Appendix
(p.283) makes provision for the Procession either at the
beginning, or immediately before the Gospel.

THE PREPARATION

2   At the entry of the ministers THIS SENTENCE may be used.

Open me the gates of righteousness:
and I will enter and give thanks to the Lord.   *Psalm 118. 19*

3   A HYMN, A CANTICLE, or A PSALM may be sung.

4   The president welcomes the people and introduces the day's
liturgy.

The Lord of glory be with you.
The Lord bless you.

Dear friends: forty days ago we celebrated the birth of our
Lord Jesus Christ. Now we recall the day on which he was
presented in the Temple, when he was offered to the
Father and shown to his people. As a sign of his coming
among us, his mother was purified, as we now come to
him for cleansing. In their old age Simeon and Anna
recognized him as their Lord, as we today sing of his glory.
In this eucharist, we celebrate both the joy of his coming
and his searching judgement, looking back to the day of
his birth and forward to the coming days of his passion.

5   GLORIA IN EXCELSIS may be used.

**Glory to God in the highest,
and peace to his people on earth.**

**Lord God, heavenly King,
almighty God and Father,
we worship you, we give you thanks,
we praise you for your glory.**

Lord Jesus Christ, only Son of the Father,
Lord God, Lamb of God,
you take away the sin of the world:
have mercy on us;
you are seated at the right hand of the Father:
receive our prayer.

For you alone are the Holy One,
you alone are the Lord,
you alone are the Most High,
Jesus Christ,
with the Holy Spirit,
in the glory of God the Father.   **Amen.**

6   The president says THE COLLECT.

Let us pray that we may know and share the light of
Christ.

Silence may be kept.

Almighty Father,
whose Son Jesus Christ was presented in the Temple
and acclaimed the glory of Israel
and the light of the nations:
grant that in him we may be presented to you
and in the world may reflect his glory;
through Jesus Christ our Lord,
who is alive and reigns with you and the Holy Spirit,
one God, now and for ever.   **Amen.**   8

THE MINISTRY OF THE WORD

7   Either two or three READINGS FROM SCRIPTURE follow, the last of
which is the Gospel.

8   **Sit**

OLD TESTAMENT READING

At the end the reader may say

This is the word of the Lord.
Thanks be to God.

9   A PSALM may be used.

10 **Sit**

NEW TESTAMENT READING (EPISTLE)

At the end the reader may say

This is the word of the Lord.
Thanks be to God.

11 A CANTICLE, A HYMN, or A PSALM may be used.

12 **Stand**

THIS ACCLAMATION may precede and/or follow the Gospel.

Today the Lord is presented in the Temple
in substance of our mortal nature.
Alleluia!

Today the Blessed Virgin comes
to be purified in accordance with the law.
Alleluia!

Today old Simeon proclaims Christ
as the light of the nations and the glory of Israel.
Alleluia! Praise to Christ, the Light of the world!

13 THE GOSPEL *Luke 2. 22-40*

When it is announced

Glory to Christ our Saviour.

At the end the reader may say

This is the Gospel of Christ.
Praise to Christ our Lord.

14 **Sit**

THE SERMON

15 **Stand**

THE NICENE CREED may be said, or an authorized AFFIRMATION
OF FAITH may be used in its place.

THE PRAYERS

16 PRAYERS OF INTERCESSION

Biddings may be given before these prayers of intercession, which are then said without interpolation. Silence may be kept after each response. Alternatively, the Prayers of Penitence and Intercession (section 15 in The Vigil for Candlemas) may take the place of sections 16 and 17 below.

Minister
Let us pray to the Father through Christ who is our Light and Life.

Father, your Christ is acclaimed as the glory of Israel:
Look in mercy on your Church, sharing his light.
Lord, have mercy.
Christ, have mercy.

Father, your Christ in his temple brings judgement on the world:
Look in mercy on the nations, who long for his justice.
Lord, have mercy.
Christ, have mercy.

Father, your Christ, who was rich, for our sakes became poor:
Look in mercy on the needy, suffering with him.
Lord, have mercy.
Christ, have mercy.

Father, your Christ is the one in whom faithful servants find their peace:
Look in mercy on the departed, who see your salvation.
Lord, have mercy.
Christ, have mercy.

Father, your Christ is revealed as the one destined to be rejected:
Look in mercy on us who now turn towards his passion.
Lord, have mercy.
Christ, have mercy.

President
Lord God, you kept faith with Simeon and Anna
and showed them the infant King.
Give us grace to put all our trust in your promises,
and the patience to wait for their fulfilment;
through Jesus Christ our Lord.   **Amen.**

17   PRAYERS OF PENITENCE may be said.

Minister
Jesus says, 'I am the light of the world.
He who follows me shall not walk in darkness,
but will have the light of life.'
Let us then bring our secret sins into his light
and confess them in penitence and faith.   *20*

Father eternal, giver of light and grace,
we have sinned against you and against our neighbour,
in what we have thought,
in what we have said and done,
through ignorance, through weakness,
through our own deliberate fault.
We have wounded your love,
and marred your image in us.
We are sorry and ashamed,
and repent of all our sins.
For the sake of your Son Jesus Christ,
who died for us,
forgive us all that is past;
and lead us out from darkness
to walk as children of light.   Amen.   *8*

President
Almighty God,
who forgives all who truly repent,
have mercy upon *you*,
pardon and deliver *you* from all *your* sins,
confirm and strengthen *you* in all goodness,
and keep *you* in life eternal;
through Jesus Christ our Lord.   **Amen.**

THE PEACE

18 **Stand**

President
In the tender compassion of our God
the dawn from on high has broken upon us,
to shine on those who dwell in darkness
and the shadow of death,
and to guide our feet into the way of peace.

The peace of the Lord be always with you
and also with you.

A minister may say

Let us offer one another a sign of peace.

and all may exchange a sign of peace.

THE PREPARATION OF THE GIFTS

19 The bread and wine are placed on the holy table.

20 The president may praise God for his gifts in appropriate
words to which all respond

Blessed be God for ever.

21 The offerings of the people may be collected and presented.
These words may be used.

Yours, Lord, is the greatness, the power,
the glory, the splendour, and the majesty;
for everything in heaven and on earth is yours.
All things come from you,
and of your own do we give you.

22 At the Preparation of the Gifts A HYMN may be sung.

THE EUCHARISTIC PRAYER

23 The president takes the bread and cup into his hands and
replaces them on the holy table.

24 The president uses one of the authorized EUCHARISTIC PRAYERS with a PROPER PREFACE of the Incarnation or one of the following.

And now we give you thanks
because by appearing in the Temple
he brings judgement on the world.
The Word made flesh
searches the hearts of all your people,
to bring to light the brightness of your splendour.

or

And now we give you thanks
because your eternal Word took our nature upon him
in the womb of Mary the Virgin.
The sword of sorrow pierced her heart
when he was lifted high on the Cross,
and by his sacrifice made our peace with you.

THE COMMUNION

25 THE LORD'S PRAYER is said in one of the following forms.

As our Saviour has taught us, so we pray

Our Father in heaven,	*or*	Our Father, who art in heaven,

Our Father in heaven,
hallowed be your name,
your kingdom come,
your will be done,
on earth as in heaven.
Give us today our daily bread.
Forgive us our sins
as we forgive those
   who sin against us.
Lead us not into temptation
but deliver us from evil.

For the kingdom, the power,
   and the glory are yours
now and for ever.   Amen.

Our Father, who art in heaven,
hallowed be thy name;
thy kingdom come;
thy will be done;
on earth as it is in heaven.
Give us this day our daily bread.
And forgive us our trespasses,
as we forgive those
   who trespass against us.
And lead us not into temptation;
but deliver us from evil.

For thine is the kingdom,
   the power, and the glory,
for ever and ever.   Amen.

26 The president breaks the consecrated bread, saying

We break the bread of life,
and that life is the light of the world.
**God here among us,
light in the midst of us,
bring us to light and life.**   *11*

27 Either here or during the distribution one of the following
ANTHEMS may be said.

**Lamb of God, you take away the sins of the world:
have mercy on us.**

**Lamb of God, you take away the sins of the world:
have mercy on us.**

**Lamb of God, you take away the sins of the world:
grant us peace.**

or

**Jesus, Lamb of God: have mercy on us.
Jesus, bearer of our sins: have mercy on us.
Jesus, redeemer of the world: give us your peace.**

28 Before the distribution the president says

The gifts of God for the people of God.
**Jesus Christ is holy,
Jesus Christ is Lord,
to the glory of God the Father.**

29 The president and people receive the Communion. Any
authorized words of distribution may be used. During the
distribution HYMNS and ANTHEMS may be sung. The Alternative
Service Book provision is followed for consecration of
additional bread and wine and for disposing of what remains.

AFTER COMMUNION

30 The president may say

This child is destined for the fall and for the rising of many in Israel, destined to be a sign that is rejected. And a sword shall pierce your own soul also.   *Luke 2. 35*

31 (If the Procession has already taken place at the beginning, the service concludes now in the form set out in the Appendix, p.283.)

THE CANDLEMAS PROCESSION

32 If the Procession is to take place now, A HYMN may be sung while the candles are lit.

33 **Stand**

The president says

Lord God, the springing source of everlasting light,
pour into the hearts of your faithful people
the brilliance of your eternal splendour,
that we, who by these kindling flames
light up this temple to your glory,
may have the darkness of our souls dispelled,
and so be counted worthy to stand before you
in that eternal temple where you live and reign,
Father, Son, and Holy Spirit,
one God, now and for ever.   **Amen.**   *3*

34 The ministers and people go in procession to the font, or to the door of the church, or to another suitable place. As they process they sing NUNC DIMITTIS in one of these forms or in another suitable version.

**A light to lighten the nations
and the glory of your people Israel.**

Now, Lord, you let your servant go in peace:
your word has been fulfilled.

**A light to lighten the nations
and the glory of your people Israel.**

My own eyes have seen the salvation:
which you have prepared in the sight of every people.

**A light to lighten the nations
and the glory of your people Israel.**

A light to reveal you to the nations:
and the glory of your people Israel.   *44*

**A light to lighten the nations
and the glory of your people Israel.**

Glory to the Father, and to the Son,
and to the Holy Spirit:
as it was in the beginning, is now,
and shall be for ever.   Amen.

**A light to lighten the nations
and the glory of your people Israel.**

or

Lord, now lettest thou thy servant depart in peace:
according to thy word.

For mine eyes have seen thy salvation:
which thou hast prepared before the face of all people;

To be a light to lighten the Gentiles:
and to be the glory of thy people Israel.

Glory be to the Father, and to the Son,
and to the Holy Ghost:
as it was in the beginning, is now, and ever shall be,
world without end.   Amen.   *41*

35   FINAL RESPONSORY

President
Father, here we bring to an end our celebration
of the Saviour's birth.
**Help us, in whom he has been born,
to live his life that has no end.**

Here we have offered the Church's sacrifice of praise.
**Help us, who have received the bread of life,
to be thankful for your gift.**

281

Here we have rejoiced with faithful Simeon and Anna.
**Help us, who have found the Lord in his temple,
to trust in your eternal promises.**

Here we have greeted the Light of the world.
**Help us, who now extinguish these candles,
never to forsake the light of Christ.**

All now extinguish their candles.

Here we now stand near the place of baptism.
**Help us, who are marked with the cross,
to share the Lord's death and resurrection.**

Here we turn from Christ's birth to his passion.
**Help us, for whom Lent is near,
to enter deeply into the Easter mystery.**

Here we bless one another in your name.
**Help us, who now go in peace,
to shine with your light in the world.
Thanks be to God!   Amen.**   *13*

36   The ministers and people depart.

APPENDIX

a   THE PROCESSION WITH CANDLES

1   If the Procession takes place earlier in the service, the
congregation assembles in a convenient place. Candles are
distributed before the Procession, which may take place at the
beginning or before the Reading of the Gospel.

2   The president welcomes the people.

May the light and peace of Jesus Christ our Lord be with
you.
The Lord bless you.

3   A HYMN or CHANT may be sung at the lighting of the candles,
and THIS ACCLAMATION may be made.

Let us give thanks to the Lord our God.
He is worthy of all thanksgiving and praise.

Blessed are you, Lord our God, King of the universe!
You make our darkness to be light.
For with you is the well of life
and in your light shall we see light.
Blessed be God for ever.   3

4   The president blesses the candles, saying

Lord God, the springing source of everlasting light,
pour into the hearts of your faithful people
the brilliance of your eternal splendour,
that we, who by these kindling flames
light up this temple to your glory,
may have the darkness of our souls dispelled,
and so be counted worthy to stand before you
in that eternal temple where you live and reign,
Father, Son, and Holy Spirit,
one God, now and for ever.   **Amen.**   3

5   Before the Procession THESE RESPONSES may be used.

We wait for your loving kindness, O Lord,
in the midst of your temple.

Open to us the gates of righteousness
that we may enter and give thanks to the Lord.

God is the Lord who has shown us light,
**Let us offer in his dwelling
an oblation with great gladness.**

6   At the Procession A HYMN or CANTICLE is sung.

At the start of the service this may be the Canticle 'Glory to
God in the highest'. If the Procession is made before the
Gospel, the Hymn 'Hail to the Lord who comes' is
appropriate. Nunc Dimittis is more suitable when the
Procession is made at the end of the service.

b   **AFTER COMMUNION**

7   When the Procession has taken place earlier in the service,
then at the end, after the Sentence and Silence, A HYMN may
be sung, or the Canticle NUNC DIMITTIS in one of these forms
or any other suitable version.

THE SONG OF SIMEON: *Nunc Dimittis*

Luke 2. 29-32

**A light to lighten the nations
and the glory of your people Israel.**

Now, Lord, you let your servant go in peace:
your word has been fulfilled.

**A light to lighten the nations
and the glory of your people Israel.**

My own eyes have seen the salvation:
which you have prepared in the sight of every people.

**A light to lighten the nations
and the glory of your people Israel.**

A light to reveal you to the nations:
and the glory of your people Israel.   *44*

**A light to lighten the nations
and the glory of your people Israel.**

Glory to the Father, and to the Son,
and to the Holy Spirit:
as it was in the beginning, is now,
and shall be for ever.   Amen.

**A light to lighten the nations
and the glory of your people Israel.**

or

Lord, now lettest thou thy servant depart in peace:
according to thy word.

For mine eyes have seen thy salvation:
which thou hast prepared before the face of all people;

To be a light to lighten the Gentiles;
and to be the glory of thy people Israel.

Glory be to the Father, and to the Son,
and to the Holy Ghost:
as it was in the beginning, is now, and ever shall be,
world without end.   Amen.   *41*

8   Either or both of the following prayers is said.

President
Lord, you fulfilled the hope of Simeon and Anna,
who did not die until they welcomed the Messiah.
May we, who have received these your gifts
    beyond words,
prepare to meet Christ Jesus when he comes
    to bring us eternal life;
for he lives and reigns with you and the Holy Spirit,
one God, now and for ever.   **Amen.**

**We thank you, Lord,
that you have fed us in this sacrament,
united us with Christ,
and given us a foretaste of the heavenly banquet
prepared for all mankind.   Amen.**   *9**

THE DISMISSAL

9   The president may say THIS BLESSING.

Christ the Son of God, born of Mary,
fill you with his grace to trust his promises
and obey his will;
and the blessing of God almighty,
the Father, the Son, and the Holy Spirit,
be upon you and remain with you always.   **Amen.**   8

10   *Minister*   Go in the light and peace of Christ.
Thanks be to God.

VII
CANTICLES AND RESPONSORIES

INTRODUCTION

This chapter includes those Canticles and Responsories which have been included in previous chapters, together with a selection of others appropriate for the season.

Responsories have their origin as extended meditative refrains in place of, or in addition to, the canticles in the Office. Their function is to turn what has been heard or read into prayer. They may be used in this way in the Office; or, alternatively, they may be used as Invitatories before the psalmody, in place of the opening versicles and responses.

At the Eucharist, Responsories may be used as psalms, canticles, or hymns in the Ministry of the Word; or they may be used to introduce a period of reflective silence before the Prayers of Penitence, or after Communion.

The Psalm Responsories have a standard form, with a refrain taken from the first verse and repeated after each subsequent verse and the Gloria. In addition to texts from the Psalter, two Songs of Isaiah have been treated in this way. Responsories drawn from other sources take various forms and are grouped seasonally, those for Epiphany and Candlemas being drawn largely from the Eastern tradition.

The number of biblical songs, hymns, and canticles is very large. While the 'Gospel Canticles' – Benedictus, Magnificat, and Nunc Dimittis – have a special place in the regular recitation of Morning, Evening, and Night Prayer, a wide range of canticles from other writings appropriate to the season is also provided.

In the Old Testament Canticles the Gloria has normally been printed at the end, and may be used if desired. In addition, the majority of canticles have a phrase at the beginning which can be used as a congregational response throughout the recitation of the canticle if so desired.

In the New Testament Canticles the Gloria has again been printed where suitable, but there are no congregational refrains. Passages printed in heavy type may suitably be said by all.

A. RESPONSORIES

1   PSALM 25

To you, O Lord, I lift up my soul:
O my God, in you I trust.
To you, O Lord, I lift up my soul:
O my God, in you I trust.

You are the God of my salvation:
in you I hope all the day long.
O my God, in you I trust.

Remember your tender mercy, O Lord:
and the love which you have shown from of old.
O my God, in you I trust.

The ways of the Lord are mercy and truth:
to those who fear him, he reveals his covenant.
O my God, in you I trust.

My eyes are always fixed on the Lord:
for he shall rescue my feet from the snare.
O my God, in you I trust.

Glory to the Father, and to the Son,
and to the Holy Spirit.
To you, O Lord, I lift up my soul,
O my God, in you I trust.

2   PSALM 80

Turn us again, O Lord God of Hosts:
shine upon us, and we shall be saved.
Turn us again, O Lord God of Hosts:
shine upon us, and we shall be saved.

O shepherd of Israel, hear us:
shine forth from your cherubim throne.
Shine upon us, and we shall be saved.

O Lord, stir up your strength:
O Lord, come to our help!
Shine upon us, and we shall be saved.

Return again, God of hosts, we pray:
look down from heaven, and see.
Shine upon us, and we shall be saved.

Visit this vine, and protect it:
the vine your right hand has planted.
Shine upon us, and we shall be saved.

Glory to the Father, and to the Son,
and to the Holy Spirit.
**Turn us again, O Lord God of Hosts:
shine upon us, and we shall be saved.**

3   PSALM 85(i)

The Lord's salvation is near those who fear him:
that glory may dwell in our land.
**The Lord's salvation is near those who fear him:
that glory may dwell in our land.**

Turn us, O God of our salvation:
and let your anger cease from us.
That glory may dwell in our land.

Will you be angry with us, for ever?
for you have covered all our sin.
That glory may dwell in our land.

Show us your mercy, O Lord:
and grant us your salvation.
That glory may dwell in our land.

Will you not restore our life once again?
that your people may rejoice in you.
That glory may dwell in our land.

Glory to the Father, and to the Son,
and to the Holy Spirit.
**The Lord's salvation is near those who fear him:
that glory may dwell in our land.**

4   PSALM 130

My soul is waiting for the Lord:
in his word is my hope.
**My soul is waiting for the Lord:
in his word is my hope.**

Out of the depths have I called to you, O Lord:
Lord, hear my voice.
In his word is my hope.

There is forgiveness with you:
therefore you shall be feared.
In his word is my hope.

My soul is longing for the Lord:
more than those who watch for daybreak.
In his word is my hope.

O Israel, trust in the Lord:
for with the Lord there is mercy.
In his word is my hope.

Glory to the Father, and to the Son,
and to the Holy Spirit.
**My soul is waiting for the Lord:
in his word is my hope.**

5   PSALM 85(ii)

The Lord's salvation is near those who fear him:
that glory may dwell in our land.
**The Lord's salvation is near those who fear him:
that glory may dwell in our land.**

Mercy and truth have met together:
righteousness and peace have kissed each other.
That glory may dwell in our land.

Truth shall spring up from the earth:
and righteousness look down from heaven.
That glory may dwell in our land.

The Lord will grant us prosperity:
and our land will yield its increase.
That glory may dwell in our land.

Righteousness shall go before him:
and peace shall be a pathway for his feet.
That glory may dwell in our land.

Glory to the Father, and to the Son,
and to the Holy Spirit.
**The Lord's salvation is near those who fear him
that glory may dwell in our land.**

6   PSALM 110

Begotten of the Father before daybreak,
you are a prince from the day of your birth.
**Begotten of the Father before daybreak,
you are a prince from the day of your birth.**

The Lord has declared the oracle of old:
Sit at my right hand, with your foes beneath your feet.
You are a prince from the day of your birth.

The Lord will wield your sceptre of power:
rule in the midst of your foes.
You are a prince from the day of your birth.

A prince from the day of your birth on the mountain:
from the womb before daybreak I begot you.
You are a prince from the day of your birth.

The Lord has sworn and will not repent:
you are a priest for ever, a priest like Melchizedek of old.
You are a prince from the day of your birth.

Glory to the Father, and to the Son,
and to the Holy Spirit.
**Begotten of the Father before daybreak,
you are a prince from the day of your birth.**

7   ISAIAH 60

Arise, shine, for your light has come:
the glory of the Lord has risen upon you.
**Arise, shine, for your light has come:
the glory of the Lord has risen upon you.**

The Lord will arise upon you:
and his glory will be seen over you.
The glory of the Lord has risen upon you.

Nations shall come to your light:
and kings to your dawning brightness.
The glory of the Lord has risen upon you.

Your gates will always be open,
shut neither by day nor by night.
The glory of the Lord has risen upon you.

The Lord will be your everlasting light:
your God will be your glory.
The glory of the Lord has risen upon you.

Glory to the Father, and to the Son,
and to the Holy Spirit.
Arise, shine, for your light has come:
the glory of the Lord has risen upon you.

8   PSALM 96

Tell it out among the nations that the Lord is king:
his salvation he has openly showed to all people.
Tell it out among the nations that the Lord is king:
his salvation he has openly showed to all people.

Sing to the Lord a new song:
sing to the Lord, all the whole earth.
His salvation he has openly showed to all people.

Sing to the Lord and bless his name:
bring offerings and come into his courts.
His salvation he has openly showed to all people.

O worship the Lord in the beauty of holiness:
let the whole earth stand in awe of him.
His salvation he has openly showed to all people.

He will rule the world in righteousness:
and judge the peoples with his truth.
His salvation he has openly showed to all people.

Glory to the Father, and to the Son,
and to the Holy Spirit.
Tell it out among the nations that the Lord is king:
his salvation he has openly showed to all people.

9   PSALM 89

I will sing for ever of your love, O Lord:
my mouth shall proclaim your faithfulness
to every generation.
I will sing for ever of your love, O Lord:
my mouth shall proclaim your faithfulness
to every generation.

I am sure that your love lasts for ever:
that your truth is firmly established in the heavens.
My mouth shall proclaim your faithfulness
to every generation.

The heavens proclaim your wonders, O Lord:
the assembly of your saints proclaims your truth.
My mouth shall proclaim your faithfulness
to every generation.

O Lord, mighty God, who is your equal?
Your truth surrounds you on every side.
My mouth shall proclaim your faithfulness
to every generation.

Justice and judgement are the pillars of your throne:
mercy and truth walk together before you.
My mouth shall proclaim your faithfulness
to every generation.

Glory to the Father, and to the Son,
and to the Holy Spirit.
I will sing for ever of your love, O Lord:
my mouth shall proclaim your faithfulness
to every generation.

10   ISAIAH 12

The Lord is my strength and my song:
the Lord has become my salvation.
**The Lord is my strength and my song:
the Lord has become my salvation.**

Behold, God is my salvation:
I will trust, and will not be afraid.
The Lord has become my salvation.

Therefore you will draw water with rejoicing:
from the wells of salvation.
The Lord has become my salvation.

You will say on that day, give thanks to the Lord:
let this be known in all the earth.
The Lord has become my salvation.

Cry aloud, inhabitants of Zion:
for great in your midst is the Holy One of Israel.
The Lord has become my salvation.

Glory to the Father, and to the Son,
and to the Holy Spirit.
**The Lord is my strength and my song:
the Lord has become my salvation.**

RESPONSORIES FOR ADVENT

11   The glory of the Lord shall be revealed,   19 †
     and all flesh shall see it.

With the Lord one day is as a thousand years
And a thousand years as one day.

The Lord is not slow about his promise,
but is forbearing towards you,
**Not wishing that any should perish,
but that all should reach repentance.**

Come, O Lord, and do not tarry;
Purge the transgressions of your people.

† Numbers in right-hand margin refer to Sources and Acknowledgements
(pp.416-419).

12   Now is the time to wake out of sleep;   *19*
now is our salvation nearer than when we first believed.

You will see the Son of Man sitting
at the right hand of power,
And coming with the clouds of heaven.

Who do you say that I am?
**Son of Man, you are the Christ,
the Son of the living God.**

The Son of Man did not come to be served, but to serve,
And to give his life as a ransom for many.

13   Our Lord says, Surely I am coming quickly.   *19*
Even so come, Lord Jesus.

Now it is full time to awake out of sleep,
For the night is far spent and the day is at hand.

Now is our salvation nearer than when we first believed,
For the night is far spent.

Let us therefore cast off the works of darkness
and put on the armour of light,
For the day is at hand.

Put on the Lord Jesus Christ
and make no provision for the flesh,
For the night is far spent and the day is at hand.

14   From afar I see the approach of the power of God   *19*
and the clouds covering all the earth.
**Let us go before him,
for he comes to rule his people.**

Are you he who is to come,
or shall we look for another?
**Let us go before him,
for he comes to rule his people.**

All inhabitants of the world,
both high and low,
rich and poor together:

Let us go before him,
for he comes to rule his people.

O Shepherd of Israel, hear us,
you who lead Joseph's flock:
shine forth from your cherubim throne.
**Let us go before him,
for he comes to rule his people.**

O gates, lift high your heads;
grow higher, ancient doors;
let him enter, the King of Glory.
**Let us go before him
for he comes to rule his people.**

RESPONSORIES FOR CHRISTMAS

15   The Word of Life which was from the beginning
we proclaim to you.

The darkness is passing away
and the true light is already shining,
the Word of Life which was from the beginning.

That which we heard, which we saw with our eyes,
and touched with our own hands
we proclaim to you.

For our fellowship is with the Father,
and with his Son Jesus Christ our Lord.
**The Word of Life which was from the beginning
we proclaim to you.**

16   See what love the Father has given us
that we should be called the children of God.

You are my sons:
this day have I begotten you.
See what love the Father has given us.

As many as received him,
to them he gave power to become the children of God.
See what love the Father has given us.

Glory to the Father, and to the Son,
and to the Holy Spirit.
See what love the Father has given us
that we should be called the children of God.

17 He created me
before the world was made.   *19*

The creator of all things gave me a commandment,
The one who created me assigned a place for my dwelling.

Make your dwelling in Jacob,
And in Jerusalem your dominion.

I took root in a people that was glorified,
in the portion of the Lord's inheritance.

He created me
before the world was made.

18 I have been found by those who did not seek me.   *19*
I have shown myself to those who did not ask for me.

They shall see, who have never been told of him,
And they shall understand, who have never heard of him.

The root of Jesse has come,
He who rises to rule the nations.

Rejoice, O nations, with his people,
And let all the peoples praise him.

RESPONSORIES FOR EPIPHANY

19 The Lord will arise upon you, O Jerusalem,   *19*
And his glory will be seen upon you.

Nations shall come to your light,
and kings to the brightness of your rising:
The Lord will arise upon you, O Jerusalem.

Your sons shall come from afar,
and your daughters shall be carried in your arms:
His glory will be seen upon you.

Everyone shall come, bringing gold and incense
and singing the praise of the Lord:
**For the Lord will arise upon you, O Jerusalem,
and his glory will be seen upon you.**

20 The Father's voice bears witness to the Son.   *34*
God the Holy Trinity has revealed himself to us.

The Son bows his head beneath the Baptist's stream.
God the Holy Trinity has revealed himself to us.

The Spirit as a dove descends from the heavens.
God the Holy Trinity has revealed himself to us.

Submitting to John's baptism,
Christ delivers us from bondage.
God the Holy Trinity has revealed himself to us.

His love is made manifest to the end of the world.
God the Holy Trinity has revealed himself to us.

21 I cannot bear the fire that consumes me.   *34*
Why turn back your waters, O Jordan?

I am filled with wonder at his humble obedience.
Why turn back your waters, O Jordan?

I am a stranger to washing one that is clean.
Why turn back your waters, O Jordan?

Christ baptized in me helps to bear the thorns of sin.
Why turn back your waters, O Jordan?

Behold the Lamb of God
who takes away the sins of the world.
Why turn back your waters, O Jordan?

22 Let the nations bless the one   *34*
who has wrought this great wonder.
The whole creation is freed from its slavery to sin.

Those who dwelt in darkness have seen a great light.
The whole creation is freed from its slavery to sin.

The Word who preserves all things
has washed away our sins.
The whole creation is freed from its slavery to sin.

Light from Light, Christ our God
has shone upon the world.
The whole creation is freed from its slavery to sin.

The heavens are astonished,
for the Prince of Life has come.
The whole creation is freed from its slavery to sin.

He grants us the peace that passes human knowing.
The whole creation is freed from its slavery to sin.

23   The one who alone is clean becomes man   *34*
and is cleansed in the Jordan.
Let us praise the greatness of God's loving purposes.

He makes the waters holy, and crushes the dragon's head.
Let us praise the greatness of God's loving purposes.

Come to the waters with faith in the Saviour of all.
Let us praise the greatness of God's loving purposes.

The grace of the Spirit of God
is poured out for us all to drink.
Let us praise the greatness of God's loving purposes.

24   He who wraps himself with light as a garment   *34*
has humbled himself to take our nature upon him.

Today he is worshipped by the Magi
who bear him costly gifts.
He has wrapped himself with light as with a garment.

Today he is baptized by John,
though he has no need of cleansing.
He has humbled himself to take our nature upon him.

Today at Cana he draws wine out of water,
a sign of the union of earth and heaven.
**He who wraps himself with light as with a garment
has humbled himself to take our nature upon him.**

25   Search the scriptures, as Christ told us in the gospels.   *34*
We find him born in our midst.
Born as a child and bound in swaddling clothes.
We find him born in our midst.
Laid in a manger and fed upon a mother's milk.
We find him born in our midst.
Presented in the temple and carried by Simeon.
We find him born in our midst.
In truth he has appeared in the world.
We find him born in our midst.

26   From the Virgin Mary shines forth Jesus, our Saviour.   *34*
Sun of Righteousness, our God for ever.
He gives light to those in darkness.
Sun of Righteousness, our God for ever.
Simeon rejoices, in old age carrying
the Redeemer of the world.
Sun of Righteousness, our God for ever.
Anna prophesies in the temple of our God.
Sun of Righteousness, our God for ever.
He is the one who offers and is offered for us.
Sun of Righteousness, our God for ever.
He bestows on us his risen power.
Sun of Righteousness, our God for ever.

27   Simeon takes in his arms the Lord of glory.   *34*
Now am I set free, for I have beheld my Saviour.
The heavenly God in mortal flesh.
Now am I set free, for I have beheld my Saviour.
He who speaks through the prophets.
Now am I set free, for I have beheld my Saviour.
Offering himself for us, in his own dwelling place.
Now am I set free, for I have beheld my Saviour.
He is fearful to all, yet his mercy knows no bounds.
Now am I set free, for I have beheld my Saviour.

28 Zion, adorn the bridal chamber.   34
    Welcome Christ the King of glory.
    Mary, the Virgin mother, has borne in the flesh
    the king of eternity.
    Welcome Christ the King of glory.
    He comes to earth and appears in the temple.
    Welcome Christ the King of glory.
    As a sword, his words are sharp with judgement.
    Welcome Christ the King of glory.
    Praise to the Lord Christ Jesus, giver of life.
    Welcome Christ, the King of glory.

B. CANTICLES

OLD TESTAMENT

1 A SONG OF PEACE
Isaiah 2. 3-5

Let us walk in the light of the Lord.

  1 Come, let us go up to the mountain of the Lord: *24**
     to the house of the God of Jacob;

  2 That he may teach us his ways:
     that we may walk in his paths.

  3 For the law shall go out from Zion:
     and the word of the Lord from Jerusalem.

  4 He shall judge between the nations:
     and settle disputes for many peoples;

  5 They shall beat their swords into ploughshares:
     their spears into pruning hooks;

  6 Nation shall not lift up sword against nation:
     nor ever again be trained for war.

  7 People of Jacob, come:
     let us walk in the light of the Lord.

     Glory to the Father, and to the Son,
     and to the Holy Spirit:
     as it was in the beginning, is now,
     and shall be for ever.   Amen.

2 A SONG OF JOY
Isaiah 9. 2-7

To us a child is born: to us a son is given.

  1 The people who walked in darkness have seen *24**
        a great light: *19*
     those who dwelt in a land of deep darkness,
        upon them the light has dawned.

2   You have increased their joy
        and given them great gladness:
    they rejoiced before you as with joy at the harvest.

3   For you have shattered the yoke that burdened them:
    the collar that lay heavy on their shoulders.

4   For to us a child is born, and to us a son is given:
    and the government will be upon his shoulder.

5   And his name will be called 'Wonderful, Counsellor,
        the Mighty God:
    the Everlasting Father, the Prince of Peace'.

6   Of the increase of his government and of peace:
    there will be no end,

7   Upon the throne of David, and over his kingdom:
    to establish and uphold it with justice
        and righteousness.

8   From this time forth and for evermore:
    the zeal of the Lord of hosts will do this.

Glory to the Father, and to the Son,
and to the Holy Spirit:
as it was in the beginning, is now,
and shall be for ever.   Amen.

3   A SONG OF PROPHECY
    Isaiah 11. 1-4a, 6

The Spirit of the Lord shall rest upon him.

1   There shall come forth a shoot   *24**
        from the stump of Jesse: *31*
    and a branch shall grow out of his roots.

2   And the Spirit of the Lord shall rest upon him:
    the spirit of wisdom and understanding,

3   The spirit of counsel and might:
    the spirit of knowledge and the fear of the Lord.

4   He shall not judge by what his eyes see:
    or decide by what his ears hear;

5   But with righteousness he shall judge the poor:
     and decide with equity for the meek of the earth.

6   The wolf shall dwell with the lamb,
     and the leopard shall lie down with the kid,

7   The calf and the young lion together,
     with a little child to lead them.

     Glory to the Father, and to the Son,
     and to the Holy Spirit:
     as it was in the beginning, is now,
     and shall be for ever.   Amen.

4   A SONG OF SALVATION
Isaiah 12. 2-6

Behold, God is my salvation.

1   Behold, God is my salvation: *24**
     I will trust and will not be afraid.   *19*

2   For the Lord God is my strength and my song:
     and he has become my salvation.

3   With joy you will draw water:
     from the wells of salvation.

4   On that day you will say:
     'Give thanks to the Lord, call upon his name.

5   Make known his deeds among the nations:
     proclaim that his name is exalted.

6   Sing praises to the Lord,
        for he has triumphed gloriously:
     let this be known in all the earth.

7   Shout and sing for joy, you that dwell in Zion:
     for great in your midst is the Holy One of Israel.'

     Glory to the Father, and to the Son,
     and to the Holy Spirit:
     as it was in the beginning, is now,
     and shall be for ever.   Amen.

5   A SONG OF THE WILDERNESS
        Isaiah 35. 1-4

The ransomed of the Lord shall return with singing.

    1   The wilderness and the dry land shall rejoice:
        the desert shall burst into song;

    2   They shall see the glory of the Lord:
        the splendour of our God.

    3   Strengthen the weary hands:
        make firm the feeble knees.

    4   Say to the anxious:
        Be strong, fear not!

    5   Your God is coming with judgement:
        coming with judgement to save you.

        Glory to the Father, and to the Son,
        and to the Holy Spirit:
        as it was in the beginning, is now,
        and shall be for ever.   Amen.

6   THE PRAYER OF HEZEKIAH
        Isaiah 38. 10-14, 17-20

You have cast all my sins behind you.

    1   I said, in the noontide of my days I must depart: *24**
        I am consigned to the gates of Sheol
           for the rest of my years.

    2   I said, I shall not see the Lord in the
           land of the living:
        I shall look no more upon the inhabitants
           of the world.

    3   My dwelling is plucked up and removed from me
           like a shepherd's tent:
        like a weaver I have rolled up my life,
           he cuts me off from the loom.

4   From day to night you bring me to an end,
      I cry for help until morning:
  like a lion he breaks all my bones;
      from day to night you bring me to an end.

5   Like a swallow or a crane I clamour,
      I moan like a dove:
  my eyes are weary with looking upward;
      O Lord, be my security.

6   Lo, it was for my welfare:
  that I had great bitterness.

7   But you have held back my life
      from the pit of destruction:
  for you have cast all my sins behind your back.

8   For Sheol cannot thank you, death cannot praise you:
  those who go down to the pit cannot
      hope for your faithfulness.

9   The living, the living, they thank you,
      as I do this day:
  the father makes known to the children
      your faithfulness.

10   The Lord will save me, and we will sing
      to stringed instruments:
  all the days of our life, at the house of the Lord.

  Glory to the Father, and to the Son,
  and to the Holy Spirit:
  as it was in the beginning, is now,
  and shall be for ever.   Amen.

7   A SONG OF A HERALD
    Isaiah 40. 9-11

Lift up your voice with strength.

1   Go up to a high mountain,   *24**
      herald of good tidings to Zion: *11*
  lift up your voice with strength,
      herald of good tidings to Jerusalem.

2   Lift it up, fear not:
      say to the cities of Judah, Behold your God!

3   See, the Lord God coming with might:
      coming to rule with his mighty arm;

4   He brings his reward with him:
      his recompense before him.

5   He will feed his flock like a shepherd:
      and gather the lambs in his arms,

6   He will hold them to his breast:
      and gently lead those that are with young.

      Glory to the Father, and to the Son,
      and to the Holy Spirit:
      as it was in the beginning, is now,
      and shall be for ever.   Amen.

8   A SONG OF THE COVENANT
Isaiah 42. 5-8

I have given you as a light to the nations.

1   Thus says the Lord who created the heavens   *24*
          and stretched them out:
      who spread forth the earth and what comes from it,

2   Who gives breath to the people upon it:
      and spirit to those who walk in it.

3   'I am the Lord, I have called you in righteousness:
      I have taken you by the hand and kept you;

4   I have given you as a covenant to the people:
      a light to the nations, to open the eyes that are blind,

5   To bring out the prisoners from the dungeon:
      from the prison, those who sit in darkness.

6   I am the Lord, that is my name:
      my glory I give to no other.'

      Glory to the Father, and to the Son,
      and to the Holy Spirit:
      as it was in the beginning, is now,
      and shall be for ever.   Amen.

9   A SONG OF THE NEW CREATION
Isaiah 43. 15-21

1   I am the Lord, your Holy One: 24
    the Creator of Israel, your King.

2   Thus says the Lord, who makes a way in the sea:
    a path in the mighty waters,

3   Remember not the former things:
    nor consider the things of old.

4   Behold, I am doing a new thing:
    now it springs forth, do you not perceive it?

5   I will make a way in the wilderness
        and rivers in the desert:
    to give drink to my chosen people,

6   The people whom I formed for myself:
    that they might declare my praise.

Glory to the Father, and to the Son,
and to the Holy Spirit:
as it was in the beginning, is now,
and shall be for ever.   Amen.

10   A SONG OF THE REDEEMER
Isaiah 49. 8-13

In the day of salvation I have helped you.

1   In a time of favour I have answered you: 24*
    in a day of salvation I have helped you.

2   I have kept you and given you as a
        covenant to the people:
    to establish the land,
        to apportion the desolate heritages,

3   Saying to the prisoners, Come forth:
    to those who are in darkness, Appear.

4   They shall feed along the ways:
    on all bare heights shall be their pasture.

5   They shall not hunger nor thirst:
      neither scorching wind nor sun shall smite them,

6   For he who has pity on them will lead them:
      and by springs of water he will guide them.

7   And I will make my mountains a way:
      and my highways shall be raised up.

8   Lo, these shall come from afar:
      and lo, these from the north and from the west.

9   Sing for joy, O heavens, and exult, O earth:
      break forth, O mountains, into singing,

10   For the Lord has comforted his people:
      and will have compassion on his afflicted.

      Glory to the Father, and to the Son,
      and to the Holy Spirit:
      as it was in the beginning, is now,
      and shall be for ever.   Amen.

11 A SONG OF THE WORD OF THE LORD
Isaiah 55. 6-11

Seek the Lord while he may be found.

1   Seek the Lord while he may be found: *24**
      call upon him while he is near.   *19*

2   Let the wicked abandon their ways:
      and the unrighteous their thoughts.

3   Turn back to the Lord, who will have mercy:
      to our God, who will richly pardon us.

4   For my thoughts are not your thoughts:
      neither are your ways my ways, says the Lord.

5   As the heavens are higher than the earth:
      so are my ways higher than your ways,
         and my thoughts than your thoughts.

6   As the rain and the snow come down from heaven:
      and return not again but water the earth,

7 Bringing forth life and giving growth:
   seed for sowing and bread to eat,

8 So is my word that goes out from my mouth:
   it will not return to me empty,

9 But it will accomplish my purpose:
   and succeed in the task I give it.

   Glory to the Father, and to the Son,
   and to the Holy Spirit:
   as it was in the beginning, is now,
   and shall be for ever.   Amen.

12 A SONG OF THE NEW JERUSALEM
    Isaiah 60. 1-3, 11, 14, 18-19

Arise, shine out, for your light has come.

1 Arise, shine out, for your light has come: 24*
   the glory of the Lord is rising upon you.   19

2 Though night still covers the earth:
   and darkness the peoples,

3 Above you the Lord now rises:
   and above you his glory appears.

4 The nations will come to your light:
   and kings to your dawning brightness.

5 Your gates will always stand open:
   shut neither by day nor by night.

6 They will call you The City of the Lord:
   Zion of the Holy One of Israel.

7 The sound of violence shall be heard
        no longer in your land:
   or ruin and devastation within your borders.

8 You will call your walls Salvation:
   and your gates Praise.

9 No more will the sun give you daylight:
   nor moonlight shine upon you.

10 But the Lord will be your everlasting light:
    your God will be your splendour.

Glory to the Father, and to the Son,
and to the Holy Spirit:
as it was in the beginning, is now,
and shall be for ever.   Amen.

13   A SONG OF THE BRIDE
Isaiah 61. 10-11; 62. 1-3

The Lord has clothed me with the garments of salvation.

1   I will greatly rejoice in the Lord: *24**
    my soul shall exult in my God,   *19*

2   For he has clothed me with the garments of salvation:
    he has covered me with the cloak of integrity,

3   As a bridegroom decks himself with a garland:
    and as a bride adorns herself with her jewels.

4   For as the earth puts forth her blossom:
    and as seeds in the garden spring up,

5   So shall the Lord God make righteousness and praise:
    blossom before all the nations.

6   For Zion's sake, I will not keep silence:
    and for Jerusalem's sake, I will not rest.

7   Until her deliverance shines forth like the sunrise:
    and her salvation as a burning torch.

8   The nations shall see your deliverance:
    and all kings shall see your glory.

9   Then you shall be called by a new name:
    which the mouth of the Lord will give.

10   You shall be a crown of glory in the hand of the Lord:
    and a royal diadem in the hand of your God.

Glory to the Father, and to the Son,
and to the Holy Spirit:
as it was in the beginning, is now,
and shall be for ever.   Amen.

14   A LAMENT OF ISAIAH
Isaiah 64. 1-7

O rend the heavens and come down.

1   O that you would rend the heavens   24*
          and come down:
    that the mountains might quake at your presence,

2   As when fire kindles brushwood:
    and the fire causes water to boil,

3   To make your name known to your adversaries:
    and that the nations might tremble at your presence.

4   When you did terrible things
          which we looked not for:
    you came down and the mountains quaked
          at your presence.

5   From of old no one has heard or perceived by the ear:
    no eye has seen a god besides you,
          who works for those who wait for him.

6   You meet him that joyfully works righteousness:
    those that remember you in your way.

7   Behold, you were angry and we sinned:
    in our sins we have been a long time,
          and shall we be saved?

8   We have all become like one who is unclean:
    and all our righteous deeds
          are like a polluted garment.

9   We all fade like a leaf:
    and our iniquities, like the wind, take us away.

10   There is no one that calls upon your name:
    that bestirs himself to take hold of you.

11   For you have hid your face from us:
    and have delivered us into the hands of our iniquities.

12   O that you would rend the heavens and come down:
    that the mountains might quake at your presence.

Glory to the Father, and to the Son,
and to the Holy Spirit:
as it was in the beginning, is now,
and shall be for ever.   Amen.

15   A SONG OF THE NEW CREATION
     Isaiah 65. 17-20, 23-25

I create new heavens and a new earth.

1   Behold, I create new heavens and a new earth: 24*
    and the former things shall not be remembered
        or come into mind.

2   Be glad and rejoice for ever in that which I create:
    for behold, I create Jerusalem a rejoicing,
        and her people a joy.

3   I will rejoice in Jerusalem, and be glad in my people:
    no more shall be heard in it the sound of weeping
        and the cry of distress.

4   No more shall there be in it an infant
        that lives but a few days:
    nor an old man who does not fill out his days.

5   They shall not labour in vain,
        or bear children for calamity:
    for they shall be the offspring of the blessed
        of the Lord, and their children with them.

6   Before they call I will answer:
    while they are yet speaking I will hear.

7   The wolf and the lamb shall feed together:
    the lion shall eat straw like the ox;
        and dust shall be the serpent's food.

8   In all my holy mountain:
    they shall not hurt or destroy, says the Lord.

Glory to the Father, and to the Son,
and to the Holy Spirit:
as it was in the beginning, is now,
and shall be for ever.   Amen.

16   A SONG OF LAMENTATION
Lamentations 1. 11b-16

Is there any sorrow like my sorrow?

1   Is it nothing to you, all you who pass by?   24*
Look and see if there is any sorrow like my sorrow
    which the Lord inflicted on the day of his fierce
    anger.

2   From on high he sent fire into my bones
    and spread a net for my feet:
he turned me back and left me stunned,
    faint all the day long.

3   My transgressions were bound into a yoke:
by his hand they were fastened together
    and set upon my back

4   The Lord caused my strength to fail:
he gave me into the hands of those whom I cannot
    withstand.

5   The Lord flouted all my mighty men
    in the midst of me:
the Lord has trodden as in a wine press
    the virgin daughter of Judah.

6   For these things I weep; my eyes flow with tears:
for a comforter is far from me,
    one to revive my courage.

Glory to the Father, and to the Son,
and to the Holy Spirit:
as it was in the beginning, is now,
and shall be for ever.   Amen.

17   A SONG OF LAMENTATION
Lamentations 3. 19-33

The steadfast love of the Lord never ceases.

1   Remember my affliction and my bitterness:
    the wormwood and the gall.

2   My soul continually thinks of it;
          and is bowed down within me:
    but this I call to mind, and there I have hope.

3   The steadfast love of the Lord never ceases:
    his mercies never come to an end.

4   They are new every morning:
    great is thy faithfulness, O Lord.

5   The Lord is my portion, therefore will I hope in him:
    the Lord is good to those who wait for him,
          to the soul that seeks him.

6   It is good that one should wait quietly:
    for the salvation of the Lord.

7   It is good for a man that he bear the yoke
          in his youth:
    let him sit alone in silence when he has laid it on him.

8   Let him put his mouth in the dust:
    there may yet be hope.

9   Let him give his cheek to the smiter,
          and be filled with insults:
    for the Lord will not cast him off for ever.

10 Though he cause grief, he will have compassion
          according to the abundance of his steadfast love:
    for he does not willingly afflict
          or grieve the sons of men.

Glory to the Father, and to the Son,
and to the Holy Spirit:
as it was in the beginning, is now,
and shall be for ever.   Amen.

Note: Because of the traditional application of these words to the sufferings of Christ in Passiontide, no attempt has been made to render the male pronouns inclusive.

18 THE SONG OF JONAH
Jonah 2. 2-8

I call to the Lord and he answers me.

1   I call to the Lord out of my distress,
        and he answers me: 24*
out of the valley of Sheol I cried,
        and you did hear my voice.

2   For you did cast me into the deep,
        into the heart of the sea:
the flood was round about me;
        all your waves and your billows passed over me.

3   Then I said, I am cast out from your presence:
how shall I again look upon your holy temple?

4   The waters closed in over me,
        the deep was round about me:
weeds were wrapped about my head
        at the roots of the mountain.

5   I went down to the land
        whose bars closed upon me for ever:
yet you did bring up my life from the pit,
        O Lord my God.

6   When my soul fainted within me,
        I remembered the Lord:
my prayer came to you, into your holy temple.

7   Those who pay regard to vain idols
        forsake their true loyalty:
but I with voice of thanksgiving
        will sacrifice to you.

8   What I have vowed I will pay:
deliverance belongs to the Lord.

Glory to the Father, and to the Son,
and to the Holy Spirit:
as it was in the beginning, is now,
and shall be for ever.   Amen.

19 THE SONG OF TOBIT
Tobit 13. 1-6

**Praise the Lord of righteousness
and exalt the King of the ages.**

1 Blessed be God, who lives for ever: *19*
   for his reign endures throughout all ages.

2 Declare his praise before the nations:
   you who are the children of Israel.

3 For if he has scattered you among them:
   there too has he shown you his greatness.

4 Exalt him in the sight of all the living:
   for he is our God and our Father for ever.

5 Though he punishes you for your wickedness:
   he will show mercy to you all.

6 He will gather you from every nation:
   from wherever you have been scattered.

7 See what the Lord has done for you
      and give thanks to him with a loud voice:
   praise the Lord of righteousness
      and exalt the King of the ages.

   Glory to the Father, and to the Son,
   and to the Holy Spirit:
   as it was in the beginning, is now,
   and shall be for ever.   Amen.

20 THE SOULS OF THE RIGHTEOUS
Wisdom 3. 1-8

The souls of the righteous are in the hand of God.

1 The souls of the righteous are in the hand of God: *11**
   no torment shall ever touch them.

2 In the eyes of the unwise they seemed to have died,
      their departure was taken for defeat:
   their going from us to be a disaster;
      but they are in peace.

3 Though they appeared to be punished,
   their hope is rich in immortality:
 small their affliction, but great their blessing.

4 God proved and found them worthy of himself:
 like gold in a furnace he tried them,
   and accepted them as an oblation.

5 In the moment of God's coming
   they shall kindle into flame:
 and run like sparks among the stubble.

6 They shall govern nations and peoples:
 and the Lord shall be their ruler for ever.

 Glory to the Father, and to the Son,
 and to the Holy Spirit:
 as it was in the beginning, is now,
 and shall be for ever. Amen.

21 A SONG OF WISDOM
 Sirach 14. 20a, 21, 27; 15. 1-6

The one who meditates on wisdom
will find gladness and a crown of rejoicing.

1 Blessed is the man who meditates on wisdom: *24*
 he who reflects in his mind on her ways
   will also ponder her secrets.

2 He will be sheltered by her from the heat:
 and will dwell in the midst of her glory.

3 The man who fears the Lord will do this:
 and he who holds to the law will obtain wisdom.

4 She will come to meet him like a mother:
 and like the wife of his youth she will welcome him.

5 She will feed him with the bread of understanding:
 and give him the water of wisdom to drink.

6 He will lean on her and will not fall:
 and he will rely on her and will not be put to shame.

7 She will exalt him above his neighbours:
and will open his mouth in the midst of the assembly.

8 He will find gladness and a crown of rejoicing:
and will acquire an everlasting name.

Glory to the Father, and to the Son,
and to the Holy Spirit:
as it was in the beginning, is now,
and shall be for ever.   Amen.

22   A SONG OF THE FAITHFUL
Sirach 34. 13-17

The eyes of the Lord are upon those who love him.

1 The spirit of those who fear the Lord will live: *24*
for their hope is in him who saves them.

2 He who fears the Lord will not be timid,
for he is his hope:
blessed is the soul of the man who fears the Lord.

3 The eyes of the Lord are upon those who love him:
a mighty protection and strong support.

4 A shelter from the hot wind
and a shade from noonday sun:
a guard against stumbling
and a defence against falling.

5 He lifts up the soul and gives light to the eyes:
he grants healing, and life, and blessing.

Glory to the Father, and to the Son,
and to the Holy Spirit:
as it was in the beginning, is now,
and shall be for ever.   Amen.

23 A SONG OF BARUCH
Baruch 5. 5-9

Arise, O Jerusalem, look to the east.

1   Arise, O Jerusalem, stand upon the height   24
        and look toward the east:
  see your children gathered from west and east,
        at the word of the Holy One.

2   For they went forth from you on foot,
        led away by their enemies:
  but God will bring them back to you,
        carried in glory, as on a royal throne.

3   For God has ordered that every high mountain
        and the everlasting hills be made low:
  that the valleys be filled up, to make level ground,

4   So that Israel may walk safely:
        in the glory of God.

5   The woods and every fragrant tree:
        have shaded Israel at God's command.

6   For God will lead Israel with joy,
        in the light of his glory:
  with the mercy and righteousness
        that come from him.

Glory to the Father, and to the Son,
and to the Holy Spirit:
as it was in the beginning, is now,
and shall be for ever.   Amen.

24 THE SONG OF THE THREE (Bless the Lord)
Song of the Three 29-34

1   Bless the Lord the God of our fathers: 8
  sing his praise and exalt him for ever.

2   Bless his holy and glorious name:
  sing his praise and exalt him for ever.

3 Bless him in his holy and glorious temple:
  sing his praise and exalt him for ever.

4 Bless him who beholds the depths:
  sing his praise and exalt him for ever.

5 Bless him who sits between the cherubim:
  sing his praise and exalt him for ever.

6 Bless him on the throne of his kingdom:
  sing his praise and exalt him for ever.

7 Bless him in the heights of heaven:
  sing his praise and exalt him for ever.

  Bless the Father, the Son, and the Holy Spirit:
  sing his praise and exalt him for ever.

25 A SONG OF GOD'S JUDGEMENT
Habbakuk 3. 2-4, 17-19

1 Lord, I have heard of your fame:
  I stand in awe of your deeds.

2 Do them again in our days,
      in our days make them known:
  in spite of your anger have compassion.

3 The glory of the Lord covers the heavens:
  and the earth is full of his praise.

4 His splendour is like the light:
  and there his power is hidden.

5 Though the fig trees do not blossom:
  nor fruit be on the vines,

6 The produce of the olive fail:
  and the fields yield no food,

7 The flock be cut off from the fold:
  and there be no herd in the stalls,

8 Yet I will rejoice in the Lord,
      and exult in God my saviour:
  God, the Lord, is my strength.

Glory to the Father, and to the Son,
and to the Holy Spirit:
as it was in the beginning, is now,
and shall be for ever.   Amen.

26   A SONG OF HOSEA
Hosea 6. 1-6

God will raise us up, that we may live in his presence.

1   Come let us return to the Lord: *24**
for he has torn us and will heal us.   *19*

2   He has stricken us:
and he will bind up our wounds.

3   After two days he will revive us:
on the third day he will raise us up,
that we may live in his presence.

4   Let us humble ourselves, let us strive
to know the Lord:
for his justice dawns like the morning light,
and its dawning is as sure as the sunrise.

5   He will come to us like the showers:
like the spring rains that water the earth.

6   O Ephraim, how shall I deal with you?
how shall I deal with you, O Judah?

7   Your love for me is like the morning mist:
like the dew that goes early away.

8   Therefore I have hewn them by the prophets:
and my judgement goes forth as the light.

9   For loyalty is my desire and not sacrifice,
and the knowledge of God
rather than burnt-offerings.

Glory to the Father, and to the Son,
and to the Holy Spirit:
as it was in the beginning, is now,
and shall be for ever.   Amen.

27   THE SONG OF HANNAH
1 Samuel 2. 1, 4-8

The Lord has filled my heart with joy.

1   My heart exults in the Lord:
    I find my strength in my God.

2   My mouth laughs at my enemies:
    as I rejoice at your saving help.
    The Lord has filled my heart with joy.

3   The bows of the mighty are broken:
    but the feeble are clothed with strength.

4   Those with plenty must labour for bread:
    but the hungry are hungry no more.

5   The barren woman has children now:
    but the fruitful wife is left forlorn.
    The Lord has filled my heart with joy.

6   It is the Lord who gives life and death:
    he sends down to the grave and raises up.

7   It is the Lord who gives poverty and wealth:
    he humbles some and makes others great.
    The Lord has filled my heart with joy.

8   The Lord lifts up the weak from the dust:
    and raises the poor from their misery.

9   He makes them companions of princes:
    and sets them on thrones of honour.

10 For the foundations of the earth are the Lord's:
    on them he has built the world.
    The Lord has filled my heart with joy.

Glory to the Father, and to the Son,
and to the Holy Spirit:
as it was in the beginning, is now,
and shall be for ever.   Amen.

NEW TESTAMENT

28 THE SONG OF ZECHARIAH – Benedictus
Luke 1. 68-79

1 Blessed be the Lord the God of Israel: 43
   for he has come to his people and set them free. 8

2 He has raised up for us a mighty saviour:
   born of the house of his servant David.

3 Through his holy prophets he promised of old:
   that he would save us from our enemies,
      from the hands of all that hate us.

4 He promised to show mercy to our fathers:†
   and to remember his holy covenant.

5 This was the oath he swore to our father Abraham:
   to set us free from the hands of our enemies,

6 Free to worship him without fear:
   holy and righteous in his sight,
      all the days of our life.

7 You, my child, shall be called the prophet
      of the Most High:
   for you will go before the Lord to prepare his way,

8 To give his people knowledge of salvation:
   by the forgiveness of all their sins.

9 In the tender compassion of our God:
   the dawn from on high shall break upon us,

10 To shine on those who dwell in darkness
      and the shadow of death:
    and to guide our feet into the way of peace.

Glory to the Father, and to the Son,
and to the Holy Spirit:
as it was in the beginning, is now,
and shall be for ever.   Amen.

† or 'forebears' if preferred

29 THE SONG OF MARY – Magnificat
Luke 1. 46-55

1 My soul proclaims the greatness of the Lord, 43
   my spirit rejoices in God my Saviour: 8
   for he has looked with favour on his lowly servant.

2 From this day all generations will call me blessed:
   the Almighty has done great things for me,
   and holy is his name.

3 He has mercy on those who fear him:
   in every generation.

4 He has shown the strength of his arm:
   he has scattered the proud in their conceit.

5 He has cast down the mighty from their thrones:
   and has lifted up the lowly.

6 He has filled the hungry with good things:
   and the rich he has sent away empty.

7 He has come to the help of his servant Israel:
   for he has remembered his promise of mercy,

8 The promise he made to our fathers:†
   to Abraham and his children for ever.

   Glory to the Father, and to the Son,
   and to the Holy Spirit:
   as it was in the beginning, is now,
   and shall be for ever.   Amen.

30 THE SONG OF SIMEON – Nunc Dimittis
Luke 2. 29-32

1 Now, Lord, you let your servant go in peace: 44
   your word has been fulfilled. 8

2 My own eyes have seen the salvation:
   which you have prepared in the sight of every people.

3 A light to reveal you to the nations:
   and the glory of your people Israel.

† or 'forebears' if preferred

Glory to the Father, and to the Son,
and to the Holy Spirit:
as it was in the beginning, is now,
and shall be for ever.   Amen.

31 THE BEATITUDES
Matthew 5. 3-12

1 Blessed are the poor in spirit,   *24**
   for theirs is the kingdom of heaven.   *11*

2 Blessed are those who mourn,
   for they shall be comforted.

3 Blessed are the gentle,
   for they shall inherit the earth.

4 Blessed are those who hunger and thirst
      for what is right,
   for they shall be satisfied.

5 Blessed are the merciful,
   for mercy shall be shown to them.

6 Blessed are the pure in heart,
   for they shall see God.

7 Blessed are the peacemakers,
   for they shall be called children of God.

8 Blessed are those who are persecuted
      in the cause of right,
   for theirs is the kingdom of heaven.

9 Blessed are you when others revile you
      and persecute you
   and utter all kinds of evil against you
      falsely for my sake.

10 Rejoice and be glad,
   for your reward is great in heaven.

Glory to the Father, and to the Son,
and to the Holy Spirit:
as it was in the beginning, is now,
and shall be for ever.   Amen.

32   THE SONG OF CHRIST'S GLORY
Philippians 2. 5-11

1   Christ Jesus was in the form of God:
    but he did not cling to equality with God.

2   He emptied himself, taking the form of a servant:
    and was born in the likeness of men;†

3   Being found in human form, he humbled himself:
    and became obedient unto death,
        even death on a cross.

4   Therefore God has highly exalted him:
    and bestowed on him the name above every name,

5   That at the name of Jesus every knee should bow:
    in heaven and on earth and under the earth;

6   And every tongue confess that Jesus Christ is Lord:
    to the glory of God the Father.

    Glory to the Father, and to the Son,
    and to the Holy Spirit:
    as it was in the beginning, is now,
    and shall be for ever.   Amen.

24*
45

33   A SONG OF REDEMPTION
Colossians 1. 13-20

1   The Father has delivered us from
        the dominion of darkness;
    and transferred us to the kingdom of his
        beloved Son,

2   In whom we have redemption:
    the forgiveness of our sins.

3   He is the image of the invisible God:
    the first-born of all creation.

4   For in him all things were created:
    in heaven and on earth, visible and invisible.

24*
19

† or 'human likeness' if preferred

328

5   All things were created through him and for him:
    he is before all things
          and in him all things hold together.

6   He is the head of the body, the Church:
    he is the beginning, the first-born from the dead.

7   For it pleased God that in him
          all fullness should dwell:
    and through him all things be reconciled to himself.

    Glory to the Father, and to the Son,
    and to the Holy Spirit:
    as it was in the beginning, is now,
    and shall be for ever.   Amen.

34   A SONG OF GOD'S GRACE
Ephesians 1. 3-10

1   Blessed be the God and Father   24*
          of our Lord Jesus Christ: 19
    who has blessed us in Christ Jesus with
          every spiritual blessing in the heavenly places.

2   He chose us in him before the foundation
          of the world:
    that we should be holy and blameless before him.

3   He destined us in love to be his sons
          through Jesus Christ:
    according to the purpose of his will.

4   To the praise of his glorious grace:
    which he freely bestowed on us in the Beloved.

5   In him we have redemption through his blood:
    the forgiveness of our sins,

6   According to the riches of his grace:
    which he lavished upon us.

7   He has made known to us in all wisdom and insight:
    the mystery of his will,

8   According to his purpose which he set forth in Christ:
    as a plan for the fullness of time,

9   To unite all things in him:
       things in heaven and things on earth.

       Glory to the Father, and to the Son,
       and to the Holy Spirit:
       as it was in the beginning, is now,
       and shall be for ever.   Amen.

35 A SONG OF THE REDEEMED
Revelation 7. 9-10, 14-17

1   Behold a great multitude: *24**
     which no one could number,   *19*

2   From every nation,
       from all tribes and peoples and tongues:
   standing before the throne and before the Lamb.

3   They were clothed in white robes
       and had palms in their hands:
   and they cried out with a loud voice,

4   'Salvation belongs to our God:
   who sits upon the throne, and to the Lamb.'

5   These are those who have come
       out of the great tribulation:
   they have washed their robes
       and made them white in the blood of the Lamb.

6   Therefore they stand before the throne of God:
   and serve him day and night within the temple.

7   And he who sits upon the throne:
   will shelter them with his presence.

8   They shall never again feel hunger or thirst:
   the sun shall not strike them,
       nor any scorching heat.

9   For the Lamb at the heart of the throne
       will be their Shepherd:
   and he will guide them to springs of living water.

       Glory to the Father, and to the Son,
       and to the Holy Spirit:
       as it was in the beginning, is now,
       and shall be for ever.   Amen.

36 A SONG OF MOSES AND OF THE LAMB
(Great and Wonderful)
Revelation 15. 3-4

1   Great and wonderful are your deeds: *24**
     Lord God the almighty.   *8*

2   Just and true are your ways:
     O King of the nations.

3   Who shall not revere and praise your name, O Lord?
     for you alone are holy.

4   All nations shall come and worship in your presence:
     for your just dealings have been revealed.

**To him who sits on the throne and to the Lamb:
be praise and honour, glory and might,
for ever and ever.   Amen.**

37 A SONG OF GOD'S JUDGEMENT
Revelation 11. 17-18; 12. 10-12

1   We give thanks to you, Lord God almighty,   *24**
          ever present and eternal: *19*
     for you have taken your great power
          and begun to reign.

2   The nations raged,
          but the day of your wrath has come:
     and the time for the dead to be judged.

3   The time has come to reward your servants
          the prophets and saints:
     and those who fear your name both small and great.

4   Now the salvation of God has come,
          his power and his glorious kingdom:
     now has come the authority of his Christ.

5   For the accuser of our brothers and sisters
          has been thrown down:
     who accuses them day and night before our God.

6 And they have conquered him
   by the blood of the Lamb:
and by their word of witness.

7 Rejoice, then, O heaven:
and you that dwell therein.

Glory to the Father, and to the Son,
and to the Holy Spirit:
as it was in the beginning, is now,
and shall be for ever.   Amen.

38   A SONG OF THE LAMB
Revelation 19. 1b, 2, 5

1 Salvation and glory and power belong to our God: *24**
his judgements are true and just.   *19*

2 Praise our God, all you his servants:
you who fear him, both small and great.

3 The Lord our God, the Almighty, reigns:
let us rejoice and exult and give him the glory.

4 The marriage of the Lamb has come:
and his bride has made herself ready.

To him who sits on the throne and to the Lamb:
be praise and honour, glory and might,
for ever and ever.   Amen.

39   A SONG OF THE HOLY CITY
Revelation 21. 1-5

1 Then I saw a new heaven and a new earth: *24**
for the first heaven and the first earth   *19*
      had passed away
      and the sea was no more.

2 And I saw the holy city, new Jerusalem,
      coming down out of heaven from God:
prepared as a bride adorned for her husband.

3 And I heard a great voice from the throne saying:
'Behold, the dwelling of God is with his people.

4   He will dwell with them and they shall be his own:
    and God himself will be with them;

5   He will wipe away every tear from their eyes:
    and death shall be no more.

6   Neither shall there be mourning
            nor crying nor pain any more:
    for the former things have passed away.'

7   And he who sat upon the throne said:
    'Behold, I make all things new.'

    Glory to the Father, and to the Son,
    and to the Holy Spirit:
    as it was in the beginning, is now,
    and shall be for ever.   Amen.

40   A SONG OF THE SPIRIT
     Revelation 22. 12-14, 17, 20

1   Behold, I am coming soon, says the Lord,   *24**
            and bringing my reward with me: *19*
    to give to everyone according to his deeds.

2   I am the Alpha and the Omega, the first and the last:
    the beginning and the end.

3   Blessed are those who do his commandments
            that they may have the right to the tree of life:
    and may enter into the city through the gates.

4   I am the root and the offspring of David:
    I am the bright morning star.

5   The Spirit and the Bride say, Come:
    and let those who hear say, Come.

6   And let those who are thirsty come:
    let those who desire
            take the water of life without price.

    'Surely, I am coming soon':
    Amen. Come, Lord Jesus!

41 THE SONG OF THE CHURCH – Te Deum

44

1 We praise you, O God,
we acclaim you as Lord;

2 all creation worships you,
the Father everlasting.

3 To you all angels, all the powers of heaven,
the cherubim and seraphim sing in endless praise:

4 **Holy, holy, holy Lord, God of power and might,
heaven and earth are full of your glory.**

5 The glorious company of apostles praise you.
The noble fellowship of prophets praise you.

6 The white-robed army of martyrs praise you.
Throughout the world the holy Church acclaims you:

7 **Father, of majesty unbounded,
your true and only Son, worthy of all praise,
the Holy Spirit, advocate and guide.**

8 You, Christ, are the King of glory,
the eternal Son of the Father.

9 When you took our flesh to set us free
you humbly chose the Virgin's womb.

10 You overcame the sting of death
and opened the kingdom of heaven to all believers.

11 You are seated at God's right hand in glory.
We believe that you will come to be our judge.

12 **Come then, Lord, and help your people,
bought with the price of your own blood,
and bring us with your saints
to glory everlasting.**

42 These versicles and responses may be added to the Te Deum
    if desired, or used independently.

Save your people, Lord, and bless your inheritance.
Govern and uphold them now and always.

Day by day we bless you.
We praise your name for ever.

Keep us today, Lord, from all sin.
Have mercy on us, Lord, have mercy.

Lord, show us your love and mercy,
for we have put our trust in you.

In you, Lord, is our hope:
let us never be put to shame.

VIII
PRAYERS

INTRODUCTION

The Collects and prayers in this chapter are drawn from various chapters in *The Promise of His Glory*, and many of them are grouped under headings which identify the season to which they most appropriately belong. These divisions are in some ways artificial, and a number of the Collects will have a use beyond their particular designation, hence their being collected together with some supplementary prayers at this point in the book.

Historically, the Collect has been a succinct prayer, prayed by the president. Such prayer has typically been offered through Christ to the Father, and the traditional fuller ending expresses our participation in the life of the Trinity. The Collect at the Eucharist is the conclusion of the Introduction to the service, and thus need not be linked thematically to the Readings which follow; indeed, it may well be appropriate that a more generally seasonal prayer is used. In the Appendix (pp.372, 380-403) some guidance is given as to the suitability of Collects for those seasons when there is no provision in the ASB or the BCP.

The Collect in the Office, or at the conclusion of a period of Intercession or a Litany, or at the end of silence following a reading and psalmody in a Vigil Service has a slightly different function. Here the Collect relates more closely to whatever precedes it. If a period of silence has been included, it is often most fruitful if it is introduced by the briefest of biddings, which is then picked up in the concluding prayer.

We have not prefaced these prayers with set biddings, because this would limit their range of application. However, the careful choice of an appropriate Collect to sum up a period of prayer or reflection is almost always more effective than the cumulation of a number of Collects with possibly overlapping petitions, and little pause for reflection.

A. FOR THE SERVICE OF LIGHT

1   Father of mercy,
     continue, we pray, your loving kindness to us all.
     May we walk in the way of righteousness before you,
     loyal to your law and clinging to good deeds.
     Keep far from us all manner of shame, grief, and care;
     and grant that peace, light, and joy
     may ever abide in our home;
     for with you is the fountain of life,
     and in your light we see light.

from Jewish eve of Sabbath devotion   46†

2   God of tender compassion and mercy,
     whose Son is the morning star
       and the sun of righteousness:
     let him shine in the darkness
       and shadows of this world,
     that we may serve you in freedom and peace;
     through Jesus Christ our Lord.

3   O Lord,
     you have set before us the great hope
       that your kingdom shall come on earth,
     and have taught us to pray for its coming:
     give us grace to discern
       the signs of its dawning,
     and to work for the perfect day
     when your will shall be done on earth
       as it is in heaven;
     through Jesus Christ our Lord.

Percy Dearmer   4

† Numbers in the right-hand margin refer to Sources and Acknowledgements
(pp.416-419).

4 Kindle, O Lord, in our hearts, we pray,
the flame of that love which never ceases,
that it may burn in us and give light to others.
May we shine for ever in your temple,
set on fire with that eternal light of yours
which puts to flight the darkness of this world;
in the name of Jesus Christ your Son our Lord.

St Columba 47

5 Yours is the day, O Lord, and yours is the night.
Let Christ the Sun of Righteousness abide in our hearts
to drive away the darkness of evil thoughts:
for he is Lord for ever and ever.

Gelasian 48

6 Grant us your light, O Lord,
that the darkness of our hearts being done away,
we may be brought at the last
 to the light which is Christ.

after Bede 49

7 Eternal Light, shine into our hearts;
eternal Goodness, deliver us from evil;
eternal Power, be our support;
eternal Wisdom, scatter the darkness of our ignorance;
eternal Pity, have mercy on us;
that with all our heart and mind and strength
 we may seek your face
and be brought by your infinite mercy
 to your holy presence;
through Jesus Christ our Lord.

Alcuin of York 4

B. FOR ALL SAINTS' TIDE

8   Almighty God,
     you have knit together your elect
     into one communion and fellowship
     in the mystical body of your Son Christ our Lord.
     Give us grace so to follow your blessed saints
     in all virtuous and godly living,
     that we may come to those unspeakable joys
     which you have prepared for those who truly love you;
     through Jesus Christ our Lord.   *8*

9   Almighty and everlasting God,
     you have kindled the flame of love
         in the hearts of the saints.
     Grant to us the same faith and power of love,
     that, as we rejoice in their triumphs,
     we may be sustained by their example and fellowship;
     through Christ our Lord.   *Gothic Missal   4*

10   O God,
     the maker and redeemer of all believers:
     grant us, with all the faithful departed,
     the sure benefits of your Son's
         saving passion and glorious resurrection;
     that in the last day,
     when you gather up all things in Christ,
     we may with them enjoy the fullness of your promises;
     through Jesus Christ our Lord.   *8*

11   Grant to us, Lord God,
     to trust you not for ourselves alone,
     but for those also whom we love
     and who are hidden from us by the shadow of death;
     that, as we believe your power to have raised
         our Lord Jesus Christ from the dead,
     so we may trust your love to give eternal life
         to all who believe in him;
     through Jesus Christ our Lord.   *4*

12 Lord God, creator of all,
    you have made us creatures of this earth,
    but have also promised us a share in life eternal.
    According to your promises,
    may all who have died in the peace of Christ
    share with your saints in the joy of heaven
    where there is neither sorrow nor pain,
    but life everlasting.   4

13 O God of grace and glory,
    we remember before you today N our *brother / sister*.
    We thank you for giving *him / her* to us
    to know and to love as a companion
    in our pilgrimage on earth.
    In your boundless compassion
    console those who mourn.
    Grant us your grace that we may see in death
       the gate of everlasting life
    and continue our course on earth in faith,
    through your Son Jesus Christ our Lord,
    the Life and the Resurrection of all
       who put their trust in him.   12

14 Be present, Spirit of God, within us,
    your dwelling place and home;
    may our darkness be dispelled by your light,
    our troubles calmed by your peace,
    all evil redeemed by your love,
    all pain transformed in the suffering of Christ,
    and all dying glorified in his risen life.
                                       Jim Cotter, amended   50

15 Grant us, Lord,
    the wisdom and the grace to use aright
    the time that is left to us here on earth.
    Lead us to repent of our sins,
    the evil we have done and the good we have not done;
    and strengthen us to follow the steps of your Son,
    in the way that leads to the fullness of eternal life;
    through Jesus Christ our Lord.   8

16 Be present, Spirit of the living God,
    and renew us in our pain and grief,
    so that we, who are wearied by the changes and
        chances of this fleeting world,
    may rest on your eternal changelessness.
    We ask this through Christ our Lord.   6

17 Lord, we confess your grace which created us;
    we praise your compassion which cares for us;
    and we worship your greatness which makes us glad,
    Lord of our death and of our life.

                                    Nestorian Liturgy, adapted   52

18 Bring us, O Lord God, at our last awakening
    into the house and gate of heaven,
    to enter into that gate and dwell in that house
    where there shall be no darkness nor dazzling,
        but one equal light;
    no noise nor silence, but one equal music;
    no fears nor hopes, but one equal possession;
    no ends nor beginnings, but one equal eternity
    in the habitations of thy glory and dominion,
    world without end.

                                                John Donne   51

19 Lord Jesus our Redeemer,
    you willingly gave yourself up to death
    so that all people might be saved
    and pass from death into a new life.
    Listen to our prayers;
    look with love on your people
    who sorrow for their departed *brother / sister.*
    Lord Jesus, you alone are holy and compassionate.
    By dying you opened the gates of life
        for those who believe in you:
    do not let our *brother / sister* be parted from you,
    but by your glorious power
        give *him / her* light, joy, and peace in heaven
    where you live for ever and ever.

                                        Roman Ritual, adapted

C. FROM ALL SAINTS' TIDE TO ADVENT

20   Grant us, Lord,
      the wisdom and the grace to use aright
      the time that is left to us here on earth.
      Lead us to repent of our sins,
      the evil we have done and the good we have not done;
      and strengthen us to follow the steps of your Son,
      in the way that leads to the fullness of eternal life;
      through Jesus Christ our Lord.   *8*

21   God and Father of our Lord Jesus Christ,
      bring us to the dwelling which your Son
      is preparing for all who love you.
      Give us the will each day
      to live in life eternal.
      Let our citizenship be in heaven
      with your blessed and beloved,
      the whole company of the redeemed;
      and with countless angels,
      praising, worshipping, and adoring him
      who sits upon the throne, for ever and ever.

22   O God,
      by whose command the order of time runs its course;
      forgive our impatience, perfect our faith,
      and, while we wait for the fulfilment of your promises,
      grant us to have a good hope because of your word;
      through Jesus Christ our Lord.

Gregory Nazianzen   *4*

23   Almighty and everlasting God,
      you have put your own eternity into our hearts,
      and desires which the world cannot satisfy.
      Lift our eyes, we pray,
      above the narrow horizons of this present world,
      that we may see the things eternal in the heavens,
      where is prepared for us
         an inheritance which never fades;
      through Jesus Christ our Lord.

The Daily Service   53

24   O God, the living God,
      you have given us a living hope
      by the resurrection of Jesus Christ from the dead:
      grant that we, being risen with him,
      may fix our desires on things heavenly
      and share life eternal;
      through the same Jesus Christ our Lord.

Daily Prayer   54

25   Stir up, O Lord,
      the wills of your faithful people;
      that richly bearing the fruit of good works,
      they may be richly rewarded;
      through Jesus Christ our Lord.

8

26   Eternal Father,
      whose Son Jesus Christ ascended to the throne of heaven
      that he might rule over all things as Lord:
      keep the Church in the unity of the Spirit
      and in the bond of his peace,
      and bring the whole created order to worship at his feet;
      who is alive and reigns with you and the Holy Spirit,
      one God, now and for ever.

8

D. FOR ADVENT

27 Almighty God,
      give us grace to cast away the works of darkness
      and put on the armour of light
      now in the time of this mortal life,
      in which your Son Jesus Christ
         came to us in great humility:
      so that, on the last day,
      when he shall come again in his glorious majesty
         to judge the living and the dead,
      we may rise to the life immortal;
      through him who is alive and reigns
         with you and the Holy Spirit,
      one God, world without end.   8

28 Lord our God,
      on the first day of creation
      you made the light that scatters all darkness.
      Let Christ, the light of lights,
      hidden from all eternity,
      shine at last on your people
      and free us from the darkness of sin.
      Fill our lives with joy
      as we go out to welcome your Son at his coming.
      We ask this in the name of Jesus the Lord.

29 Merciful Father and eternal Judge,
      whose Son will come to bring to light
         things hidden in darkness
      and to reveal the secrets of all hearts:
      by your grace make us trustworthy and true servants,
      so that we may be found worthy of your praise
      on the day of Jesus Christ.

30 Be to us, Lord, a crown of glory
    on the day when you come
       to judge the world by fire;
    that in your grace and mercy
    you may clothe us now in this life
       with the robe of righteousness,
    and in the life hereafter
       with the perfection of a glorious liberty;
    for with the Father and the Holy Spirit
    you are one God, now and for ever.

Monarchic   55

31 O Christ our God,
    who will come to judge the world
    in the humanity that you have assumed:
    sanctify us wholly,
    that on the day of your coming
    our whole spirit, soul, and body
    may so rise to a fresh life in you,
    that we may live and reign with you for ever.

Mozarabic   56

32 Almighty God,
    you sent your Son to redeem the world,
    and will send him again to be our judge.
    May we so imitate him
    in the humility and purity of his first coming,
    that, when he comes again,
    we may be ready to greet him
    with joyful love and firm faith;
    through the same Christ our Lord.

4

33 Stir up your power, Lord,
    and with great might come among us;
    and, because we are sorely hindered by our sins,
    let your bountiful grace
       speedily help and deliver us;
    through Jesus Christ our Lord.

Gelasian   4

34 O Lord our God,
   make us watchful and keep us faithful
   as we await the coming of your Son our Lord;
   that, when he shall appear,
   he may find us not sleeping in sin,
   but active in his service and joyful in his praise;
   for the glory of your holy name.

Gelasian 4

35 Keep us, O Lord,
   while we tarry on this earth,
   in a serious seeking after you,
   and in an affectionate walking with you,
   every day of our lives;
   that when you come,
   we may be found not hiding our talent,
   nor serving the flesh,
   nor yet asleep with our lamp unfurnished,
   but waiting and longing for our Lord,
   our glorious God for ever.

Richard Baxter 4

36 O Lord Christ,
   before whose judgement seat we must all appear:
   keep us steadfast and faithful in your service,
   and enable us so to judge ourselves in this life,
   that we may not be condemned
       on the day of your appearing;
   for your tender mercy's sake.

William Bright 4

37 We implore you, O Lord, to come to us day by day
   and cleanse our consciences;
   so that when your Son our Lord comes in his glory
   he may find in us a place ready for his dwelling;
   through the same Jesus Christ our Lord.

Gelasian

38 Almighty God,
    as your blessed Son Jesus Christ
        first came to seek and to save the lost;
    so may he come again to find in us
        the completion of his redeeming work;
    for he is now alive and reigns
        with you and the Holy Spirit,
    God for ever and ever.

Scottish Prayer Book 1929, adapted 7

39 Eternal God,
    you have warned us
    that your Son the Bridegroom will come at midnight,
    at an hour when we are least aware.
    Let us ever hear the cry,
    'The bridegroom is coming',
    so that we may never be unprepared to meet him,
    our Lord and Saviour Jesus Christ.

Lancelot Andrewes

40 O Lord Jesus Christ,
    before whose judgement seat we must all appear,
    and give account of the things done in the body:
    grant that, when the books are opened on that day,
    we may stand with confidence through your merits,
    for you are our blessed Saviour.

41 Grant us, Lord,
    the wisdom and the grace to use aright
    the time that is left to us here on earth.
    Lead us to repent of our sins,
    the evil we have done and the good we have not done;
    and strengthen us to follow the steps of your Son,
    in the way that leads to the fullness of eternal life;
    through Jesus Christ our Lord.   8

42 Almighty and everlasting God,
    whose servant and prophet John the Baptist
    bore witness to the truth as a burning and shining lamp:
    lead us to bear witness to your Son,

who is the eternal light and truth,
and lives and reigns with you and the Holy Spirit,
now and for ever.

43   Almighty God,
who sent your servant John the Baptist
to prepare your people for the coming of your Son:
inspire the ministers and stewards of your truth
to turn our disobedient hearts to the law of love;
that when he comes again in glory,
we may stand with confidence before him as our judge;
who is alive and reigns with you and the Holy Spirit,
one God, now and for ever.   *8*

44   Almighty God,
you make us glad with the yearly remembrance
of the birth of your Son Jesus Christ.
Grant that, as we joyfully receive him for our redeemer,
we may with sure confidence behold him
when he shall come to be our judge;
who is alive and reigns with you and the Holy Spirit,
one God, now and for ever.   *8*

45   Father, you made us in your image
and your Son accepted death for our salvation.
Help us to keep watch in prayer at all times.
May we be free from all sin
when we leave this world,
and rejoice in peace with you for ever;
through Jesus Christ our Lord.   *4*

46   Come, Lord Jesus, do not delay;
give new courage to your people
who trust in your love.
By your coming, raise us
to the joy of your kingdom,
where you live and reign
with the Father and the Spirit,
one God for ever and ever.

For Collects for The Blessed Virgin Mary, see section G,
nos. 88-94.

E. FOR CHRISTMAS AND
THE NEW YEAR

47   Almighty God,
you have shed upon us
the new light of your incarnate Word,
giving us gladness in our sorrow,
your presence in our isolation.
Fill our lives with your light
until they overflow with gladness and praise;
through Christ our Lord.   *4*

48   Holy Jesus,
to deliver us from the power of darkness
you humbled yourself to be born among us
    and laid in a manger.
Let the light of your love always shine in our hearts,
and bring us at last
    to the joyful vision of your beauty;
for you are now alive and reign
    with the Father and the Holy Spirit,   *4*
God for ever and ever.   *57**

49   Father of lights,
from whom comes every good and perfect gift:
keep us in the light of Christ,
to shine in your world,
that all may believe in you
through Jesus Christ our Lord.

50   Eternal God,
who made this most holy night
to shine with the brightness of your one true light:
bring us, who have known the revelation
    of that light on earth,
to see the radiance of your heavenly glory;
through Jesus Christ our Lord.   *8*

51   All praise to you,
     Almighty God and heavenly king,
     who sent your Son into the world
     to take our nature upon him
     and to be born of a pure virgin.
     Grant that, as we are born again in him,
     so he may continually dwell in us
     and reign on earth as he reigns in heaven
     with you and the Holy Spirit,
     now and for ever.   *8*

52   To you, O Christ, Word of the Father,
     we offer our lowly praises and humble thanks.
     For love of our human race
     you most wonderfully chose to be made man,
     and to take our nature as nevermore to lay it by;
     so that we might be born again by your Spirit
     and restored in the image of God;
     to whom, one blessed Trinity,
     be given all honour, might, majesty, and power,
     now and for ever.   *32*

53   We pray you, Lord, to purify our hearts
     that they may be worthy to become your dwelling-place.
     Let us never fail to find room for you,
     but come and abide in us,
     that we also may abide in you;
     for as at this time you were born into the world for us,
     and live and reign, King of kings and Lord of lords,
     now and for ever.

                              William Temple   *33*

54   Eternal God,
     to deliver us from the power of darkness
     your Son deigned to be born in human form
     and laid in a manger.
     Let the light of your love always shine in our hearts,
     and bring us at last to the joyful vision of his beauty;
     for he is alive and reigns with you and the Holy Spirit,   *4*
     God for ever and ever.   *57**

351

55 Eternal Father,
   whose Son Jesus
   was in the fullness of his power most gentle,
   and in his greatness most humble:
   bestow his mind and spirit upon us,
   who have no cause for pride;
   that, clothed in true humility,
   we may be exalted to true greatness.
   Hear our prayer through the same Jesus,
   who is now Lord and Christ.

56 Father of mercy,
   whose Son Jesus deigned to take our nature,
   to be the sharer of our sorrows,
   the companion of our journeys,
   the light of our ignorance,
   and the remedy of our weakness:
   fill us with the grace of your Spirit,
   that, as he has been born in our likeness,
   so we may grow into his;
   through the same Jesus Christ our Lord.

57 God and Father,
   whose Son our Lord Jesus Christ was rich
   yet became poor for our sake,
   to make us rich out of his poverty:
   by your grace let our lives overflow
   in a wealth of generous service
   to you and to our neighbour;
   through the same Jesus Christ our Lord.

58 Merciful and most loving God,
   by whose will and generous gift
   Jesus Christ our Lord
   humbled himself to exalt our human race,
   took our flesh to restore in us your image,
   and was born of the Virgin to raise up the lowly:
   grant to us the inheritance of the meek,
   perfect us in your likeness,

and bring us at the end
to rejoice in the vision of your beauty,
and with all your saints to glorify your grace;
through the same Jesus Christ our Lord.

Gallican

59 Eternal God,
whose only Son shares your glory
and yet was born in human flesh of the Virgin Mary:
strengthen us in our proclaiming and witnessing,
that we may be unharmed in conflict
and come to everlasting joy;
through Jesus Christ our Lord.

after Leo

60 Heavenly Father,
whose blessed Son shared at Nazareth
    the life of an earthly home:
help us to live as the holy family,
united in love and obedience,
and bring us at last to our home in heaven;
through Jesus Christ our Lord.   8

61 Almighty God,
who wonderfully created us in your own image
and yet more wonderfully restored us
in your Son Jesus Christ:
grant that, as he came to share our human nature,
so we may be partakers in his divine glory;
who is alive and reigns with you and the Holy Spirit,
one God, now and for ever.   8

62 Almighty God,
whose blessed Son was circumcised
in obedience to the law for our sake
and given the Name that is above every name:
give us grace faithfully to bear his Name,
to worship him in the freedom of the Spirit,
and to proclaim him as the Saviour of the world,
who is alive and reigns with you and the Holy Spirit,
one God, now and for ever.   8

353

63   God and Father of our Lord Jesus Christ,
       whose years never fail,
       and whose mercies are new each returning day:
       let the radiance of your Spirit renew our lives,
       warming our hearts and giving light to our minds;
       that we may pass the coming year
       in joyful obedience and firm faith;
       through him who is the beginning and the end,
       your Son Christ our Lord.   4

Mozarabic 56

64   O God,
       by whose command the order of time runs its course:
       forgive our impatience, perfect our faith,
       and, while we wait for the fulfilment of your promises,
       grant us to have a good hope because of your word;
       through Jesus Christ our Lord.

Gregory Nazianzen 4

65   Eternal Lord God,
       we give you thanks for bringing us
          through the changes of time
       to the beginning of another year.
       Forgive us the wrong we have done
          in the year that is past,
       and help us to spend the rest of our days
       to your honour and glory;
       through Jesus Christ our Lord.

F. FOR EPIPHANY AND CANDLEMAS

66   Almighty and everlasting God,
you have revealed the incarnation of your Son
by the bright shining of a star,
which led the wise men to offer costly gifts in adoration.
Let the star of your justice give light to our hearts,
that we may give as our treasure
    all that we possess and all that we are;
through Jesus Christ our Lord.

Gelasian   4

67   Eternal God,
who by the shining of a star
led the wise men to the worship of your Son:
guide by his light the nations of the earth,
that the whole world may behold your glory;
through Jesus Christ our Lord.   8

68   Almighty God,
who anointed Jesus at his Baptism with the Holy Spirit
and revealed him as your beloved Son:
give to us who are born of water and the Spirit
the will to surrender ourselves to your service,
that we may rejoice to be called your children;
through Jesus Christ our Lord.   8*

69   Almighty God,
in Christ you make all things new.
Transform the poverty of our nature
    by the riches of your grace,
and in the renewal of our lives
make known your heavenly glory;   8
through Jesus Christ our Lord.   58

70   Grant us, Lord, who behold your glory,
        to drink from the waters of the new creation
        flowing from the river of life at your baptism.
        Give us the wings of the Spirit
        that we may hasten to meet you at your coming,
        and praise you, with the Father and the Holy Spirit,
        now and for ever.

71   Almighty God,
        who at the baptism of your blessed Son Jesus Christ
          in the river Jordan
        revealed the glory of his divine nature:
        let the light of his presence shine in our hearts,
        and his glory be shown forth in our lives;
        through the same Jesus Christ our Lord.

Scottish Prayer Book   7

72   Lord Jesus, our Master, go with us
        while we travel to the heavenly country;
        that, following your star,
        we may not wander in the darkness of this world's night,
        while you, who are our Way and Truth, and Life,
        shine within us to our journey's end;
        for your mercy's sake.   *Mozarabic* 56

73   Lord God, heavenly King,
        whose only Son is the Lamb
        born to take away the sins of the world:
        show us your mercy and goodness
        by turning us from our sins,
        that we may live in your peace
        and give you glory for ever;
        through Jesus Christ, our Saviour and Redeemer.

74   Living God,
        whose Son the Lord Christ
        came to share our mortal nature:
        grant that by the grace and power
          of your immortal Spirit

we may live on earth
  as those whose true home is in heaven,
where he is alive and reigns
  with you and the same Spirit,
one God, world without end.

75   Almighty and everlasting God,
     who drew the Gentiles to your brightness
     and made known to them the one who is our true light,
     the bright and morning star:
     fill the whole world, we pray, with your glory,
     and by the radiance of your splendour
     reveal yourself to your faithful people;
     through Jesus Christ our Lord.

76   Almighty God,
     who at the baptism of Jesus in the river Jordan
     declared him to be your eternal and beloved Son,
     your chosen one, the Messiah:
     Let your Spirit rest upon us,
     that we may serve you with justice,
     and bring light and freedom
       to those who dwell in darkness;
     through Jesus Christ our Lord.

77   Almighty God,
     in our baptism you have consecrated us
     to be temples of your Holy Spirit.
     May we, whom you have counted worthy,
     nurture your indwelling Spirit with a lively faith,
     and worship you with upright lives;
     through Jesus Christ.

78   God our Father,
     whose Son was revealed to Simeon and Anna
     as the light of the nations, and the glory of Israel:
     grant that, guided by your Holy Spirit,
     we may live by the light of faith
     until we come to the light of glory;
     through Christ our Lord.   *8**

79 O Lord, you have given us your word
for a light to shine upon our path.
Grant us so to meditate on that word,
and to follow its teaching,
that we may find in it the light
that shines more and more until the perfect day;
through Jesus Christ our Lord.   4

80 Lord God almighty,
you have given us the vision of your holiness,
and thereby of our own unworthiness to be your witnesses.
Touch, we pray, our lips with your cleansing fire;
that so cleansed and hallowed, we may go out into the world
with the authority of your commission;
for Jesus Christ's sake.   54

81 O God, who in the work of creation
commanded the light to shine out of darkness:
we pray that the light of the glorious gospel of Christ
may shine into the hearts of all your people,
dispelling the darkness of ignorance and unbelief,
and revealing to them the knowledge of your glory
    in the face of Jesus Christ our Lord.   4

82 Almighty God,
whose Son revealed in signs and miracles
the wonder of your saving love:
renew your people with your heavenly grace,
and in all our weakness sustain us by your mighty power;   8
through Jesus Christ our Lord.   58

83 God of hope,
by your Spirit you make known your truth.
Remember the many who, though created in your image,
have known neither you nor the dying of your Son,
their Saviour Jesus Christ;
and grant that by the prayers and labours of your Church
they may be delivered from ignorance and unbelief
and brought to worship you;
through him who is the resurrection and the life of all,
Jesus Christ our Lord.

84 Almighty God,
who called your Church to witness
that you were in Christ reconciling the world to yourself:
help us so to proclaim the good news of your love
that all who hear it may be reconciled to you;
through him who died for us and rose again
and reigns with you and the Holy Spirit,
one God, now and for ever.   8

85 Almighty Father,
whose Son Jesus Christ was presented in the Temple
and acclaimed the glory of Israel
and the light of the nations:
grant that in him we may be presented to you
and in the world may reflect his glory;
through Jesus Christ our Lord.   8

G. FOR SAINTS' DAYS

86 Almighty God,
     who chose your servant *N* to be an apostle,
     that he might bring those who were wandering
          in darkness and error
     to the true light and knowledge of your word:
     let us so walk in that light,
     that we may come at last
          to the light of everlasting life;
     through the merits of Jesus Christ
     your Son our Lord.

   Note: For Feasts of Martyrs, Evangelists, Witnesses, etc.
   substitute the appropriate word in line 2 and use 'he', 'she',
   or 'they' in line 3.

87 Almighty God,
     who gave such grace to your apostles
     that they readily obeyed the call of your Son:
     give us, who are called by your holy Word,
     grace to follow without delay
     and to tell the good news of your kingdom;
     through Jesus Christ our Lord.   8*

THE BLESSED VIRGIN MARY

88 Almighty and everlasting God,
     you have stooped to raise fallen humanity
     through the child-bearing of blessed Mary.
     Grant that we who have seen your glory
          revealed in our human nature,
     and your love made perfect in our weakness,
     may daily be renewed in your image,
     and conformed to the pattern of your Son,
     Jesus Christ our Lord.   4

89 Almighty and eternal God,
    who prepared the blessed Virgin Mary
    to be the mother of your Son:
    grant that, as with her we look
    for his first coming as our Saviour,
    so we may be ready to greet him
    when he comes again as our Judge;
    for he is alive and reigns
    with you and the Holy Spirit,
    one God, now and for ever.   7

                                        Franciscan   8

90 Almighty God,
    with singular grace
    you have made the blessed Virgin Mary
    to be the mother of your only Son.
    By the same grace
    hallow our bodies in chastity
    and our souls in humility and love;
    through Jesus Christ our Lord.

                          Scottish Prayer Book   7*

91 Almighty God,
    who by your grace called the blessed Virgin Mary
    and opened for all the door
    of infinite mercy and eternal light:
    fill us with your grace,
    that, through our obedience and faith,
    the world may rejoice in your mercy
    and walk in your light;
    for the sake of Jesus Christ our Lord.

92 God and Father of our Lord Jesus Christ,
    whose virgin mother was blessed in bearing him,
    but still more blessed in keeping your word:
    give the will to us,
    who honour the lifting up of her lowliness,
    to follow the example of her faith and obedience;
    through the same Jesus Christ our Lord.

                                                361

93 Heavenly Father,
    who chose the Virgin Mary, full of grace,
    to be the mother of our Lord and Saviour:
    fill us with your grace,
    that in all things we may accept your holy will
    and with her rejoice in your salvation;
    through Jesus Christ our Lord.   8

94 We beseech you, O Lord,
    to pour your grace into our hearts;
    that as we have known the incarnation
        of your Son Jesus Christ
    by the message of an angel,
    so by his cross and passion
    we may be brought to the glory of his resurrection;
    through Jesus Christ our Lord.   8

ST MARTIN 11 November

95 Lord God,
    you called Martin from among
        the armies of the world
    to be a faithful soldier of Christ.
    Give us grace to follow him
    in his love and compassion as a pastor
    and in his zeal to spread the good news;
    through Jesus Christ our Lord.

                              Franciscan Office Book 19

ST NICHOLAS 6 December

96 Almighty Father, lover of souls,
    who chose your servant Nicholas
        to be a bishop in the Church,
    that he might give freely
        out of the treasures of your grace;
    make your people mindful
        of the needs of others,
    and as they have themselves received,
    so teach them also to give;
    through Jesus Christ our Lord.

                                  Cloud of Witnesses 59

ST THOMAS OF CANTERBURY 29 December

97   Lord God,
you gave grace to your servant Thomas Becket
to put aside the fear of man
and to be faithful even to death.
Grant that we, disregarding worldly honours,
may fight all wrong, uphold your rule,
and serve you to our life's end;
through Jesus Christ our Lord.

Franciscan Office Book   19

ST BASIL OF CAESAREA, ST GREGORY OF NAZIANZUS AND ST GREGORY OF NYSSA 2 January

98   Lord God,
whose servants Basil and Gregory
proclaimed the mystery of your Word made flesh,
to build up your Church in wisdom and strength:
grant that we may rejoice in his presence among us,
and so be brought with them to know
the power of your unending love;
through Jesus Christ our Lord.

THE CONFESSION OF ST PETER 18 January

99   Almighty God,
who inspired your apostle Saint Peter
to confess Jesus as Christ and Son of the living God:
build up your Church upon this rock,
that in unity and peace
it may proclaim one truth and follow one Lord,
your Son our Saviour Jesus Christ,
who is alive and reigns with you and the Holy Spirit,
one God, now and for ever.

8

H. GENERAL

PEACE

100 God, the God of eternal peace,
    whose reward is the gift of peace,
    and whose children are the peacemakers;
    Pour your peace into our hearts
    that conflict and discord may vanish,
    and our love and desire be always for your peace;
    through Jesus Christ our Lord.   *Mozarabic*   56

101 Almighty God,
    from whom all thoughts of truth and peace proceed:
    kindle, we pray, in every heart the true love of peace;
    and guide with your pure and peaceable wisdom
    those who take counsel for the nations of the earth;
    that in tranquillity your kingdom may go forward,
    till the earth is filled with the knowledge of your love;
    through Jesus Christ our Lord.   8

102 Almighty God,
    whose will it is to restore all things
      in your beloved Son, the king of all:
    govern the hearts and minds of those in authority,
    and bring the families of the nations,
    divided and torn apart by the ravages of sin,
    to be subject to his just and gentle rule;
    who is alive and reigns with you and the Holy Spirit,
    one God, now and for ever.   8

KNOWLEDGE OF GOD

103 Living God,
    in whom is the fountain of life:
    so teach us to know you through Jesus Christ
    that we may share the power of his eternal life,
    and that our whole life may be brought
      into obedience to his holy will;
    through the same Jesus Christ our Lord.   *Eric Fenn*   60

PERSEVERANCE

104 God of compassion,
   you have willed that the gate of mercy
      should always stand open for your people.
   Look upon us with your mercy,
   that we who are following the path of your will
   may continue in it to the end of our lives;
   through Jesus Christ our Lord.

Leonine   61

VICTORY

105 Almighty God,
   in whose presence is fullness of joy,
   and whose power is made perfect in our weakness:
   grant us so to dwell in your presence,
   that we may ever be glad of heart,
   and so to rest on your strength,
   that we may have victory over evil;
   through Jesus Christ our Lord.

New Every Morning   62

FREEDOM

106 Set us free, O Lord God,
   from the bondage of sin and fear;
   that in your service we may find our freedom,
   and in your will our peace;
   through Jesus Christ our Lord.

TRUE VALUES

107 Grant us, O Lord,
   not to be taken up with earthly things,
   but to love things heavenly;
   and even now, while we live among things
      which are passing away,
   to cling to what shall abide;
   through Jesus Christ our Lord.

Leonine Sacramentary   61

UNION WITH THE SAINTS

108 O Lord,
    feed your people with your grace,
    and deliver us from the death of sin;
    that, filled with your mercy,
    we may be united with the joys of the saints;
    through Jesus Christ our Lord.

Sarum Breviary   63

UNITY

109 Eternal God and Father,
    whose Son at supper
        prayed that his disciples might be one,
    as he is one with you;
    draw us closer to him,
    that in common love and obedience to you
    we may be united to one another
    in the fellowship of the one Spirit,
    that the world may believe that he is Lord,
    to your eternal glory;
    through the same Christ our Lord.

After William Temple   33*

110 Heavenly Father,
    you have called us
        in the Body of your Son Jesus Christ
    to continue his work of reconciliation
    and reveal you to the world.
    Forgive us the sins which tear us apart;
    give us the courage to overcome our fears
    and to seek that unity
    which is your gift and your will;
    through Jesus Christ our Lord.

8

111 O God the Father of our Lord Jesus Christ,
   our only Saviour, the Prince of Peace:
   give us grace seriously to lay to heart
   the great dangers we are in
       by our unhappy divisions.
   Take away all hatred and prejudice,
   and whatever else may hinder us
       from godly union and concord:
   that, as there is but one Body, and one Spirit,
   and one hope of our calling,
   one Lord, one faith, one baptism,
   one God and Father of us all;
   so we may henceforth be all of one heart,
       and of one soul,
   united in one holy bond of peace,
       of faith and charity,
   and may with one mind and one mouth glorify you;
   through Jesus Christ our Lord.

*Accession Service   41**

DEDICATION FESTIVAL

112 Almighty God,
   to whose glory we celebrate
       the dedication of this house of prayer:
   we praise you for the many blessings
   you have given to those who worship here;
   and we pray that all who seek you in this place
       may find you
   and being filled with the Holy Spirit
   may become a living temple acceptable to you;
   through Jesus Christ our Lord.

8

APPENDIX

A SUGGESTED CALENDAR AND LECTIONARIES

PREFATORY NOTE

The Calendar and Lectionaries set out in this Appendix provide the framework within which the services and prayers are to be understood as an integral whole. Because this publication is an attempt to provide a unified approach to the whole season, some consequent adjustments to the Calendar are necessary, as well as a consistent Lectionary provision.

Such a Calendar and Lectionary are provided in this Appendix. Because they cover significant parts of the Church's year, they require full Synodical authorization.

It will be for the General Synod, in the light of experience gained by using the material in Chapters I to VIII, to decide whether to authorize such provision in addition to that of the BCP and ASB.

NOTE
The material in this Appendix does not have authorization for liturgical use in the Church of England.

AN ALTERNATIVE CALENDAR

The Last Sunday of October [1]
ALL SAINTS' DAY
Commemoration of the Faithful Departed
The First Sunday of November [1] [2]

Dedication Festival
1 November [2]
2 November
All Saints

THE SUNDAYS OF THE KINGDOM [3]

First Sunday of the Kingdom
Second Sunday of the Kingdom [4]
Third Sunday of the Kingdom

Remembrance Sunday

The Kingship of Christ

THE SUNDAYS OF ADVENT

First Sunday in Advent
Second Sunday in Advent
Third Sunday in Advent
Fourth Sunday in Advent

The Forerunner
The Blessed Virgin Mary

CHRISTMASTIDE

Christmas Eve
CHRISTMAS DAY
First Sunday after Christmas
   St Stephen the First Martyr
   St John the Evangelist
   The Holy Innocents
   Fifth Day after Christmas
   Sixth Day after Christmas
Seventh Day after Christmas
THE NAMING OF JESUS
   or The Circumcision of Christ
Second Sunday after Christmas
THE EPIPHANY OF CHRIST

24 December
25 December

26 December
27 December
28 December
St Thomas Becket

New Year's Day

6 January

THE SUNDAYS OF EPIPHANY

THE BAPTISM OF CHRIST
Second Sunday of Epiphany
Third Sunday of Epiphany
Fourth Sunday of Epiphany
THE PRESENTATION OF CHRIST [5]

First Sunday of Epiphany

2 February

NOTES

1 These Sundays are Sundays after Pentecost, and may be kept as such, in which case the proper for the Last Sunday after Pentecost in the ASB may be used on the first Sunday in November (see below).

The last Sunday in October may be kept as the Dedication Festival, unless it is kept on a known date. Or it may be kept as Reformation Sunday, as in the Lutheran tradition, with particular thanksgiving for the Bible as the Word of God; or as the Sunday in One World Week, or in the Week of Prayer for World Peace (see Note 2 on p.374, and the provision on pp.380-381). The last Sunday in October may, on occasion, be the feast of St Simon and St Jude.

2 When All Saints' Day is not kept on 1 November, it may be kept on 31 October, if a Sunday (in this case the 'Last Sunday of October' is 24 October), or on the Sunday following.

When All Saints' Day is kept on 1 November, the Sunday following may be kept as the Sunday in All Saints' Tide, using another set of propers from the provision. Alternatively, this Sunday may be the Last Sunday after Pentecost. This provision may also be used during the week following.

3 Suggested Collects for these and other Sundays are listed in the Table below, and are noted in Lectionary 1 under the appropriate Sunday or festival.

4 When Advent Sunday falls as early as 27 or 28 November, and All Saints' Day is kept on the Sunday following 1 November, there will be only two Sundays of the Kingdom. In these years, the provision for the second Sunday of the Kingdom is omitted.

5 The Presentation of Christ may be transferred to the nearest Sunday if not kept on 2 February.

A TABLE OF COLLECTS

FOR USE WITH AN ALTERNATIVE CALENDAR

INTRODUCTION TO THE LECTIONARIES

LECTIONARY 1

Lectionary 1 makes general provision for the period from the end of October until the beginning of Lent, and particular provision for both Sundays and Festivals from the third Sunday before Advent – the First Sunday of the Kingdom – until the Festival of the Presentation of Christ in the Temple, and also for each day from 17 December until the Festival of the Baptism of Christ on the First Sunday of the Epiphany.

Lectionary 1 is designed for use in conjunction with either of the currently authorized lectionaries. Once adopted it should be used continuously for the whole period, except that units from Lectionary 2 may be used from the Second Sunday of Epiphany.

Among other features it includes the three-year lectionary which is widely used in Anglican and other churches throughout the world. It aims to offer a wide freedom in the use of options so that local needs and traditions may take their place within a broad framework. This freedom is expressed in the provision of long and short versions of passages, in the permission to transpose readings, or courses of readings, from one service to another or from one year to another, and in the occasional provision for selection from a range of alternatives.

The period from the First Sunday of the Kingdom (the third Sunday before Advent) until the Second Sunday in Advent is devoted to prophetic, apocalyptic, and eschatological themes, together with a course of readings from the Books of the Maccabees reflecting, as do the psalms for Morning Prayer from 17 to 23 December, the occurrence of the Festival of Hanukkah and its Messianic associations. The period from the Third Sunday in Advent to the Presentation of Christ in the Temple is provided with material which prefigures or reflects the Incarnation, with a particular emphasis on annunciation material just before Christmas.

Greater Festivals are afforded a full provision which includes psalms and readings for the eve when they are required. Some Lesser Festivals and Commemorations are included because they relate to the main season, either by theme or coincidence of date.

This provision is an alternative to the two main options open to parishes: the Book of Common Prayer family of lectionary provisions, and the Alternative Service Book lectionary. For that reason we do not offer a canonical alternative to every apocryphal reading , but, where there is limited scope for avoiding apocryphal material, we have ensured that a canonical alternative is readily available by transfer from another service and/or another year.

NOTES TO LECTIONARY 1

1 **Versions of the Bible**

The references in the lectionary are from the Revised Standard Version of the Bible and the Psalter of the Alternative Service Book.

2 **Point of Departure**

This lectionary begins at the third Sunday before Advent, the First Sunday of the Kingdom. Those using the ASB lectionary will be left with two Sundays between the end of the previous cycle and the beginning of this. They may provide psalms and readings for these Sundays by either

(a) selecting from the ASB provision material not required after Epiphany or after Pentecost,

or

(b) observing
the Dedication of a Church (p.380)
or Reformation Sunday (p.381)
or the Sunday in One World Week (p.381)
or the Festival of St Simon and St Jude, when the Sunday falls on 28 October
or the Festival of All Saints, when the Sunday falls on 31 October.

3 **The Three-Year Lectionary**

The lectionary is presented as a three-year cycle. Year 1 begins with The First Sunday of the Kingdom, 1989 et seq. Nevertheless, pastoral consideration may require the adoption of the provision for another year.

4 **Transfer of Psalms and Readings**

Psalms and readings may be interchanged with those provided for other services on the same day, or with those set for another year, always provided that, where sequential courses are set, the whole sequence is followed.

5 Options

Where options are provided (especially those designated A B C) the groups of psalms and readings are intended to be used together. Nevertheless, pastoral need may require that such groups be broken up. One group may be used every year, or the options may be treated as a three-year cycle.

6 Adaptation of Length

On some occasions a longer or shorter form of a psalm or reading is provided. Pastoral need may require similar adaptation of other psalms and readings at the discretion of the minister.

7 Editing of Readings

Some readings are presented as a selection of verses which are designed to offer a brief and continuous piece suitable for public reading. Care should be taken in the selection of the translation to be used at the service, and in editing it. Particular attention should be given to the use of proper names, nouns, and pronouns to identify the speaker.

8 Selection of Psalms and Readings

This provision offers a wide selection together with considerable discretion for the minister. This discretion should be used within the various options. However, local circumstances and pastoral need may occasionally require the choice of other psalms and readings.

9 Invitatories

In addition to the provision in the Alternative Service Book of the Venite, Jubilate, and Easter Anthems as invitatories at Morning Prayer, Psalm 24 is appropriate during Advent and Psalm 67 during Christmastide and Epiphanytide.

10 The Gospel Canticles

It is strongly recommended that the Gospel Canticles, Benedictus and Magnificat, be used at some point during Morning and Evening Prayer during the whole season from Advent to The Presentation of Christ. If Night Prayer is not said, the Nunc Dimittis should also be given prominence after Christmas. While the Alternative Service Book locates the Gospel Canticles as a bridge between the Old and New Testament readings, an alternative tradition uses them after the New Testament reading as a Gospel climax to the service.

11 Other Canticles

In addition to the provision of additional canticles in the ASB, a
further selection is to be found in Chapter VII.

12 Apocrypha

In accordance with established custom the readings from the
Apocrypha are generally provided with a canonical alternative.
Attention should be paid to the principle of the Thirty-nine Articles
(Article 6) that the Apocrypha should not be applied to 'establish
doctrine'. On the First Sunday after Christmas, when a reading
from Ecclesiasticus 3 is provided, the minister will need to bear this
in mind as he chooses from the options and decides which
translation is to be used.

13 The First Reading at the Holy Communion

While the normal provision for readings at the Holy Communion
is:

> Old Testament
> Gradual Psalm
> New Testament
> Gospel

it is on occasion appropriate to use an additional New Testament
passage, from either the Acts of the Apostles or the Revelation to
John, in place of the Old Testament reading. While this usage is
most commonly associated with Eastertide, provision is made here
for this possibility:

> New Testament (Acts or Revelation)
> Gradual Psalm
> New Testament
> Gospel

in Alternative A on All Saints' Day, on the Conversion of Saint
Paul, and on the Confession of Saint Peter. It may also be
appropriate for the minister similarly to adapt the provision for
Saints Timothy and Titus.

14 Patronal Festivals

If no provision is made in this order, psalms and readings for the
festival of the patron saint of a church or a diocese and its eve may
be chosen at the discretion of the minister. The festival may be
transferred to the preceding or following Sunday, except a Sunday
between Advent 1 and Epiphany 1: The Baptism of Christ. In this

instance the festival may be observed by substituting the collect of the title or patron saint for that of the day, as well as by the use of appropriate hymns and references in the intercession. In Eucharistic Prayers 1, 2, and 3 the saint might be named at a suitable point.

LECTIONARY 2

In the tradition of the Church the public reading of scripture has been organized broadly on two different principles.

(a) **Thematic reading**   Passages are chosen to present a particular scriptural theme. In the synagogue and the patristic Church this principle was used for festivals, as is seen in the traditional readings of Lent and Easter, Advent, Christmas, and Epiphany. The length of the festival seasons has varied in different parts of the Church. It may be that the preferred length of a season is partly determined by social factors.

(b) **Semi-continuous reading**   Chosen books are read through on a selective basis in order to allow the major concerns of the book to be heard. In Jesus' time the Torah was read through continuously over a period of about three and a half years. Often, in the period of the early Church, books were chosen locally outside the festival seasons, and then read at successive services. Many of the biblical sermons of the early church fathers will have been preached in this way.

This lectionary option is designed to provide for the semi-continuous reading of scripture outside the high point of the period from Advent 3 to Epiphany 1. During this latter period it is more appropriate that the great scriptural themes of this season should unite the Church. The lectionary provision for this period should be taken from the ASB or from Lectionary 1.

An attempt has been made to do justice to the theological and literary balance of the particular books being read. In each case a gradual psalm and a gospel reading is provided. The traditional use of a gospel reading serves to emphasize that the primary witness of the scriptures is to Jesus Christ.

HOW TO USE LECTIONARY 2

1 This lectionary may be adopted for appropriate periods between 1 September and Advent 3 and from Epiphany 2 to the seventh Sunday before Easter. In the autumn period local factors will decide when the change from existing lectionaries should be made.

If the change to this lectionary is made after the Last Sunday after Pentecost it may be preferable to continue with the ASB provision for the Sundays after Pentecost until the change is made.

2 It is possible to transfer from this lectionary to Lectionary 1 on the seventh Sunday before Christmas (First Sunday of the Kingdom) in order to make use of the seasonal material provided there.

3 In the chosen period particular Sundays will be earmarked for locally determined special services or for celebrations such as Saints' Days, Harvest, All Saints, or Remembrance Day. Scripture readings for this latter group, and rules governing their occurrence, are to be found in the ASB and in Lectionary 1.

4 Scripture readings for the remaining Sundays in the designated period are then chosen from Lectionary 2. The lectionary of the ASB regards the Sundays before Christmas as an appropriate time to read the Old Testament. An older tradition read the Old Testament in preparation for Easter. Parishes may choose when they wish to read particular books. Care needs to be taken to retain a balance and flow through the year.

When different units are being combined, the same or similar gospel readings or psalms may recur. If this happens other suitable gospels or psalms should be chosen.

Where the chosen units do not fit the period available they may be shortened. In deciding which set of readings to omit, care should be taken to preserve the balance of the readings. For some units supplementary Sundays are indicated by [ ].

5 Many of the collects of the ASB were chosen to illustrate the theme present in the readings and will not be suitable for use in this option. Other collects should be chosen from the Prayers of Chapter VIII, from the ASB, or from the Book of Common Prayer. It should be borne in mind that the purpose of the opening collect is to gather the attention of the assembly and to prepare them for what is to follow.

If a unit is being continued into the first two Sundays in Advent a collect should be used that acknowledges that Advent has begun.

6 One or more introductory sentences are provided with each unit. Other sentences may also be used.

7 On occasion verses have been omitted in order to enable an extended story or argument to be included in one reading. It may not be helpful for the reader to begin with a detailed announcement of the verses to be read.

8 The references in the lectionary are from the Revised Standard Version of the Bible and the Psalter of the Alternative Service Book. Where different translations are used care will need to be taken and minor alterations may need to be made. Particular attention should be given to the use of proper names, nouns, and pronouns. On some occasions a longer or shorter form of a reading is provided; pastoral need may require similar adaptation of other psalms and readings at the discretion of the minister.

9 Churches may also wish to design their own reading scheme on similar principles to the units in Lectionary 2. Where they do so they should ensure that an adequate amount of scripture is chosen; that justice is done to the balance of the book and to the general teaching of scripture; and that appropriate gospel passages are chosen for the Eucharist.

10 It may be appropriate for the use of this option to be planned with members of the church.

LECTIONARY 1

Table 1
All Saints' Tide to the Presentation of Christ

Collects and Lectionary for Sundays and Major Festivals

Where not otherwise indicated, the Lectionary is arranged in columns as follows:

MORNING PRAYER	THE HOLY COMMUNION	EVENING PRAYER	NIGHT PRAYER

THE DEDICATION FESTIVAL

This festival of the anniversary of a church may be observed on any of the following days:
(a) the date of the anniversary, (b) the Sunday nearest to the anniversary, (c) the Sunday before All Saints' Day, (d) the first Sunday in October.
If the festival coincides with a Sunday between Advent 1 and the Baptism of Christ, it is transferred to a suitable weekday.

Collect 110		Ps.93,99 Jer.7.1-11 Heb.10.19-31	Ps.147 Heb.12.22-24
Ps.132 1 Chron.29.6-19 Jn.2.13-22	**A** 2 Chron.5.6-11, 13–6.2 Ps.122 Rev.21.9-14, 22-end Jn.4.19-24	Ps.48 Hag.2.1-9 Eph.2.8-end	Ps.147 Heb.12.22-24
	B 1 Kings 8.22-30 Ps.84.1-7 1 Pet.2.1-10 Matt.21.12-16		
	C Gen.28.10-17 (18-end) Ps.24 1 Cor.3.9-13, 16-17 Lk.19.1-10		

SUNDAY IN THE WEEK OF PRAYER FOR WORLD PEACE

When the last Sunday in October is kept as a Sunday in the Week of Prayer for World Peace, it is appropriate to use the prayers, psalms and readings for The Peace of the World, ASB pp.912-914.

REFORMATION SUNDAY

When it is desired to celebrate the last Sunday in October as Reformation Sunday (see Note 2) suitable provision may be made from the psalms and readings below. These may also be suitable for a Bible Sunday, which has no specific place in our provision for Advent.

Collects 80,82

Psalms	Old Testament	New Testament	Gospel
19.1-6 *or* 7-14	Deut.30.15-20	Rom.10.9-18	Matt.7.21-29
46	Isa.49.1-6	Rom.15.4-13	Lk.4.14-21
119.97-112	Isa.55.6-11	Gal.2.15–3.9	Lk.11.14-28
or 105-112	Isa.64.1-7	2 Tim.3.14–4.2	Jn.6.63-69
or 129-152			

SUNDAY IN ONE WORLD WEEK

When it is desired to keep the last Sunday in October with a particular emphasis on the fulfilment of creation, pointing forward to the goal and end of all things, then this material for the Sunday in One World Week may provide suitable readings.

Collects 81,84,101

Psalms	Old Testament	New Testament	Gospel
34,67	Gen 1.1-3,24-31a	Acts 14.8-18	Matt.5.1-16
72,82	Lev.19.9-18	Acts 17.22-31	Matt.5.38-end
85,100	Isa.2.1-5	Rom.8.18-25	Lk.10.25-37
	Isa.65.17-25	Rev.21.1-7	Lk.16.19-end

SAINTS SIMON AND JUDE

When the last Sunday in October is observed as the Festival of SS. Simon and Jude, the following provision should be used.

MORNING PRAYER	THE HOLY COMMUNION	EVENING PRAYER	NIGHT PRAYER
		Ps.119.1-16	Ps.119.97-112
		Isa.43.10-15	Eph.4.7-16
		Jn.14.15-end	
Ps.66	Isa.28.9-16	Ps.116	Ps.119.97-112
Isa.45.18-end	Ps.19.1-6	1 Macc.2.42-66	Eph.4.7-16
Rev.21.9-14	Eph.2.19-end	*or* Jer.3.11-18	
	Lk.6.12-19	Jude 1-8,17-end	

ALL SAINTS' DAY: 1 November

When this Festival falls on a Sunday it is observed on that day. When it falls on a weekday it may be transferred to a Sunday between 31 October and 7 November.

Readings for the Vigil Service are to be found in Chapter I, C.1. If the Vigil Service is not celebrated, the psalms and readings for Evening Prayer and Night Prayer are as follows:

Collect 8,(9)

Ps.113,116.1-9	Ps.91	
Ecclus.44.1-10, 13-14	Isa.56.3-8	
or Isa.43.1-7		
Heb.11.32–12.2		

The following sets of propers are for use at any time during All Saints' tide. This includes the Festival itself, the Sunday following, the days which fall between them, and 8 November (The Saints and Martyrs of England). One set should be chosen for each day. During the week following the Sunday in All Saints' Tide, the propers for the Last Sunday after Pentecost are appropriate.

MORNING PRAYER	THE HOLY COMMUNION	EVENING PRAYER	NIGHT PRAYER
	A		
Ps.33	Rev.7.2-4,9-14	Ps.97,149.1-5	Ps.116.11-end
Ecclus.44.1-10, 13-14	Ps.24.1-6	Wis.3.1-9	117
or Isa.43.1-7	1 Jn.3.1-3	*or* Isa.65.17-end	Rom.8.28-30
Lk.9.18-27	Matt.5.1-12	Rev.21.1-4,22–22.5	
	B		
Ps.34	2 Esd.2.42-end	Ps.111,112	
Jer.31.31-34	*or* Isa.66.20-23	Wis.5.1-5(6-13)14-15	
Phil.3.7-end	Ps.15	*or* Jer.31.10-14	
	Heb.12.18-24a	2 Cor.4.5-12	
	Matt.5.1-12		
	or Lk.6 20-23		
	C		
Ps.145	Ecclus.2.7-11	Ps.89.5-18	
Isa.61.4-9	*or* Isa.40.27-end	Ecclus.51.1-12	
Jn.17.(9-17) 18-23	Ps.1	*or* Jer.15.15-21	
	Rev.19.1,4-10	Eph.1.11-end	
	Matt.5.1-12		
	or Jn.15.15-21		

THE COMMEMORATION OF THE FAITHFUL DEPARTED:
2 November

This commemoration may be observed on 2 November even if that day falls on a Sunday. However, Evening Prayer of the eve is that of All Saints' Day. In any year it may be transferred to a suitable day between the observance of All Saints' Day and the following Sunday.

Collects 10,11,(12)(24)

MORNING PRAYER	THE HOLY COMMUNION	EVENING PRAYER	NIGHT PRAYER
Ps.90	Isa.25.6-9	Ps.121,130	Ps.139
Job 19.21-27a	or Lam.3.17-26,	Dan 12.1-3	Jn.14.1-6,27
2 Cor.4.16–5.10	31-33	1 Thess.4.13-end	
	Ps.27.1,4,5,9,16-end		
	or Ps.23		
	Rom.5.5-11		
	or 1 Pet.1.3-9		
	Jn.6.37-40		
	or Jn.20.1-9		
	or		
(Year 1)	Matt.11.25-end		
(Year 2)	Mk.15.33-39;		
	16.1-4		
(Year 3)	Lk.7.11-17		

FIRST SUNDAY OF THE KINGDOM : The Third Sunday before Advent

YEAR ONE	Collect 22		
Ps.37.1-22	2 Macc.7.1-2,	Ps.37.23-end	Ps.86
Isa.33.17-22	7-14,20-23	Mic.4.1-7	Isa.30.15
2 Tim.3.14–4.8	Ps.17.1-2,5-6,8,16	1 Cor.15.50-end	
	2 Thess.2.16–3.5		
	Lk.20.27-38		

YEAR TWO	Collect 33		
Ps.37.1-22	Wis.6.12-16	Ps.37.23-end	Ps.86
Isa.45.8-23	Ps.63.1-9	Zeph.3.14-end	Isa.30.15
1 Tim.6.11-16	1 Thess.4.13-end	Lk.12.35-48	
	Matt.25.1-13		

YEAR THREE	Collect 34		
Ps.37.1-22	1 Kings 17.8-16	Ps.37.23-end	Ps.86
Jer.23.1-8	Ps.146.5-end	Jer.29.1-14	Isa.30.15
or 5-8	Heb.9.24-end	Phil.3.7-end	
1 Pet.4.7-11	Mk.12.38-end	or 17-end	

REMEMBRANCE SUNDAY

Additional Psalms and Readings

The psalms and readings provided in course for the First Sunday of the Kingdom are generally appropriate to the themes of peace, suffering and the fallen, and should normally be used at the Holy Communion and Morning and Evening Prayer. Nevertheless the additional material, provided for other services, may be used where circumstances require it.

Psalms	Old Testament	New Testament	Gospel
46,47,93,130	Isa.10.33–11.9	Rom.8.31-end	Matt.5.1-12
	Isa.32.1-2,12-18	Eph.2.13-18	Jn.14.23-29
	Ezek.37.1-14	1 Tim.2.1-6	Jn.15.9-17
	Micah 4.1-7	Jas.3.13-end	Jn.16.23a-end
	Ecclus.51.1-12		

SECOND SUNDAY OF THE KINGDOM: Second Sunday before Advent

MORNING PRAYER	THE HOLY COMMUNION	EVENING PRAYER	NIGHT PRAYER
YEAR ONE	**Collect** 30		
Ps.25	Mal.4.1-2a	Ps.122,126	Ps.86
1 Macc.1.5-15,	*or* 3.16–4.2a	Amos 1.1-2;	Isa.30.15
41-43,54-57,	Ps.98.6-end	3.1-8, 13-end	
62-end	2 Thess.3.7-12	1 Cor.3.1-9a	
Rev.4	Lk.21.5-19		
YEAR TWO	**Collect** 29		
Ps.25	Prov.31.10-16,	Ps.122,126	Ps.86
Isa.51.4-11	19-20,	Dan.1.1-6,8-20	Isa.30.15
Rev.1.1-8	30-31	Lk.17.22-end	
2.1-7	Ps.128		
	1 Thess.5.1-6		
	Matt.25.14-30		
YEAR THREE	**Collect** 32		
Ps.25	Dan.12.1-3	Ps.122,126	Ps.86
Zech.2.1-5,	Ps.16.5-end	Isa.2.1-11	Isa.30.15
10-end	Heb.10.11-14	*or* 2.2-5	
Rev.19.1-16	Mk.13.24-32	Jn.8.12-20	

THIRD SUNDAY OF THE KINGDOM: The Sunday before Advent

This may be observed as the Feast of the Kingship of Christ. If it is observed in this way, psalms and readings for Evening Prayer of the eve should be used.

	Ps.110,113	Ps.29
	Isa.10.33–11.9	1 Tim.3.16
	Matt.28.16-end	

MORNING PRAYER	THE HOLY COMMUNION	EVENING PRAYER	NIGHT PRAYER
YEAR ONE	Collect 26		
Ps.146,149.1-5	2 Sam.5.1-3	Ps.72.1-8(9-end)	Ps.29
1 Macc.2.15-29	Ps.122	Amos 5.14-24	1 Tim.3.16
Rev.5 or 5.1-10	Col.1.11-20	Lk.19.29-38	
	Lk.23.35-43		
YEAR TWO	Collect 26 or 25		
Ps.146,149.1-5	Ezek.34.11-12,	Ps.72.1-8(9-end)	Ps.29
Isa.52.1-12	15-17	Dan.2.31-45	1 Tim.3.16
Rev.3.7-end	Ps.23	Matt.21.1-9	
	1 Cor.15.20-26,28		
	Matt.25.31-end		
YEAR THREE	Collect 26 or 39		
Ps.146,149.1-5	Dan.7.13-14	Ps.72.1-8(9-end)	Ps.29
Zech.6.9-end	Ps.93	Isa.4.2-6	1 Tim.3.16
Rev.20.11–22.7	Rev.1.4-8	or 4.2–5.7	
	Jn.18.33-37	Mk.11.1-10	

FIRST SUNDAY OF ADVENT

Readings for Vigil Services in Advent are to be found in Chapter I, C.2, 3, 4, 5.

YEAR ONE	Collect 27		
Ps.68.1-20	Isa.2.1-5	Ps.18.1-32	Ps.130
or 1-6	Ps.122	or 6-14	Mk.13.35-end
1 Macc.3.1-2,	Rom.13.11-end	Amos 6.1-10	
10-26	Matt.24.37-44	or 4-8	
Rev.12.1-12		1 Cor.3.9b-15	
or 1-6			
YEAR TWO	Collect 27 or 28		
Ps.68.1-20	Isa.63.16-17;	Ps.18.1-32	Ps.130
Isa.54.1-10	64.1,3-8	Dan.5.1-6,13-14,	Mk.13.35-end
or 1-5	Ps.80.1-2,	16-17,22-28	
Rev.2.8-17	14-end	Lk.20.27-40	
	1 Cor.1.3-9		
	Mk.13.33-end		
YEAR THREE	Collect 27 or 46		
Ps.68.1-20	Jer.33.14-16	Ps.18.1-32	Ps.130
Zech.8.1-8,	Ps.25.3-9,14	Isa.25.1-9	Mk.13.35-end
20-end	1 Thess.3.12–4.2	or 6-9	
Rev.21.22–22.5	Lk.21.25-28,	Jn.11.17-27	
	34-36		

385

SECOND SUNDAY OF ADVENT

MORNING PRAYER	THE HOLY COMMUNION	EVENING PRAYER	NIGHT PRAYER
YEAR ONE	**Collect** 29		
Ps.94	Isa.11.1-10	Ps.50	Ps.130
or 1-2,12-15,22	Ps.72.1-2,7-8,	*or* 1-6	Mk.13.35-end
1 Macc.4.36-37.	12-13,18-19	Amos 7.1-9	
52-59	Rom.15.4-9	(10-end)	
Rev.14.1-5 (14-end)	Matt.3.1-12	1 Cor.3.16-end	
YEAR TWO	**Collect** 30		
Ps.94	Isa.40.1-5,9-11	Ps.50	Ps.130
or 1-2,12-15,22	Ps.85	*or* 1-6	Mk.13.35-end
Isa.55.6-11	2 Pet.3.8-14	Dan.7.2-14	
Rev.2.18–3.6	Mk.1.1-8	Lk.21.25-36	
YEAR THREE	**Collect** 43		
Ps.94	Bar.5	Ps.50	Ps.130
or 1-2,12-15,22	*or* Isa.35.1-6,10	*or* 1-6	Mk.13.35-end
Zec.13.7-end;	Ps.126	Isa.26.1-6	
14.6-9	Phil.1.1,3-11	*or* 1-19	
Rev.22.12-13,	Lk.3.1-6	Jn.16.1-11	
16-17,20			

THIRD SUNDAY OF ADVENT

YEAR ONE	**Collect** 42		
Ps.11,14	Isa.35.1-6,10	Ps.80	Ps.130
Jer.1.4-10	Ps.146.5-end	Amos 8.1-6,9-12	Mk.13.35-end
Lk.1.1-25	Jas.5.7-10	1 Cor.4.1-5	
or 5-17	Matt.11.2-11		
YEAR TWO	**Collect** 41		
Ps.11,14	Isa.61.1-2a,	Ps.80	Ps.130
Isa.49.1-13	10-end		
or 1-6	Magnificat	Dan.7.15-27	Mk.13.35-end
Lk.1.1-25	1 Thess.5.16-24	1 Pet.1.3-12	
or 5-17	Jn.1.6-8,19-28	*or* 8-12	
YEAR THREE	**Collect** 35,(37)		
Ps.11,14	Zeph.3.14-18	Ps.80	Ps.130
Mal.3.1-5; 4	Song of Isaiah	Isa.32.1-8	Mk.13.35-end
Lk.1.1-25	(Isa.12.2-end)	Jude 1-4,17-end	
or 5-17	Phil.4.4-7		
	Lk.3.10-18		

FOURTH SUNDAY OF ADVENT

MORNING PRAYER	THE HOLY COMMUNION	EVENING PRAYER	NIGHT PRAYER
YEAR ONE	**Collect** 89		
Ps.40	Isa.7.10-14	Ps.89.1-4,19-38	Ps.130
Isa.42.1-12	Ps.24	2 Sam.7.1-5,	Mk.13.35-end
Heb.10.1-10	Rom.1.1-7	8-14a,16	
	Matt.1.18-end	Lk.1.26-38	
YEAR TWO	**Collect** 90		
Ps.45	2 Sam.7.1-5,	Ps.86	Ps.130
Gen.3.8-15	8-14a,16	Mic.5.1-4	Mk.13.35-end
Rom.1.1-7	Ps.89.1-4,27-29	Lk.1.39-45	
	Rom.16.25-end		
	Lk.1.26-38		

At Evening Prayer the Magnificat must follow the second reading.

YEAR THREE	**Collect** 92		
Ps.146	Mic.5.1-4	Ps.24	Ps.130
Isa.11.1-9	Ps.80.1,14-end	Isa.7.10-14	Mk.13.35-end
Rom.16.25-end	Heb.10.1-10	Matt.1.18-end	
	Lk.1.39-45		

17 DECEMBER

Ps.111,112	Gen.49.2,8-10	Ps.120,121	Ps.139.1-18,
Gen.3.8-15	Ps.72.1-5,20-end	Isa.45.2-8	23-end
Jn.3.16-21	Matt.1.1-17	Heb.10.23-end	Rev.1.1-8

18 DECEMBER

Ps.113,114	Jer.23.5-8	Ps.122,123,124	Ps.139.1-18,
Jer.29.10b-14	Ps.72.1,6-8,	Isa.51.1-11	23-end
Jn.3.22-end	20-end	2 Pet.3.8-13	Rev.21.1-7
	Matt.1.18-24		

19 DECEMBER

Ps.115	Judg.13.2-7,	Ps.125,126	Ps.139.1-18,
Jer.30.18-22	24-end	Isa.52.1-12	23-end
Jn.4.19-26	Ps.71.3-8	Jude	Rev.21.9-10,
	Lk.1.5-25	*or* 1-6,17-end	22-end

20 DECEMBER

Ps.116,117	Isa.7.10-14	Ps.127,128	Ps.139.1-18,
Jer.33.11-16	Ps.24	Isa.54.1-13	23-end
Jn.5.24-37a	Lk.1.26-38	1 Cor.1.3-9	Rev.22.1-5

21 DECEMBER

MORNING PRAYER	THE HOLY COMMUNION	EVENING PRAYER	NIGHT PRAYER
Ps.118	S of S 2.8-14	Ps.129,130	Ps.139.1-18,
S of S 2.8-14	or Zeph.3.14-18	Isa.55	23-end
or Zeph.3.14-18	Ps.33.1-4,11-12,	Jas.5.7-9	Rev.22.6-11
Jn.6.1-14	19-end		
	Lk.1.39-45		

22 DECEMBER

Ps.135	1 Sam.1.24-end	Ps.132	Ps.139.1-18,
Sam.1.1-20	Song of Hannah	Isa.56.1-8	23-end
Jn.6.35-51	(1 Sam.2.1-10)	Phil.1.3-11	Rev.22.12-17
	or Ps.113		
	Lk.1.46-56		

23 DECEMBER

Ps.145	Mal.3.1-4;	Ps.131,133,134	Ps.139.1-18,
Dan.9.17-19	4.5-end	Isa.58.1-12	23-end
Jn.7.37-43	Ps.25.3-10	Phil.4.4-8	Rev.22.18-end
	Lk.1.57-66		

CHRISTMAS EVE

YEAR ONE

Ps.89.5-18	2 Sam.7.1-5,
Isa.32.1-8	8-14a,16
Rom.16.25-end	Ps.89.1-4,27-29
	Lk.1.67-end

YEAR TWO

Ps.89.5-18	2 Sam.7.1-5,
Isa.32.1-8	8-14a,16
Heb.10.1-10	Ps.89.1-4,27-29
	Lk.1.67-end

YEAR THREE

Ps.89.5-18	2 Sam.7.1-5,
Isa.32.1-8	8-14a,16
Rom.1.1-7	Ps.89.1-4,27-29
	Lk.1.67-end

CHRISTMAS DAY: 25 December

Readings for the Vigil Service are to be found in Chapter I, C.6, 7, 8, and 9.
Night Prayer is not said if the Midnight Eucharist is celebrated.

MORNING PRAYER	THE HOLY COMMUNION	EVENING PRAYER	NIGHT PRAYER

	Vigil Eucharist
	Isa.62.1-5
	Ps.89.1-4,27-29
	Acts 13.16-17,
	      22-25
	Matt.1.18-end
		Ps.89.1-4,19-30
		Isa.62.1-5
		Acts 13.16-17,
		      22-25
		or Matt.1.18-end
			Ps.85
			or 123,131
			Wis.18.14
			or a reading from the midnight provision

		If there is a Vigil Eucharist: Ps.85 Isa.61.10-end Phil.2.5-11	

The following psalms and readings provided for the Holy Communion may be interchanged according to pastoral need.

Collect 50	*Midnight Eucharist* Isa.9.2-7 Ps.96.1-3,11-end Titus 2.11-14 Lk.2.1-14		
Collect 51 Ps.19 Zech.2.10-end 1 Jn.4.7-16 or if there is no early morning Eucharist, a selection from that provision	*Early Morning Eucharist* Isa.62.11-end Ps.97.1,6,11-12 Titus 3.4-7 Lk.2.15-20		
Collect 51	*Daytime Eucharist* Isa.52.7-10 Ps.98.1-7 Heb.1.1-6 Jn.1.1-14(15-18) *or* 1.1-5,9-14	Ps.8,110 Isa.65.17-end 1 Jn.1.1-9	Ps.85 Wis.18.14 *or* 2 Cor.8.9

The week after Christmas Day is first and foremost a celebration of the Incarnation of our Lord. These festivals, which are provided with psalms and readings which reflect the season, may be observed on their days when they fall on the First Sunday after Christmas, or they may be transferred to the next available weekday. Evening Prayer of the eve is that of the preceding day. Evening Prayer of the day may be of the festival, or of Christmas.

SAINT STEPHEN, MARTYR: 26 December

MORNING PRAYER	THE HOLY COMMUNION	EVENING PRAYER	NIGHT PRAYER
Ps.13,57	2 Chron.24.20-22	Ps.119.17-24;	Ps.85
Jer.26.1-9,12-15	Ps.31.3-6,17-18	161-168	Wis.18.14
Acts 6.1-7	Acts 6.8-10;	Wis.4.7-15	or 2 Cor.8.9
	7.54-end	or Gen.4.1-10	
	Matt. 10.17-22	Matt.23.34-end	
		or	
		Ps.19	
		Isa.41.1-5	
		Jn.12.20-26	

SAINT JOHN, APOSTLE AND EVANGELIST: 27 December

Ps.92	Exod.33.18-end	Ps.21	Ps.85
Ex.33.7-11a	Ps.97.1-2,5-6,	Isa.6.1-8	Wis.18.14
Jn.13.21-35	11-12	1 Jn.5.1-12	or 2 Cor.8.9
	1 Jn.1.1-4	or	
	Jn.20.2-8	Ps.45	
		Isa.41.8-16	
		Jn.12.27-33	

THE HOLY INNOCENTS: 28 December

Ps.36	Jer.31.15-17	Ps.123,126	Ps.85
Bar.4.21-27	Ps.124	Isa.49.14-25	Wis.18.14
or Isa.54.1-13	1 Jn.1.5–2.2	Matt.18.1-14	or 2 Cor.8.9
1 Pet.4.12-end	Matt.2.13-18	or	
		Ps.132	
		Isa.41.17-20	
		Jn.12.34-37	

29 DECEMBER

Ps.146	1 Jn.2.3-11	Ps.96,97	Ps.85
Mic.2.12-13	Ps.96.1-4	Isa.7.10-14	Wis.18.14
Gal.4.1-7	Lk.2.22-35	Jn.12.37-43	or 2 Cor.8.9

30 DECEMBER

MORNING PRAYER	THE HOLY COMMUNION	EVENING PRAYER	NIGHT PRAYER
Ps.147	1 Jn.2.12-17	Ps.98,99	Ps.85
Mic.4.1-5	Ps.96.7-10	Isa.10.33–11.10, 12	Wis.18.14
2 Cor.8.7-9	Lk.2.36-40	Jn.12.44-end	or 2 Cor.8.9

31 DECEMBER

Ps.149,150	1 Jn.2.18-21
Mic.5.2-5a	Ps.96.1,11-end
Eph.3.14-end	Jn.1.1-18

FIRST SUNDAY AFTER CHRISTMAS
The Holy Family

The psalms and readings not required on Christmas Day may be used. When the Naming of Jesus falls on the following day, Evening Prayer is either of the eve of the festival, or from the provision for New Year.

The Festival of the Holy Family may be observed on the Sunday after Christmas. When the Naming of Jesus is observed on that day, this festival, with the psalms and readings of Christmas 1, may be observed on 30 December. When this day is the Feast of Title, readings for the eve may be chosen from those not required on the day.

YEAR ONE	Collect 54 or 60		
Ps.132	Ecclus.3.2-6, 12-14	Ps.84,122	Ps.85
Isa.35	or Prov.4.1-6	Isa.41.21-end	Wis.18.14
Col.1.1-20	Ps.128	Phil.2.1-11	or 2 Cor.8.9
or Lk.2.41-end	Col.3.12-21	or Lk.2.22-40	
	Matt.2.13-15, 19-end		

YEAR TWO	Collect 54 or 60		
Ps.132	Ecclus.3.2-6, 12-14	Ps.84,122	Ps.85
Isa.35	or Prov.4.1-6	Isa.41.21-end	Wis.18.14
Col.1.1-20	Ps.128	Phil.2.1-11	or 2 Cor.8.9
or Matt.2.12-15, 19-end	Col.2.12-21 or Gen.15.1-6; 21.1-3	or Lk.2.41-end	
	Ps.105.1-9		
	Heb.11.8,11-12, 17-19		
	Lk.2.22-40		

391

MORNING PRAYER	THE HOLY COMMUNION	EVENING PRAYER	NIGHT PRAYER
YEAR THREE	**Collect** 54 *or* 60		
Ps.132	Ecclus.3.2-6,	Ps.84,122	Ps.85
Isa.35	12-14	Isa.41.21-end	Wis.18.14
Col.1.1-20	*or* Prov.4.1-6	Phil.2.1-11	*or* 2 Cor.8.9
or Lk.2.22-40	Ps.128	*or* Matt.2.12-15,	
	Col.3.12-21	19-end	
	or 1 Sam.1.20-22,		
	24-end		
	Ps.84.1-4,9-12		
	1 Jn.3.1-2,21-end		
	Lk.2.41-end		

The psalms and readings not required on Christmas Day may be used.

THE NAMING OF JESUS: 1 January

When this festival falls on the First Sunday after Christmas, it is observed on that day, and the Sunday is omitted.

Collect 63		Ps.103	Ps.62 *or* 90
		Gen.17.1-12a,	Jn.16.23b-27
		15-16	*or* Lk.21.25-36
		Col.2.8-15	
		or	
		Ps.90	
		Isa.65.15b-25	
		Rev.21.1-6a	
Ps.148	Num.6.22-end	Ps.115	Ps.87
Isa.9.2-7	Ps.67	Jer.23.1-6	Mal.1.11
Acts 3.1-16	Gal.4.4-7	Acts 4.8-12	
	Lk.2.16-21		

NEW YEAR

Additional Psalms and Readings

The psalms and readings provided may be used at special services to mark the New Year. While it is not normally appropriate to substitute them for the psalms and readings provided for the Holy Communion, and for Morning and Evening Prayer, on 1 January or on either Sunday after Christmas, they are suitable for use at Evening and Night Prayer on 31 December.

Readings for the Vigil Service are to be found in Chapter I, C.10.

Collects 63,64,65

Psalms	Old Testament	New Testament	Gospel
Ps.49.1-16, 62,	Gen.1.14-18	1 Cor.7.29-31	Matt.25.31-end
90.1-12(13-end)	Ex.34.1-10	Col.2.1-7	Mk.6.31-34
	Deut.30.1-14	James 4.13-15	Lk.12.35-40
	(15-end)	Rev.21.1-6a	Lk.21.25-36
	Eccles.3.1-13		
	Isa.65.15b-25		

SECOND SUNDAY AFTER CHRISTMAS

When Saint Stephen, Saint John, the Holy Innocents, or the Naming of Jesus is observed on the First Sunday after Christmas, the psalms and readings displaced may be used on the Second Sunday.

Collects 47,61

MORNING PRAYER	THE HOLY COMMUNION	EVENING PRAYER	NIGHT PRAYER
Ps.19	Ecclus.24.1-4,	Ps.85,87	Ps.87
Isa.46.3-end	12-16	Isa.12	Mal.1.11
Rom.15.8-21	*or* Isa.62.11-12	1 Jn.4.7-end	
	Ps.147.12-end		
	Eph.1.2-6,15-18		
	Jn.1.1-18		
	or Jn.1.1-5,9-14		

2 JANUARY

Ps.33	1 Jn.2.22-28	Ps.66	Ps.87
Isa.42.1-9	Ps.98.1-4	Isa.43.1-13	Mal.1.11
Eph.1.1-14	Jn.1.19-28	Matt.11.2-6	

3 JANUARY

Ps.45	1 Jn.2.29–3.6	Ps.46	Ps.87
Isa.42.11-17	Ps.98.1-7	Isa.44.1-8	Mal.1.11
Eph.1.15-end	Jn.1.29-34	Mk.3.31-end	

4 JANUARY

Ps.89.5-18	1 Jn.3.7-10	Ps.89.1-4,19-38	Ps.87
Isa.42.18-end	Ps.97.1,8-end	Isa.49.14-end	Mal.1.11
Eph.2.1-10	Jn.1.35-42	Lk.10.21-24	

5 JANUARY

Ps.132	1 Jn.3.11-21
Isa.33.17-end	Ps.100
Eph.2.11-end	Jn.1.43-end

THE EPIPHANY OF CHRIST: 6 January

Readings for the Vigil Service are to be found in Chapter I, C.11. If the Vigil Service is not celebrated, the psalms and readings for Evening Prayer and Night Prayer are as follows:

Collect 67

		Ps.98,113	Ps.138
		Bar.4.36–5-end	1 Tim.3.16
		or Isa.41.8-20	
		Rev.21.22–22.5	
Ps.2,110	Isa.60.1-6	Ps.96,97	Ps.138
Isa.49.1-6	Ps.72.1-2,7-13	Isa.49.7-13	1 Tim.3.16
John 1.29-34	Eph.3.2-3a,5-6	John 2. 1-11	
	Matt.2.1-12		

The following provision is used until the Baptism of Christ (Epiphany 1) only.

7 JANUARY

Ps.111,112	1 Jn.3.22–4.6	Ps.145	Ps.138
Isa.60.8-end	Ps.2.6-end	Isa.64	1 Tim.3.16
Eph.4.1-16.	Matt.4.12-17, 23-end	Col.1.1-14	

8 JANUARY

Ps.113,114	1 Jn.4.7-10	Ps.146	Ps.138
Isa.61.1-9	Ps.72.1-8	Isa.65.8-16	1 Tim.3.16
Eph.4.17-end	Mk.6.34-44	Col.1.15–2.7	

9 JANUARY

Ps.115	1 Jn.4.11-18	Ps.147	Ps.138
Isa.61.10–62.5	Ps.72.1,10-13	Isa.65.17-end	1 Tim.3.16
Eph.5.1-14	Mk.6.45-52	Col.2.8-end	

10 JANUARY

Ps.116,117	1 Jn.4.19–5.4	Ps.148	Ps.138
Isa.62.6-end	Ps.72.1,18-end	Isa.66.1-2,5-16	1 Tim.3.16
Eph.5.15-end	Lk.4.14-22	Col.3	

11 JANUARY

Ps.118	1 Jn.5.5-13	Ps.149,150	Ps.138
Isa.63.1-6	Ps.147.12-end	Isa.66.18-22	1 Tim.3.16
Eph.6.1-9	Lk.5.12-16	Col.4	

12 JANUARY

Ps.135	1 Jn.5.14-end
Isa.63.7-end	Ps.149.1-5
Eph.6.10-end	Jn.3.22-30

THE BAPTISM OF CHRIST: First Sunday of Epiphany

This festival is observed on the First Sunday of Epiphany; but if the Epiphany itself is celebrated on that day for pastoral reasons, the Feast of the Baptism of Christ may be observed on the Second Sunday of Epiphany.

Readings for the Vigil Service are to be found in Chapter I, C.12. If the Vigil Service is not celebrated, the psalms and readings for Evening Prayer and Night Prayer are as follows:

		Ps.36	Ps.30
		Josh.3	2 Cor.4.3-6
		Gal.3.23-end; 4.4-7	
YEAR ONE	Collect 68		
Ps.89.1-4,19-38	Isa.42.1-4,6-7	Ps.89.5-18	Ps.30
1 Sam.16.1-13a	Ps.29	Isa.61	2 Cor.4.3-6
Eph.2.1-10	Acts 10.34-38	Lk.3.15-22	
	Matt.3.13-17		
YEAR TWO	Collect 68 or 71		
Ps.89.1-4,19-38	Isa.42.1-4,6-7	Ps.89.5-18	Ps.30
1 Sam.16.1-13a	Ps.29	Isa.61	2 Cor.4.3-6
Eph.2.1-10	Acts 10.34-38	Matt.3.1-17	
	Mk.1.7-11		
YEAR THREE	Collect 68 or 76		
Ps.89.1-4,19-38	Isa.42.1-4,6-7	Ps.89.5-18	Ps.30
1 Sam.16.1-13a	Ps.29	Isa.61	2 Cor.4.3-6
Eph.2.1-10	Acts.10.34-38	Mk.1.1-11	
	Lk.3.15-16,21-22		

SECOND SUNDAY OF EPIPHANY

YEAR ONE	Collect 73		
Ps.15,16	Isa.49.3,5-6	Ps.46,47	Ps.4
Eccles.1.2-11	Ps.40.1-3,8-11	Ruth 1	1 Pet.5.6-7
John 3.1-15	1 Cor.1.1-9	or 1.1-7,	
or 2.1-12	Jn.1.29-34	14-18,22	
		2 John	
		or 2 Jn.4-9	
YEAR TWO	Collect 67		
Ps.15,16	1 Sam.3.3-10,19	Ps.46,47	Ps.4
Prov.3.27-34	Ps.40.1-3,8-11	Wis.1 or 1.1-7	1 Pet.5.6-7
Jn.6.30-40	1 Cor.6.13-15,	Titus 1.1-9	
or 2.1-12	17-20		
	Jn.1.35-42		

MORNING PRAYER	THE HOLY COMMUNION	EVENING PRAYER	NIGHT PRAYER
YEAR THREE	**Collect 69**		
Ps.15,16	Isa.62.1-5	Ps.46,47	Ps.4
Mic.2	Ps.96.1-3,7-10	1 Sam.1.1-20	1 Pet.5.6-7
or 2.1-5	1 Cor.12.4-11	2 Tim.1.1-3,6-12	
Jn.8.1-20	John.2.1-12		
or 8.12-20			

THIRD SUNDAY OF EPIPHANY

YEAR ONE	**Collect 75**		
Ps.33	Isa.8.23–9.3	Ps.135	Ps.4
Eccles.3.1-11	Ps.27.1-5,16-end	Ruth 2.1-3,8-11;	1 Pet.5.6-7
John 3.16-21	1 Cor.1.10-13,17	4.13-17	
	Matt.4.12-23	3 John *or*	
	or 12-17	3 Jn.5-8	
YEAR TWO	**Collect 80**		
Ps.33	Jonah 3.1-5,10	Ps.135	Ps.4
Prov.21.1-6,	Ps.25.1-9	Wis.6.1-21	1 Pet.5.6-7
10-13	1 Cor.7.29-31	*or* 1-11	
Jn.6.44-51	Mk.1.14-20	Titus 2.1-8,11-14	
YEAR THREE	**Collect 81**		
Ps.33	Neh.8.2-6,8-10	Ps.135	Ps.4
Mic.6.1-4,6-8	Ps.19.7-end	1 Sam.1.21–2.11	1 Pet.5.6-7
John 8.21-30	1 Cor.12.12-30	2 Tim 2.8-15	
	or 12-14,17		
	Lk.1.1-4;4.14-21		

FOURTH SUNDAY OF EPIPHANY

YEAR ONE	**Collect 82**		
Ps.34	Zeph.2.3;3.12-13	Ps.42,43	Ps.4
Eccles.11.9–12end	Ps.146.5-end	Hab.1.12–2.4	1 Pet.5.6-7
Jn.3.25-end	1 Cor.1.26-end	Philemon	
or 31-end	Matt.5.1-12	*or* 1-16	
YEAR TWO	**Collect 77**		
Ps.34	Deut.18.15-20	Ps.42,43	Ps.4
Prov.30.5-9	Ps.95.1-9	Wis.7.15–8.1	1 Pet.5.6-7
Jn.6.52-59	1 Cor.7.32-35	*or* 7.22–8.1	
	Mk.1.21-28	Titus 3.1-11	
		or 1-7	

MORNING PRAYER	THE HOLY COMMUNION	EVENING PRAYER	NIGHT PRAYER
YEAR THREE	**Collect 84**		
Ps.34	Jer.1.4-5,	Ps.42,43	Ps.4
Mic.7.14-15	17-19	1 Sam.3	1 Pet.5.6-7
or 14-end	Ps.71.1-6,	2 Tim.3.10–4.8	
Jn.8.31-42	17-19		
	1 Cor.12.31–		
	13 end		
	or 13.4-end		
	Lk.4.21-30		

THE PRESENTATION OF CHRIST: 2 February

This festival, traditionally a bridge between Epiphanytide and Passiontide, is rich in potential to become a major observance. It is a most appropriate occasion for the celebration of the Feast of Title of a church dedicated to Our Lord (Christ Church or Christ the Saviour, for example). It may be transferred to, or include, the preceding or following Sunday. It always has Evening Prayer of the eve, and is given a wide selection of readings, including a vigil. Sundays after the Presentation should be designated Sundays before Easter.

Readings for the Vigil Service are to be found in Chapter I, C.15. If the Vigil Service is not celebrated, the psalms and readings for Evening Prayer and Night Prayer are as follows:

		Ps.40	Ps.113
		Ex.12.51-end;	Rom.12.1-8
		13.1-2,11-16	
		Heb.10.1-10	

Collect 85 *or* 78

A

Ps.118	Mal.3.1-5	Ps.48	Ps.42,43
Ezek.43.27–44.4	Ps.24.7-end	Prov.9.1-11	Jn.8.31-36
Heb.7.7-17	Heb.2.14-end	Heb.2.14-end	
	or 4.11-13	*or* 4.11-end	
	Lk.2.22-40		

B

Ps.48	Ezek.43.27–44.4	Ps.24	Ps.84
Prov.9.1-11	Ps.118.19-26	Mal.3.1-5;	Rom.8.14-21
Heb.2.14-end	Heb.7.7-17	4.1-3	
or 4.11-end	Lk.2.22-40	Heb.2.14-end	
		or 4.11-end	

MORNING PRAYER	THE HOLY COMMUNION	EVENING PRAYER	NIGHT PRAYER
C			
Ps.24 *or* 87,110	Prov.9.1-11	Ps.118	Ps.147.12-end
Mal.3.1-5;	*or* 9.1-6	Ezek.43.27–44.4	1 Jn.3.1-8
4.1-3	Ps.48.9-end	Heb.7.7-17	
Heb.2.14-end	Heb.2.14-end		
or 4.11-end	*or* 4.11-end		
	Lk.2.22-40		

When the festival is transferred to a Sunday, the psalms and readings not required may be used on 2 February.

When the festival is observed on 2 February, the provision below may be used on the Sunday following, provided that the Ninth Sunday before Easter (Septuagesima) has not been reached.

Ps.42,43	1 Sam.1.20-end	Ps.84	Ps.46,87
Jer.7.1-11	Ps.122	Hag.2.1-9	Rom.8.14-21
Jn.8.31-36	Gal.4.4-7	Jn.4.9-26	
	Lk.2.41-end	*or* 1 Jn.3.1-8	
	or Jn.2.13-22		

LECTIONARY 1
Table 2
Festivals and Commemorations

SAINTS AND MARTYRS OF ENGLAND: 8 November

This festival is not observed on a Sunday. A selection of psalms and readings is provided for the Holy Communion. Psalms and readings for Morning and Evening Prayer may be drawn from that provision, or from those not required on All Saints' Day.

Collect ASB p.837

Ecclus.44.1-15
or Isa.61.4-9
Ps.1,15,34,
or 89.1-8(-18)
2 Cor.4.5-15
or Rev.19.6-10
Lk.6.17-23
or Jn.17.18-23

Provision for Morning and Evening Prayer may be made from this selection, or from that for All Saints' Day.

SAINT MARTIN, BISHOP: 11 November

This festival is not observed on a Sunday. If it is the patronal festival of a church, it is transferred to the preceding Saturday or to the first suitable day following. The psalms and readings provided reflect both the coincidence of this festival with one of the traditional dates for beginning Advent, and the arrangement of this lectionary for a change of direction on the First Sunday of the Kingdom. The psalms and readings provided for the Holy Communion may be used at the discretion of the minister, but the additional psalms and readings are only to be used at Morning and Evening Prayer if this is the Patronal Festival of the church.

Collect 95

Isa.61.1-3a
Ps.89.1-4,21-22,27-28
1 Thess.5.1-11
Matt.25.34-end

Additional Psalms and Readings

Psalms	*Old Testament*	*New Testament*	*Gospel*
1,15,27,99,112	Isa.58.6-12	Acts 20.28-35	Matt.24.42-46
	Ezek.34.11-16	2 Cor.4.1-10	Lk.11.33-36
	Mal.2.5-7	Phil.4.4-9	
		1 Pet.5.1-4	

DAY OF PRAYER FOR MISSION: 29 November

Psalms and readings are provided for the Holy Communion only. A selection from that provision may be used at Morning or Evening Prayer if special services are held.

Collect ASB p.907

> Isa.49.1-6
> *or* Isa.61.1-3 (4-end)
> Ps.100
> *or* Ps.117
> Acts 16.6-15
> *or* Eph.2.13-end
> Matt.28.16-end
> *or* Jn.4.31-38

SAINT ANDREW, APOSTLE AND MARTYR: 30 November

This festival is not observed on a Sunday. If it is the patronal festival of a church, it is transferred to the preceding Saturday or to the first suitable day following. The psalm and readings for Evening Prayer of the eve are only used when this day is the patronal festival, or for a service of prayer for Mission.

MORNING PRAYER	THE HOLY COMMUNION	EVENING PRAYER	NIGHT PRAYER
Collect ASB p.815		Ps.92	Ps.139.1-18
		Deut.30.11-14	Acts 5.12-14
		or Ecclus.14.	*or* of Advent
		20-end	
		1 Cor.4.9-16	
Ps.96,98	Zech.8.20-end	Ps.47,48	Ps.139.1-18
Isa.49.1-9a	Ps.19.1-6	Ezek.47.1-12	Acts 5.12-14
Jn.1.35-42	*or* Ps.87	Jn.12.20-32	*or* of Advent
	Rom.10.9-18		
	Matt.4.18-22		

SAINT NICHOLAS, BISHOP: 6 December

This festival is not observed on a Sunday. If it is the patronal festival of a church, it is transferred to the preceding Saturday or to the first suitable day following. Psalms and readings are provided for the Holy Communion and special services which are connected with this commemoration. They are only used at Morning and Evening Prayer if this day is the patronal festival.

MORNING PRAYER	THE HOLY COMMUNION	EVENING PRAYER	NIGHT PRAYER

Collect 96

Psalms	Old Testament	New Testament	Gospel
1,15,23,40,96,99,	Isa.6.1-8	1 Cor.4.1-6	Matt.24.42-44
107.23-30, 110	Isa.52.7-10	1 Tim.4.1-5	Matt.25.14-30
	Isa.61.1-3	1 Tim.6.6-11	Mk.10.13-16
	Ezek.34.11-16	1 Pet.5.1-4	Lk.10.1-9
	Mal.2.5-9		

THE CONCEPTION OF THE BLESSED VIRGIN MARY: 8 December

This festival, appointed in the BCP, is not observed on a Sunday. Psalms and readings are recommended for the Holy Communion. Psalms and readings for Morning and Evening Prayer may be chosen from the additional provision. The whole provision is appropriate to the season of Advent.

Collect 89   Gen.3.9-15,20
                     Ps.98.1-5
                     Eph.1.3-6,11-12
                     Lk.1.26-38

Additional Psalms and Readings

Psalms	Old Testament	New Testament	Gospel
46,85,87,113,122	Prov.8.22-31	Rom.5.12-19	Matt.1.18-end
127,147.12-end	Isa.61.10–62.5	Rom.8.28-30	
	Zeph.3.14-17	1 Cor.1.26-30	
	Ecclus.24.17-22	Rev.11.19–12.6,10	

ADVENT ORDINATION AND EMBER DAYS

Jer.1.4-10 *or* Isa.45.1-8
Ps.80.14-end *or* 84.8-end
1 Pet.4.7-11 *or* 1 Cor.4.1-5
Lk.3.1-6,15-17 *or* Lk.12.35-43

SAINT THOMAS BECKET, BISHOP AND MARTYR: 29 December

The psalms and readings provided for the Holy Communion may be used at the discretion of the minister. When this day is observed as a patronal festival, the psalms and readings for Morning and Evening Prayer may also be used.

Collect 97

Ps.2,110	Jer.3.15-17	93,97
Ecclus.51.1-8	Ps.23	Isa.52.1-12
or	Col.1.24-29	Matt.10.28-33
Ezek.34.11-16	Lk.22.24-30	
Jn.10.1-16		
or 10.11-16		

THE CONFESSION OF ST PETER: 18 January

This festival, which begins the Week of Prayer for Christian Unity, is not observed on a Sunday. It is observed in the Episcopal (Anglican) Church of the U.S.A. as a celebration parallel to that of the Conversion of Saint Paul. The two apostles thus begin and close the week. A psalm and readings are provided for the Holy Communion. Psalms and readings for Morning and Evening Prayer may be chosen from the additional provision.

Collect 99	Ezek.3.4-11
	or Acts 4.8-13
	Ps.23
	1 Pet.5.1-4
	Matt.16.13-19

Additional Psalms and Readings

Psalms	Old Testament	New Testament	Gospel
30,34,71,145	Ezek.2.1-7	Acts 9.36-end	Matt.14.22-33
	Ezek.34.11-16	Acts 11.1-18	Jn.21.15-22
		Acts 12.1-17	

WEEK OF PRAYER FOR CHRISTIAN UNITY: 18-25 January

The psalms and readings provided may be used at any service during the week.

Psalms	Old Testament	New Testament	Gospel
100	Deut.30.1-4	Eph.4.1-6	Lk.9.49-56
106.1-6,49-end	Eccles.4.9-12	Eph.4.30–5.2	Jn.11.45-52
118,122,133	Jer.33.4-9a	Col.3.9-17	Jn.17.11b-19
	Ezek.37.15-19,	1 Jn.4.9-15	Jn.17.20-end
	21-22,		
	26-end		
	Zeph.3.16-end		

SUNDAY IN THE WEEK OF PRAYER FOR CHRISTIAN UNITY

If the Sunday in the Week of Prayer for Christian Unity is not kept as a Sunday of Epiphany, then it is appropriate to use the prayers, psalms and readings for The Unity of the Church, ASB pp.904-906.

THE CONVERSION OF ST PAUL, APOSTLE: 25 January

This festival may be observed on its date when it falls on a Sunday, or it may be transferred to the first suitable weekday. When it is observed on a Sunday the psalms and readings for Evening Prayer of the eve may be used.

MORNING PRAYER	THE HOLY COMMUNION	EVENING PRAYER	NIGHT PRAYER
Collect ASB p.754		Ps.66,67	Ps.18.22-35
		1 Kings 19.15-end	1 Cor.15.8-10
		Matt.19.23-end	*or* Acts 26.9-21
Ps.119.41-56	Acts 22.3-16	Ps.119.89-112	
Josh.5.13-15	Ps.117	Ecclus.39.1-10	
or Isa.45.18-end	Gal.1.11-end	*or* Isa.56.1-8	
Gal.1.11-end	*or*	Phil.3.4b-14	
or Col.1.24–2.7	Josh.5.13-15		
	Ps.117		
	Acts 9.1-23		
	Mk.16.15-18		

SAINTS TIMOTHY AND TITUS, BISHOPS: 26 January

This festival is only observed on a Sunday when it is the Patronal Festival. A psalm and readings are provided for the Holy Communion. The additional provision may be used at Morning and Evening Prayer.

> Isa.61.1-3
> Ps.96.1-10
> 2 Tim.1.1-8
> *or* Tit.1.1-5
> Lk.10.1-9

Additional Psalms and Readings

Psalms	*Old Testament*	*New Testament*	*Gospel*
97,98,99,	Num.27.15-end	Acts 20.17-35	Mk.16.14-end
100,101	Jer.1.4-10	Gal.2.1-10	Lk.4.14-19
		1 Tim.6.11-16	

LECTIONARY 2

1. GOD AND THE WORLD: GENESIS 1-11

God is not far from each one of us; in him we live and move and have our being. (Acts 17.27,28)

Wk 1	Gen.1.1-2, 1.24–2.3	Ps.33.1-9	Matt.6.25-30
Wk 2	Gen.2.4-9 (10-14) 15-end	Ps.104.15-25	Matt.19.3-5
Wk 3	Gen.3.1-19	Ps.139.1-11	Jn.8.31-36
Wk 4	Gen.4.2b-16	Ps.6	Matt.5.21-24
Wk 5	Gen.5.1-4 6.9-14,22	Ps.53	Lk.12.16-20
Wk 6	Gen.11.1-9	Ps.87	Matt.8.5-13

2. NOAH

Noah walked with God. (Gen.6.9b)

As were the days of Noah, so will be the coming of the Son of man. (Matt.24.37)

Wk 1	Gen.6.5-end	Ps.26	Mark 7.14-23
Wk 2	Gen.7.11-end	Ps.29	Matt.24.36-42
Wk 3	Gen.8.13,20-end 9.1-13	Ps.24.1-6	Mark 14.22-25

3. ABRAHAM

Abraham believed God and it was counted to him as righteousness.(Gen.15.6)

It is people of faith who are children of Abraham. (Gal.3.7)

Wk 1	Gen.11.31–12.7	Ps.22.28-end	Mark 1.16-20
[Wk 2	Gen.13.1-18	Ps.131	Matt.20.20-23]
Wk 3	Gen.17.1-7, (8-14) 15-21	Ps.105.7-15	Jn.8.51-end
Wk 4	Gen.18.1-15	Ps.105.1-6	Lk.24.28-31
Wk 5	Gen.18.17-33	Ps.145.13-20	Jn.15.14-16
[Wk 6	Gen.20	Ps.118.4-9	Lk.12.1-7]

4. SARAH

You are Sarah's daughters if you do what is right and do not give way to fear.
(1 Pet.3.6)

| Wk 1 | Gen.16 | Ps.13 | Jn.7.1-9 |
| Wk 2 | Gen.18.9-15; 21.1-7 | Ps.98 | Jn.12.44-50 |

5. HAGAR

The Lord has heard your cries of distress. (Gen.16.11)

| Wk 1 | Gen.21.9-21 | Ps.30 | Jn.10.14-16 |

6. REBEKAH

Cast your cares upon God for he cares for you. (1 Pet.5.7)

Wk 1	Gen.24.42-end	Ps.32.8-12	Jn.14.1-6
Wk 2	Gen.25.19-28	Ps.113	Jn.16.20-24
Wk 3	Gen.27.1-17	Ps.37.3-8	Lk.6.12-16

7. JACOB

In the womb Jacob grasped his brother's heel: as an adult he wrestled with God. (Hos.12.3)

Blessed is he whose help is the God of Jacob. (Ps.146.5)

Wk 1	Gen.25.19-34	Ps.105.4-11	Lk.1.26-33
Wk 2	Gen.27.11-19	Ps.50.16-end	Mark 3.31-35
Wk 3	Gen.28.10-22	Ps.119.17-24	Jn.1.47-51
Wk 4	Gen.29.15-30	Ps.146.3-9	Lk.15.11-14
Wk 5	Gen.32.22– 33.4(-11)	Ps.34.3-8	Matt.5.3-9

8. LEAH AND RACHEL

The eyes of the Lord are toward the righteous, and his ears toward their cry. (Ps.34.15)

| Wk 1 | Gen.29.31–30.24 | Ps.120 | Lk.1.36-38 |
| Wk 2 | Gen.35.9-20 | Ps.17.8-16 | Lk.20.34-38 |

9. JOSEPH

All things work together for good to those who love God, who are called according to his purpose. (Rom.8.28)

God sent me before you to preserve life. (Gen.45.5)

Wk 1	Gen.37.3-13, 18-24 (31-33)	Ps.57.1-7	Jn.7.1-6
Wk 2	Gen.39.1-15, 20-end	Ps.138	Matt.5.27-30
Wk 3	Gen.41.15-25 29-40	Ps.105.16-23	Lk.12.27-31
Wk 4	Gen.42.6-25 29-30, 35-36	Ps.103.1-12	Matt.21.28-32
Wk 5	Gen.44.1-4,14-18; 44.24–45.9	Ps.32	Matt.5.23-26
Wk 6	Gen.50.1-15	Ps.128	Lk.10.23-24

10. WOMEN IN THE MESSIANIC LINE

A record of the genealogy of Jesus Christ, the son of David, the Son of Abraham. (Matt.1.1)

Wk 1 – Tamar

Judah fathered Perez and Zerah, whose mother was Tamar. (Matt.1.3)

	Gen.38.11-27	Ps.63.1-9	Mark 7.25-30

Wk 2 – Rahab

Salmon fathered Boaz, whose mother was Rahab. (Matt.1.4)

	Josh.2.1-21	Ps.25.1-9	Jn.10.7-9

Wk 3 – Ruth

Boaz fathered Obed, whose mother was Ruth. (Matt.1.5)

	Ruth 1.1-18	Ps.68.4-10	Mark 10.28-31

Wk 4 – Bathsheba

David fathered Solomon, whose mother had been Uriah's wife. (Matt.1.6)

	1 Kings 1.15-31	Ps.51.1-17	Mark 2.13-17

Wk 5 – Mary

Jacob fathered Joseph, the husband of Mary; of her was born Jesus who is called Christ. (Matt.1.16)

	Deut.22.13-21	Ps.40.1-10	Matt.1.18-25

11. DAVID

I love you, O Lord my strength: the Lord is my rock, my fortress and my deliverer. (Ps.18.1,2)

I have found in David a man after my own heart. (Acts 13.22)

Wk 1	1 Sam.16.1-13	Ps.2.6-11	Mark 1.9-11
[Wk 2	1 Sam.17.19-49	Ps.18.33-39	Matt.17.18-20]
[Wk 3	1 Sam.17.57–18.16	Ps.23	Mark 1.35-38]
[Wk 4	1 Sam.22.1–1; 2 Sam.23.8-19	Ps.70	Mark 3.13-19]
[Wk 5	2 Sam.1.11-27	Ps.62.1-8	Jn.11.32-36]
Wk 6	2 Sam.5.1-10	Ps.48 or 132.13-18	Lk.13.31-35
Wk 7	2 Sam.7.1-17	Ps.89.1-4 or 89.29-38	Matt.22.41-46
[Wk 8	2 Sam.11.1-15; 12.1-7a	Ps.51.1-17	Matt.5.27-30]
[Wk 9	2 Sam.15.7-22	Ps.57	Jn.11.5-16]

12. AMOS

Let justice roll down like a river, and righteousness like an ever-flowing stream. (Amos 5.24)

Wk 1	Amos 1.1-10	Ps.82	Lk.4.22-28
Wk 2	Amos 2.1–3.2	Ps.10	Lk.19.1-10
Wk 3	Amos 4.1-13	Ps.123	Lk.8.1-3
Wk 4	Amos 6.1-12	Ps.49	Lk.6.20-26
Wk 5	Amos 7.(1-9) 10-17	Ps.52	Lk.13.31-35
[Wk 6	Amos 8.1-12	Ps.119.25-32	Lk.16.19-31]

13. HOSEA

Come let us return to the Lord; for he has torn that he may heal us. (Hos.6.1)

The word of the Lord that came to Hosea: I will heal their faithlessness. (Hos.1.1;14.4)

Wk 1	Hos.1.1–2.1	Ps.95.6-11	Matt.23.37-39
Wk 2	Hos.4.1-14	Ps.81.10-16	Lk.6.43-45
Wk 3	Hos.5.13–6.6	Ps.80.1-7	Matt.11.25-30
[Wk 4	Hos.8	Ps.115.2-8	Mark 12.1-9]
Wk 5	Hos.11.1-11	Ps.81.1-9	Jn.13.1-9
[Wk 6	Hos.14	Ps.37.27-35	Lk.15.3-7]

14. ISAIAH 1

O house of Jacob, come, let us walk in the light of the Lord. (Isa.2.5)

Wk 1	Isa.1.1-4,9-20	Ps.50.7-15	Matt.15.4-11
[Wk 2	Isa.5.1-10,18-23	Ps.80.8-15	Lk.16.10-15]
Wk 3	Isa.6	Ps.93	Jn.12.36-41
Wk 4	Isa.8.9–9.7	Ps.118.81-88	Matt.4.12-17
Wk 5	Isa.11.1-11	Ps.72.1-11	John 12.31-33

15. ISAIAH 2

You shall go out in joy, and be led forth in peace. (Isa.55.12)

Wk 1	Isa.40.1-17, 27-end	Ps.102.12-22	Mark 1.1-4
Wk 2	Isa.42.1-12(-17)	Ps.110	Matt.12.9-23
[Wk 3	Isa.43.1-13(-19)	Ps.111	Lk.24.44-49]
Wk 4	Isa.52	Ps.122	Mark 1.14-15
Wk 5	Isa.55	Ps.21.1-6	Jn.4.13-15

16. ISAIAH 3

The Spirit of the Lord God is upon me, because he has anointed me to preach good news to the poor. (Lk.4.18)

Wk 1	Isa.56.1-8	Ps.84	Matt.21.12-16
Wk 2	Isa.58	Ps.41.1-4, 11-13	Matt.25.34-40
Wk 3	Isa.60.11-6, 10-end	Ps.138	Matt.2.1-11
Wk 4	Isa.61.10–62.7	Ps.45.1-9	Matt.9.35-38
[Wk 5	Isa.65.17-end	Ps.45.10-17	Mark 10.28-31]

17. JEREMIAH 1

Before you were born I consecrated you; I appointed you a prophet to the nations. (Jer.1.5)

Your words came and I ate them; they were my joy and my heart's delight. (Jer.15.16)

Wk 1	Jer.1	Ps.119.9-16	Matt.10.16-20
[Wk 2	Jer.16.1-18	Ps.119.33-40	Matt.19.8-12]
Wk 3	Jer.20.7-18	Ps.119.25-32	Mark 10.35-40
[Wk 4	Jer.28	Ps.119.41-48	Lk.10.16]
Wk 5	Jer.36.1-10,14-28	Ps.119.49-56	Matt.5.14-18
Wk 6	Jer.38.1-23	Ps.119.17-24	Matt.10.41-42

18. JEREMIAH 2

The heart is deceitful above all things and desperately corrupt; who can understand it? (Jer.17.9)

The prophets prophesy lies, the priests rule at their direction; and my people love to have it so. What will you do when the end comes? (Jer.5.31)

Wk 1	Jer.2.1-13	Ps.78.33-40	Mark 2.18-19
Wk 2	Jer.8.8–9.3	Ps.19.7-end	Matt.15.12-14
Wk 3	Jer.18.1-17	Ps.28.1-5	Matt.12.33-37
Wk 4	Jer.23.16-32	Ps.74.9-12	Jn.5.37-44
Wk 5	Jer.29.1,4-14	Ps.137.1-6	Lk.11.9-13
[Wk 6	Jer.31.31-37	Ps.51.8-13	Mark 14.22-25]

19. EZEKIEL

A new heart I will give you and a new spirit I will put within you. (Ezek.36.26)

Say to them, 'Thus says the Lord God' whether they listen or refuse to listen. (Ezek.3.11)

Wk 1	Ezek.1.1-14, 22-end	Ps.29	Jn.1.14-18
[Wk 2	Ezek.8.1-18	Ps.101	Mark 9.43-47]
Wk 3	Ezek.33.7-20	Ps.32	Matt.20.1-16
Wk 4	Ezek.34.1-24	Ps.23	Jn.10.11-18
Wk 5	Ezek.36.16-32	Ps.51.10-14	Jn.7.37-39
[Wk 6	Ezek.47.1-12	Ps.46	Jn.17.20-23]

20. DANIEL

Blessed be the name of God for ever and ever, to whom belong wisdom and might. (Dan.2.20)

Wk 1	Dan.1.1-20	Ps.101.1-8	Matt.5.13-16
Wk 2	Dan.2.1-6,25-35, 37-47	Ps.96.1-10	Matt.16.15-18
[Wk 3	Dan.3.1,8-12, 16-25	Ps.16	Lk.12.4-12]
Wk 4	Dan.5.1,5-8,17-30	Ps.75	Matt.6.19-23
Wk 5	Dan.6.4-23	Ps.27.1-8	Matt.5.10-12

21. VISIONS OF DANIEL

I saw in the night visions, and behold with the clouds of heaven there came one like a son of man. (Dan.7.13)

Wk 1	Dan.7.2-18	Ps.80.14-end	Lk.22.66-70
Wk 2	Dan.9.1-7 17-23(-27)	Ps.122	Matt.24.15-31
Wk 3	Dan.10.2-20	Ps.34.1-9	Jn.14.25-31
Wk 4	Dan.12	Ps.44.21-end	Jn.16.29-33

22. JONAH

As Jonah became a sign to the men of Nineveh, so will the Son of man be to this generation. (Lk.11.30)

Wk 1	Jonah 1	Ps.139.1-11 *or* Jonah 2.2-9	Lk.9.7-62
Wk 2	Jonah 2.10–3.10	Ps.2.6-11	Lk.11.29-32
Wk 3	Jonah 4	Ps.8	Matt.9.10-13

23. ROMANS 1

By one man's obedience many will be made righteous. (Rom.5.19)

I am not ashamed of the gospel; it is the power of God for salvation to every one who believes. (Rom.1.16)

You must consider yourselves dead to sin and alive to God in Christ Jesus. (Rom.6.11)

Wk 1	Rom.1.13-25; 2.12-16	Ps.106.20-24	Matt.3.4-12
Wk 2	Rom.3.9-end	Ps.72.1-7	Mark 10.17-21
Wk 3	Rom.5.1-17	Ps.103.8-14	Mark 10.42-45
Wk 4	Rom.6.1-4,12-end	Ps.32	Jn.8.2-11
[Wk 5	Rom.8.1-4, 9-11, 18-27	Ps.98	Matt.19.23-29]
[Wk 6	Rom.8.28-end	Ps.84	Jn.10.27-29]

24. ROMANS 2

The same Lord is Lord of all and bestows his riches upon all who call on him. (Rom.10.12)

Wk 1	Rom.11.1-6,11-24	Ps.107.1-9	Matt.15.21-28
Wk 2	Rom.12	Ps.116.1-9	Lk.6.27-36
[Wk 3	Rom.13	Ps.94.14-23	Lk.20.19-25]
Wk 4	Rom.14.1-6,13-23	Ps.133	Matt.7.1-5
Wk 5	Rom.15.7-21	Ps.117	Jn.17.20-23

25. EPHESIANS

Once you were darkness, but now you are light in the Lord. (Eph.5.8)

Wake, O sleeper, rise from the dead, and Christ will give you light. (Eph.5.14)

For by grace you have been saved through faith; and this is not your own doing, it is the gift of God. (Eph.2.8)

Wk 1	Eph.1.1-14 (15-23)	Ps.145.1-9	Jn.1.14-16
Wk 2	Eph.2.1-10	Ps.116.1-9	Lk.23.39-43
Wk 3	Eph.2.11-22; 3.8-13	Ps.87	Matt.28.16-end
[Wk 4	Eph.4.1-16	Ps.133	Matt.16.13-18]
Wk 5	Eph.4.22–5.14	Ps.5.1-7	Matt.6.19-23
[Wk 6	Eph.6.10-20	Ps.44.5-9	Lk.10.17-20]

26. 1 THESSALONIANS

He who calls you is faithful and he will do it. (1 Thess.5.24)

Wk 1	1 Thess.1	Ps.115.1-8	Matt.13.45-46
Wk 2	1 Thess.2.1-13	Ps.34.11-end	Matt.23.1-12
[Wk 3	1 Thess.3.12–4.12	Ps.15	Lk.19.11-27]
Wk 4	1 Thess.4.13–5.11	Ps.98	Jn.3.17-21
[Wk 5	1 Thess.5.12-end	Ps.105.1-8	Jn.17.11-18]

27. 2 THESSALONIANS

May the Lord direct your hearts towards the love of God and the perseverance of Christ. (2 Thess.3.5)

Wk 1	2 Thess.1	Ps.95	Matt.22.1-14
Wk 2	2 Thess.2.1-15	Ps.97	Matt.24.23-27
Wk 3	2 Thess.3	Ps.98	Mark 4.2-9

28. 1 JOHN

God is light, and in him is no darkness at all. (1 Jn.1.5)

The darkness is passing away and the true light is already shining. (1 Jn.2.8)

Wk 1	1 Jn.1.1–2.6	Ps.36	Jn.3.19-21
Wk 2	1 Jn.2.18–3.3	Ps.1	Jn.1.9-13
Wk 3	1 Jn.3.4-10, 3.19–4.6	Ps.43	Jn.8.42-47
Wk 4	1 Jn.4.7–5.5	Ps.67	Jn.1.14-18
[Wk 5	1 Jn.5.6-end	Ps.2.6-end	Jn.16.7-15]

29. REVELATION 1

Blessed are those who are invited to the marriage supper of the Lamb. (Rev.19.9)

The Spirit and the Bride say, 'Come'. Whoever is thirsty let him come, let him take the free gift of the water of life. (Rev.22.17)

Wk 1	Rev.1.4-end	Ps.45.1-9	Matt.17.1-8
Wk 2	Rev.3	Ps.7.9-18	Matt.16.15-18
Wk 3	Rev.12	Ps.47	Jn.12.31-36
Wk 4	Rev.21.1-14	Ps.45.10-17	Jn.6.35-40

30. REVELATION 2

The world and its desires pass away, but whoever does the will of God lives for ever. (1 Jn.4.17)

The one who is in you is greater than the one who is in the world. (1 Jn.4.4)

Wk 1	Rev.4.1-2;5	Ps.118.19-26	Jn.1.25-29
Wk 2	Rev.6	Ps.44.19-27	Mk.13.5-13
Wk 3	Rev.13	Ps.52	Jn.15.19-25
Wk 4	Rev.18.21–19.9	Ps.49.12-21	Lk.6.20-26
Wk 5	Rev.21.10-14; 21.22–22.5	Ps.66.1-8	Matt.25.1-13

HISTORICAL COMMENTARY

The development of the liturgical calendar was a gradual process, though today it is no longer possible to maintain the view popularized by Dom Gregory Dix that only in the fourth century did historicization take place. From very early times there existed a tension between eschatology and history, and it was this tension which produced the liturgical calendar.

'If Christ has not been raised, then our preaching is in vain and your faith is in vain' (1 Corinthians 15. 14). Paul rightly saw that at the heart of Christianity lies the resurrection of Jesus, which was commemorated and celebrated weekly on the First Day of the week, and annually at Paschaltide. Sunday and Easter are the core of the liturgical calendar. Nevertheless, at an early date interest was focused on the divine nature of Jesus, both its public disclosure at his baptism, and the more private disclosure in the events surrounding his birth. This is already clear in St Mark's Gospel which begins with the baptism, and in St John with the Baptist's declaration that this is the Lamb of God; and in the complex structures of the birth narratives of Matthew and Luke. This dual interest in the proclamation of Sonship/Messiahship at the baptism, and the birth of the Son of the Most High, seems to be the basis of two festivals in close proximity – Christmas and Epiphany.

The reason why these two festivals are so close seems to be that although they have become two separate and distinct celebrations, originally they were simply the Western and Eastern dates for celebrating the one mystery of the incarnation. The West, perhaps being more concerned with history, concentrated on the birth of Christ on 25 December, whereas in the East 6 January, the Epiphany, was concerned with the wider mystery of incarnation in terms of the birth, the visit of the Magi, the baptism, and the wedding of Cana – the showing forth of the divinity through a number of events. Gradually East and West accepted each other's festivals in addition to their own, and the incarnation/birth themes tended to cluster around 25 December. In the West, 6 January tended to concern itself mainly with the visit of the Magi, but in the East the baptism and the wedding at Cana continued to be the main themes. Even today, in the Eastern Churches, 6 January is the more important festival, and the Armenian

Church has never adopted 25 December; on 6 January that Church still celebrates all the incarnational mysteries.

But why these particular dates? On this question there are two schools of thought. The older view is that these two dates represent Christian adaptation of the respective winter solstice dates in the West and East, which were already important pagan festivals. Those who hold this view cite the celebrations connected with Apollo, Mithras, and Dionysus with their themes of birth and rebirth, and the coming of the deity to dwell with his followers. In Rome by AD 274 the winter solstice was a public holiday in honour of Sol Invictus, the unconquered sun. In the East a slightly different calendar was followed, and the winter solstice was 6 January. It is suggested that in Egypt there was on this date an ancient festival of water, and in Alexandria the celebration of the virgin birth of Aion from Kore; in Syria, so it is argued, there were celebrations of miracles of water changed into wine. It is argued, therefore, that these pagan festivals were taken over and christianized. The birth of the sun of righteousness (Malachi 4. 2), the Dayspring from on high (Luke 1. 78) replaced Sol Invictus, and in the East the Virgin Birth, the baptism, and the wedding of Cana replaced (or were even suggested by) their pagan counterparts.

Although this view is still very common, it has been seriously challenged by what may be called the 'calculation' theory. This view stresses that in Judaism, which was the cradle of Christianity, there was pressure to believe that important events in salvation history happened – and will happen – on the same date. Some Rabbis argued that on 14 Nisan the world was created, the patriarchs were born, the Exodus took place, and that the Day of the Lord would also happen on this date. Christians dated the Pascha to 14 Nisan, but in the Roman calendar this was estimated at 25 March in the West, and in the East, where there was a different calendar in use, 6 April. By a strange process of exegesis of the Bible (strange by modern methods, that is) several of the Fathers calculated that the conception of Jesus (in the sixth month) took place on the same day as his passion, 25 March or 6 April. By calculating the birth as a perfect nine months (for God is perfect) they arrived at 25 December in the West and 6 January in the East. Furthermore, much of the 'evidence' for pagan festivals has been challenged. There is evidence to suggest that in the Roman Church 25 December was observed as the feast of the incarnation before that date was chosen to celebrate Sol Invictus. It is also questionable whether 6 January was the date of various Eastern festivals – the 4th or 5th seems to be the important date for some Egyptian celebrations. Certainly recent studies on the calendar have seriously weakened the older 'adaptation' view, and need to be taken seriously.

Whatever the precise origin, the Church is left with two major festivals within the space of twelve days. The secular world greatly inflates and distorts the first and in England, at least, totally ignores the second. In order to give 6 January a separate identity, *The Promise of His Glory* has emphasized the older Eastern themes of the baptism of Christ and the wedding at Cana. Since the renewal of baptismal vows at Easter only dates from 1951 in the Roman Catholic Church, it is hardly an ancient tradition. Epiphany is an equally good occasion.

The origin of Advent is even more mysterious than the question of Christmas and the Epiphany, though, as with the season of Lent in relation to Easter, it is a later development. A major problem is that the historical evidence relating to Advent is conflicting and inconclusive. In some traditions it had and has overtones of being a Fast, though the reason for this and the length of the season differed from place to place. At Rome in the fourth century it was the end of the year (the new year began with 25 December) and there it seems to have concentrated on eschatology. In the East it came to be concerned with biblical annunciations, leading up to that of Christ, and the length of the season varies in the Eastern Churches, some having four Sundays and others having five. In the West in some places it lasted only one Sunday, in others six or seven. At Rome itself there is evidence that it was once six weeks in duration, then five, and finally four. Most Western Churches had adopted this Roman four-Sunday scheme by the tenth century, though even today the rite of Milan has a six-Sunday Advent. Thus there seems to have been a mixture of themes – eschatology, penitence, annunciation, and preparation. The length of the season varies – and thus is still variable if it is thought desirable.

FOR FURTHER READING

Robert F Taft, 'Historicism Revisited', in *Beyond East and West*. Pastoral Press, Washington, 1984

Raymond Brown, *The Birth of the Messiah*. Doubleday, New York, 1977

Adolf Adam, *The Liturgical Year*. Pueblo, New York, 1981

Thomas J Talley, *The Origins of the Liturgical Year*. Pueblo, New York, 1986

SOURCES AND
ACKNOWLEDGEMENTS

Thanks are due to many whose names are listed below, for permission to include copyright texts in *The Promise of His Glory*.

The number which precedes each item in the list of sources is used throughout the book to identify the material to which the permission relates. The numbers appear in the right-hand margin. An asterisk indicates that the text has been adapted, sometimes substantially. A number in parentheses in the list below indicates an attributed text which is believed to be out of copyright.

It has not always been possible to identify the owners of copyright in prayers and similar material in their original form, and the Central Board of Finance apologizes in advance to any whose copyright may have been overlooked.

1   Malling Abbey: a translation of 'O gladsome light'.

2   GIA Publications Inc., Chicago, Illinois: two songs by James A Melloh from *Praise God in Song*.

3   Portsmouth Cathedral.

4   Mowbray, a Cassell imprint: *Prayers for use at the Alternative Services*, compiled by David Silk (1980, revised 1986).

5   The Provost and Scholars of King's College, Cambridge: A Bidding Prayer.

6   *The Prayer Book as Proposed in 1928*: copyright administered by the Central Board of Finance of the Church of England.

7   Scottish Episcopal Church: *Scottish Prayer Book 1929*.

8   *The Alternative Service Book 1980*, copyright © The Central Board of Finance of the Church of England.

9   Methodist Publishing House: *The Methodist Service Book*.

10 Excerpts from the English translation of *The Roman Missal*, © 1973 International Commission on English in the Liturgy Inc. All rights reserved.

11 Anglican Church of Canada: *The Book of Alternative Services*, © The General Synod of the Anglican Church of Canada 1985.

(12) Episcopal Church of the USA: *The Book of Common Prayer* according to the use of the Episcopal Church of the USA (1979). (The ECUSA Prayer Book is not subject to copyright.)

416

13 The Revd Michael Perham.

14 *Service for Remembrance Sunday*, © SPCK 1968, 1984 for the compilers.

15 Westminster Abbey: A Bidding Prayer.

16 Christ Church, Oxford: A Bidding Prayer (E W Heaton).

17 St George's, Oakdale.

18 English Hymnal Company Ltd: 'O come, O come, Emmanuel' from *New English Hymnal*.

19 The Society of St Francis: Daily Office SSF.

20 Mowbray, a Cassell imprint: *In Penitence and Faith: Texts for Use with the Alternative Services*, compiled by David Silk (1988).

(21) The full version of the Dies Irae is from *The English Hymnal*; the short version by Richard Crashaw is from *The Cambridge Hymnal*.

22 Westcott House, Cambridge.

22a Mowbray, a Cassell imprint: *After Communion*, C L MacDonnell, 1985.

23 *Memorials upon Several Occasions*.

24 The Revised Standard Version of the Bible, copyright 1946, 1952, © 1971, 1973 The Division of Christian Education of the National Council of the Churches of Christ in the USA.

25 The Rt Revd Timothy Dudley-Smith: A Christingle Hymn, 'God whose love is everywhere', © Timothy Dudley-Smith 1988. USA © Hope Publishing Company, Carol Stream, IL 60188, USA.

26 The Children's Society: the Christingle Service Prayer by John Bradford.

27 The Revd Dr Kenneth Stevenson.

28 Holy Trinity Church, Wealdstone.

29 Jubilee Hymns: *Church Family Worship*, edited by Michael Perry, Hodder and Stoughton 1986, © 1986 Jubilee Hymns Ltd.

30 The Church Literature Association.

31 Church of the Province of New Zealand: *A New Zealand Prayer Book – He Karakia Mihinare o Aotearoa*, © The Church of the Province of New Zealand 1989.

32 *After the Third Collect*, Eric Milner-White, © 1959.

33 Archbishop William Temple (1881-1944).

34 Inspired by, or derived from, hymns of the Byzantine Rite: a semi-official English translation is available in *The Festal Menaion*, Faber 1969.

34a The Iona Community, Wild Goose Publications.

35   Saint Andrew Press: *Worship Now Book 1.*

36   *Lent, Holy Week, Easter: Services and Prayers,* copyright © The
Central Board of Finance of the Church of England 1984, 1986.

37   Harper Collins Publishers, New York: *The Wideness of God's Mercy.*

38   The Lima Liturgy (World Council of Churches 1983 Vancouver
Assembly), from *One Lord, One Faith, One Baptism,* © British Council
of Churches.

39   From *La prière oecuménique.*

40   Coventry Cathedral.

41   Extracts from the Book of Common Prayer of 1662, the rights in which
are vested in the Crown in perpetuity within the United Kingdom, are
reproduced by permission of the Crown's Patentee, Cambridge
University Press.

(42)   A translation by Robert Bridges (1844-1930) from the *Yattendon
Hymnal.*

43   English version © 1975 International Consultation on English Texts
(ICET).

44   English version © 1988 English Language Liturgical Consultation
(ELLC).

45   Church of the Province of Southern Africa (Anglican): *An Anglican
Prayer Book 1989.*

46   From a Jewish eve of Sabbath devotion.

47   St Columba.

48   Triangle/SPCK: *The Edge of Glory,* © 1985 by David Adam.

49   After Bede.

50   Cairns Publications, Sheffield: *Prayer at Night* by Jim Cotter, 4th edn
1988.

(51)   John Donne (1572-1631).

52   Adapted from the Nestorian Liturgy.

53   *The Daily Service.*

54   Oxford University Press: *Daily Prayer,* compiled by Eric Milner-White
and G W Briggs (1941).

55   Monarchic.

56   Mozarabic.

57   Hodder and Stoughton Ltd: *Parish Prayers,* compiled and edited by
Frank Colquhoun, 1967.

418

58 *Modern Collects*, Church of the Province of Southern Africa.

59 William Collins Sons & Co Ltd: *The Cloud of Witnesses*, © 1982 G B Timms.

60 Eric Fenn.

61 Leonine (Leonine Sacramentary).

62 BBC Books: *New Every Morning, A Book of Daily Services*, new edition 1973.

63 Sarum Breviary.

Collects not from *The Alternative Service Book 1980* are mostly new adaptations of ancient collects, many of them derived from Bright's *Ancient Collects*. Many of the scripture passages are in versions prepared by the Liturgical Commission after consulting a number of the published versions. Considerable use has been made of The Revised Standard Version of the Bible (24 above), and The Jerusalem Bible, © 1966 by Darton Longman & Todd Ltd and Doubleday and Company, Inc.